The Book of Kells

DR CAROL FARR is a former Associate Professor of Art History, University of Alabama in Huntsville. She now lives in London and is continuing her research on early medieval art. Her previous publications include contributions on the art of the Book of Kells in *Minorities and Barbarians in Medieval Life and Thought* (edited by S. Ridyard and R. Benson, 1996); *From the Isles of the North: Early Medieval Art in Ireland and Britain* (edited by C. Bourke, 1995); *The Book of Kells: Proceedings of a Conference at Trinity College, Dublin, 6–9 September 1992* (edited by F. O'Mahony, 1994); and *Studies in Insular Art and Archaeology* (edited by R. Farrell and C. Karkov, 1991).

THE BOOK OF KELLS

Its Function and Audience

Carol Farr

THE BRITISH LIBRARY

AND

UNIVERSITY OF TORONTO PRESS

1997

FIRST PUBLISHED 1997 BY
THE BRITISH LIBRARY
GREAT RUSSELL STREET
LONDON WCIB 3DG

British Library Cataloguing in Publication Data
A catalogue record for this title is available from the British Library

ISBN 0 7123 0499 1 (cloth)
ISBN 0 7123 4576 0 (paper)

PUBLISHED IN NORTH AMERICA IN 1997 BY
UNIVERSITY OF TORONTO PRESS INCORPORATED
TORONTO AND BUFFALO

Canadian Cataloguing in Publication Data
is available from University of Toronto Press

ISBN 0 8020 4337 2 (cloth)
ISBN 0 8020 8157 6 (paper)

DESIGNED AND TYPESET BY
A.H. JOLLY (EDITORIAL) LTD.
YELVERTOFT. NORTHANTS NN6 7LF.

PRINTED IN GREAT BRITAIN.

CONTENTS

Chapter Four
Conclusion

Appendices

Appendix One

Appendix Two

LIST OF ILLUSTRATIONS

ILLUSTRATION ACKNOWLEDGEMENTS

I am most grateful to the following institutions for supplying photographic illustrations, and for granting permission for them to be used here: Bibliothèque Nationale, Paris (Figs 24, 25, 26, 30); Biblioteca Apostolica, Vatican (Figs 15, 27); Biblioteca Medicea Laurenziana, Florence, by permission of the Ministero per i Beni Culturali e Ambientali (Fig. 2); Bodleian Library, Oxford (Figs 11, 12, 13, 14, 23); The British Library, London (Figs 7, 8, 9, 10, 16, 17, 18, 19, 20, 21); The British Museum (Fig. 3); Dean and Chapter of Durham, Cathedral (Fig. 22); The Trustees of Trinity College Library, Dublin (PLATES I, II, III, IV, V, VI, VII, VIII; Figs 5, 6, 28, 29); Yale University Art Gallery, Dura Europos Archive (Fig. 1). Fig. 4 is by the author.

PREFACE

WHEN A STUDENT I began asking some questions about certain figures depicted in Insular art and the objects they were holding. The questions coalesced and snowballed, nearly glaciating, into a mass that, over many years, moved inexorably into a Master's thesis, Ph.D. dissertation, several conference papers and articles, and finally this book. Due to the lengthy duration of research for this study, I emphasise that I am not just making an obligatory statement of gratitude when I say that, if this book is any good at all, it is because of the help that so many people and institutions have given to me. I hope that this book in some way shows itself to be deserving of all the kindness its author has received.

An extremely important part of the help and kindness was given to me during my time as Assistant and Associate Professor at the University of Alabama in Huntsville. The funding I received there to pay for photographs and slides and for travel to libraries to examine original manuscripts enabled the advancement of my work beyond the level of a Ph.D. dissertation. For their generous and enlightened support, I offer my sincerest thanks to Richard Moore, Johanna Shields, and their assistant, Ann Lee, of the UAH Humanities Center, and to Dr. Kenneth Harwell and his staff at the UAH Research Institute.

The British Library and Trinity College Library, Dublin, deserve much thanks also for their assistance with costs of photographs to illustrate my book.

The long list of individuals who have helped me in nearly every way possible must be headed by two people. First, I thank S. M. Alexander, my master's thesis and Ph.D. dissertation adviser, for her many years of guidance and especially for her incomparable teaching which has led me and numerous others onto questions and curiosity about Insular art. In terms of chronology, Michelle Brown is second. I thank her for her extraordinary generosity both as friend and professional colleague. Her involvement in this book reaches much greater depths than her support of its publication, her deft editorial skills, and her indispensable aid in obtaining access to manuscripts in the British Library.

David Way and Anne Young of British Library publishing staff were also marvellously helpful, sympathetic, and patient. They made my first experience with book publication a pleasant one.

I thank George Hardin Brown for his expert help in polishing the English translations of Latin texts, as well as for suggesting some published translations. Unless indicated otherwise, the translations of Latin exegesis are my own, with Professor Brown's assistance. For English translations of the Vulgate, the Douay Version was used, except in a few instances where its wording was inappropriate to the images in the Book of Kells.

Many others have helped in conversations and correspondence on the Book of Kells and Insular culture, as well as by providing access to materials. In particular I wish to thank Éamonn Ó Carragáin, Jennifer O'Reilly, Henry Mayr-Harting, Jonathan Alexander, Bernard Meehan, Nancy Netzer, Catherine Karkov, Bob Farrell, Rosemary Cramp, Richard Bailey, Jane Hawkes, Carol Neumann de Vegvar, Peter Harbison, Doug MacLean, Sue Youngs, Niamh Whitfield, Cormac Bourke, Paul Meyvaert, Colmán Etchingham, Tom Reese, Stuart Ó Seanóir, David Ganz, Leonard Boyle, Roger Stalley, Liz Teviotdale, Eric Cambridge, Cathy Swift, Heather Buchanan, Cecil Brown, Terry O'Reilly, Charles Wright, Bill Munson, Patricia Stirnemann, Roger Norris, Martin Kauffmann, Louis Mackey, George Greenia, Richard Pfaff, Roger Reynolds, Fred Orton, Joan Holladay, and Eleanor Greenhill. With such help, one wonders how mistakes could occur in this book; the surviving errors, therefore, are certainly my own.

Finally, I dedicate this book to Richard Buchanan as a gift to begin our marriage.

Carol Farr
May 1997

THE BOOK OF KELLS

INTRODUCTION

The Book of Kells and the Insular Gospel Books

THE BOOK OF KELLS (Dublin, Trinity College Library, MS 58) is an elaborately decorated copy of the Gospels. It and the other decorated gospel manuscripts created in Ireland and the British Isles in the seventh to ninth centuries represent perhaps the most eloquent witnesses to the Christianisation of northern Europe. The Gospels were the word of God, upon which doctrine was built, and they provided for believers the spiritual truth read publicly in the liturgy. The text's divine and authoritative nature provided the main reason for creating large, impressively decorated copies of it.

Despite the gospel books' fame and the status of some as much-studied objects, questions of their function and audience remain substantially unaddressed in modern scholarship. The usual sources and approaches have proved uninformative on these counts, but the manuscripts' physical evidence can still be looked at in new ways to glean information from which may be deduced possible functions. It is equally important that knowledge of the manuscripts be enriched by considering their decoration and textual presentation within political, social, and historic as well as religious contexts. Even if the audience was 'only God' or if the book served only as the focus of individual contemplation, the concepts of sanctity expressed in visual art can be shown to have been constructed by early medieval Celtic and Anglo-Saxon society in ways that were socially and politically significant. To what extent and in which ways were the decoration, illustrations, and textual presentation of luxury gospel manuscripts, such as the Book of Kells, determined by their function and audience? The major, if not the only, component of that audience may have been virtually identical with the book's creators: the Insular monastic and clerical élite. The Book of Kells, famed for its pure visual splendour, may become even more alive and meaningful in our imaginations if we begin to learn how it may have functioned as a gospel manuscript within the larger context of the Christian élite and the early medieval western Church.

During the fourth to seventh centuries, the gospel text, like the rest of the Bible, was brought to the Celts of Ireland, Britain, Wales, and Scotland and to the Anglo-Saxons in a language foreign to them, a circumstance crucial to the development of verbal and visual interpretive forms with which they overlaid and surrounded Scripture. Moreover, Christianity and the things which accompanied it – books themselves, an extensive literacy, and new types of literature, art, and architecture – were products of the urbanized, Late Roman culture of the Mediterranean. In the wake of the northern, tribal migrations that had arrived in western Europe from the third century AD, the Christian culture of the Mediterranean was reshaping the political and social forms of continental Europe, beginning to re-establish the concept of the centralized, territorial state and putting in place the Christian world view of history as the story of Fall and Redemption. Emerging in the late sixth and seventh centuries from their own periods of change and turmoil, the Irish and Anglo-Saxons recognised the virtue of emulating, synthesizing, and participating in the culture accompanying the Gospels. Many of the visual and graphic features of the Book of Kells and other Hiberno-Saxon luxury gospel books not only reflect this cultural mixing but also indicate the participation of gospel manuscripts in the emerging medieval Christian world.[1] The Celtic and Anglo-Saxon élite who controlled textual and artistic production created in the medium of manuscript decoration visual and graphic interpretive figures and signs to link indigenous society with a prestigious, authoritative international system, Christianity, as well as to make Christian text and Latin language relevant to themselves and their tradition of learning. The gospel book served both as object of interpretation and interpretative object.

Modern art history usually places the Book of Kells at the end of a line tracing development of the Insular or Hiberno-Saxon style of manuscript decoration.[2] Michelle Brown has recently pointed out, however, that the Book of Kells also presents important palaeographical and stylistic relationships to the display scripts and decoration of late eighth- and ninth-century southern Anglo-Saxon (Southumbrian) manuscripts such as the Book of Cerne and the Barberini Gospels.[3] Although the manuscript's connections with the seventh- and early eighth-century art of Northumbria, Ireland, and Scotland are extremely significant, the prevalent lopsided view of the Book of Kells as a terminus rather than a turning point is limiting and artificial. It arises more from the way in which art historians and palaeographers have studied Insular manuscripts than from an understanding of the continuum of history in Ireland and the British Isles. The primary concern of art historians has been to determine the origins of the Hiberno-Saxon style, in tandem with efforts to place the most impressive manuscripts within the historical construct by date and place of origin. Did the origins of the Hiberno-Saxon style lie primarily in Ireland, Northumbria, or Scotland? When and in which scriptorium in which of these places was the Book of Kells made?[4] Moreover, answers to the preferred questions have been distorted and limited not only by modern political differences and cultural desires, but also by the nature of the available textual sources of evidence.[5]

The debate, because it concerns origins, tends to focus on the seventh century and the early years of the eighth, the period during which the Hiberno-Saxon stylistic synthesis of Celtic, Anglo-Saxon, and Mediterranean art took place. The well-known large format gospel books, other than Kells, date from this time: the Book of Durrow, the Lindisfarne Gospels, and the Echternach Gospels, as well as the Durham A.II.17 gospel fragments. Current opinions place the Book of Kells later, somewhere between the mid-eighth and early ninth centuries, with a date around 800 and origin at Iona enduring in popularity.[6] As a result, much of the discussion of Hiberno-Saxon art has shed only indirect light on it. The

Book of Kells postdates, moreover, the major contemporary source for Insular history, Bede's *Historia Ecclesiastica*, completed in 731. The terminal date of Bede's *Historia* seems to have effected a bias in historical studies of pre-Viking Anglo-Saxon England, favouring the seventh and early eighth centuries. Irish studies, also, focus on the seventh century because it is the earliest from which written sources are plentiful enough to allow informative study. It represents for scholars of Hiberno-Latin and Old Irish texts the period in which themes and forms were set down.[7] Thus, for example, recent ground-breaking discussion of the Book of Armagh, a firmly dated and placed early ninth-century manuscript presenting artistic and palaeographical connections with the Book of Kells, has focused on the seventh- and early to mid eighth-century period of compilation of its Patrician texts.[8] Besides these difficulties, one sees also the effect of Bede's romanizing, Northumbrian agenda and his disfavour directed at Celtic regions,[9] inhibiting modern understanding of the interplay of British, Irish, Anglo-Saxon, and Mediterranean contributions.[10] Moreover, the sheer difficulty of the Old Irish material and the obscurity of Hiberno-Latin texts have been an obstacle. Serious misunderstanding of such important documentation as the law tracts and a romanticized view of early Irish literary culture in general have only recently begun to be reversed.[11] A further historiographic problem has been created by the tendency, in particular in the realm of art historical scholarship, to shift attention from the late eighth-century Insular context to the contemporary continental development of Charlemagne's imperial culture.[12]

While it is true that the dates and origins of two great seventh-century gospel manuscripts, the Book of Durrow and the Echternach Gospels, remain subjects of dispute,[13] the lacunae in discussion of Insular art and culture seem to have had a yet more crucial impact on our understanding of the Book of Kells. Even though it is the most famous of all Insular codices and is much studied as art object and manuscript, much historical, art historical, and palaeographical discussion does not address its probable chronological context.[14] Scholarship has only begun recently to turn from a rigidly constructed Irish and Anglo-Saxon dichotomy sited in Northumbria, specifically at Lindisfarne, to a more precise, flexible view offering some hope of insight into not only when and where it was made but also why it was made and how it may have generated meaning – and what those meanings may have been – when its Insular audience read, viewed, or otherwise used it. Given the current state of knowledge, an unequivocal declaration of the date and origin of the Book of Kells is impossible, but an overview of its general historical background is still essential to an understanding of its function and meaning in Insular culture of the late eighth and early ninth centuries.

The Historical Background

The Book of Kells presents features unique or new among extant gospel books of the last half of the eighth and early ninth centuries, but it also looks back to archaic traditions. It shares with early manuscripts from Ireland, such as the early seventh-century Gospels called Codex Usserianus Primus (Dublin, Trinity College Library MS 55), text written in long lines instead of columns, graphic articulation or punctuation that merges with decorative forms, use of crosses and cross shapes in decoration to introduce or end major sections of gospel text, and an early series of textual divisions. These and other archaic features of the Codex Usserianus Primus are linked with the context of early Irish book production, a tradition thought by modern palaeographers to have preserved the methods and forms of a Late Antique, provincial industry inherited from Britain and possibly Gaul, although limited contact with Rome cannot be ruled out, as suggested by certain historical evidence.[15]

Conventional history and palaeography view the origins of literacy in Ireland as occurring under the impetus of Christian conversion in the late fourth and fifth centuries. Recently Stevenson and Harvey have shown the possibility of a pre-Christian transmission of limited literacy through trade channels with Roman Britain and Gaul.[16] This small-scale literacy would have facilitated the interests of the native élite during the period of Christianisation and could, Stevenson argues, explain Ireland's exceptionally early development of vernacular writing, established by the seventh century.

Christianity, however, brought more extensive literacy than the earlier trade contacts could. It also brought book production to answer its need for manuscripts for liturgy, preaching, and study. Exactly when Christianity first arrived in Ireland is unknown. Although the Irish had contact with the Roman Empire,[17] they were never under Roman administration and, therefore, were not Christianised directly under Rome as the British had been. A Christian community, however, existed in Ireland by 431, when Pope Celestine sent Palladius to serve as bishop to the 'Irish who believe in Christ,' according to Prosper of Aquitane.[18] Patrick, the traditional apostle of Ireland, probably arrived on his mission later, perhaps after 460, from Britain. A literate, Christian, Roman citizen of privileged background, Patrick had come earlier to Ireland as a captive and slave. After escaping his captors to make his way back to his home in Britain, he returned years later to evangelize and serve Christians in Ireland as their bishop. Patrick's story, preserved in the Book of Armagh, gives a glimpse of the late- and sub-Roman world in which Irish and British cultural interaction took place. Patrick seems to have taken up his mission on his own, without papal or episcopal sanction, and he claimed to have funded himself.[19] The picture is consistent with the comparative tendency towards isolation of Ireland and Britain in the last half of the fifth century, after the Roman withdrawal from Britain and before the Christianisation of the Franks, who were establishing kingdoms on the other side of the Channel. Literacy and book production in this context may well have been small-scale, local, and private, in contrast with the well-established literacy and luxury book production of the wealthy, urbanized Mediterranean where a large audience participated directly in Graeco-Roman culture and manuscripts were produced under the centralized authority of the Church.[20]

Julian Brown has related features of early Irish script, such as that found in the Codex Usserianus Primus, with this early, 'low-end' book production, showing its origins in the cursive half-uncial script of marginal notations and the educated individual's personal use.[21] The Codex Usserianus Primus shares its single-column, long-line block text layout with the earliest Insular luxury gospel manuscripts (Durrow and Durham A.II.10), as well as Late

Antique manuscripts written in *scriptio continua*, or continuous lines of letters without word divisions.[22] The block format served the compression of text. The amount of page space used was minimized, but graphic articulation – word division, punctuation, hierarchies of letter size – facilitated access to the information contained in the text. These concerns for optimal use of materials and access to information speak on the one hand of a small scale operation with limited resources and on the other of a particular kind of literacy which led the Irish to their concern for Late Antique grammatical systems and methods of punctuation. Knowledge of Latin grammar and development of punctuation, which effectively structured sense and grammatical units, provided them with the means of articulating structure in Latin texts and thus of facilitating and controlling the Insular audience's understanding, including their interpretation, of them.[23]

Textual articulation in early Irish manuscripts was accomplished by layout of text in combination with punctuation and decoration in the form of colour in-fills, enlarged letters, and decorative patterns. The Irish viewed punctuation and decoration as 'two aspects of the same thing', as 'inextricably linked' forms of graphic articulation facilitating access to information in a text.[24] The repeated 7-shaped commas marking sense units and chapter divisions in Usserianus can be seen to have been 'translated' in later gospel books to enlarged, sometimes coloured or decorated, initial letters and, in the Book of Kells, figural decoration of varying elaborateness.[25] The division between the Gospels of Luke and Mark in the Old Latin text of Usserianus is emphasized with a cross in the form of the monogram of Christ (Xp) flanked with the letters *alpha* and *omega*, the whole placed within borders composed of shapes resembling punctuation marks and the letter s.[26] The cross itself is outlined with a contour of dots, a device used in Late Antique manuscripts to bestow decorative emphasis upon selected initial letters. The decorative and punctuation forms merge into a symbol of Christ to structure the text. Similar use of the decorated cross appears in three early continental manuscripts dating from the fifth to seventh centuries, including two gospel manuscripts.[27] The cross monogram has been compared in its design, placement, and structural function with the cross carpet pages of later manuscripts, such as the Lindisfarne Gospels,[28] but also it could be compared with the cross form of the four-symbols pages in the Book of Kells and other Insular manuscripts. The repeated 7-shaped commas divide Usserianus's text into sections resembling the chapter divisions of an Old Latin Gospel series, which also may have influenced some of the decorative textual articulation in the Book of Kells.[29]

The gospel book was an important part of the equipment of evangelisation, essential to Christian education at every level. In the Book of Armagh, a short collection of notes, which may be displaced from a seventh-century text by Tírechán, begins with a list of the books and liturgical objects which Patrick distributed to fifty new churches. The list includes the Gospels but not the Psalter although the importance of the Psalter in the early Christian culture of the Scotti, or Irish Celts, is evident in Adomnán's account of the life of St Columba, whose last known writing was a manuscript of the Psalms.[30] Survival of the early to mid seventh-century 'Cathach of St Columba' (Dublin, Royal Irish Academy, s.n.)

further proves the existence of early book copies of the psalms, even though members of monastic communities undoubtedly knew the text by heart from their daily recitation of psalms in the monastic cycle of daily prayer.[31]

St Columba lived during the sixth century, by which time the aristocracy of Ireland had largely accepted Christianity, although the entire society was not yet Christianised.[32] By the beginning of the century the powerful kings of the Irish tribes, such as the Uí Néill, had established colonies along the west coast of Britain, one of the most notable of these being the extension of Dal Riata into western Scotland, whose king eventually became ruler of the colonial Scotti and another group to the East, the Picts.[33] Kings and aristocracy in sixth-century Ireland and Scotland gave financial and political support to the establishment of monastic communities.[34] An aristocrat of the Cenél Conaill branch of the Uí Néill, whose kinsmen became kings of Tara, Columba had been raised for priesthood, and he dedicated his life to spreading monasticism and evangelizing. In 563, following events that suggest his political partisanship, Columba went to Britain on religious exile (*peregrinatio*) where the son of the king of Dal Riata gave him the island of Iona for his monastic community.[35] Columba founded additional communities for anchorites and penitents in Britain and also the monastery at Durrow amongst his Irish foundations. His monasteries were centres of learning and evangelisation, some of them being perhaps what might be called training centres for monastic and clerical leaders.[36] Columba thus began one of the most influential monastic networks (*paruchiae*) of the early Middle Ages, shaping the culture which directly or indirectly became the environment in which the Book of Kells was created.[37]

The abbacy of Iona remained in the hands of the Cenél Conaill. With relatively few exceptions, Iona's leaders came for centuries from Columba's branch of the Uí Néill. In 623, one of the strongest of the Cenél Conaill abbots, Ségéne, assumed leadership of Iona.[38] Ségéne's conservative commitment to the Columban traditions and promotion of the saint's influence can be seen to lie at the root of his three most important actions. In an act benefiting the interests of Iona and also the prestige of his royal relatives, he collected stories of Columba's holiness and possibly commissioned Cumméne, his nephew and later abbot, to write them up.[39] Cumméne's text, which does not survive, provided the source, in the 680s, for Adomnán's *Vita Columbae*, an extant text.[40] Ségéne thus began the Columban community's hagiographic commemoration of its founding saint. This same conservative commitment led him to take an active part in the controversy over the calculation of the date of Easter. The method used by the Columban community differed from that of Churches following the Roman calculation, used in Anglo-Saxon kingdoms and southern Ireland, whose position Ségéne is known to have criticized.[41] For Ségéne, departure from Columba's traditional calculation would have represented a betrayal of his saintly relative and royal house. Even more importantly, Ségéne expanded Iona's political and missionary interests in Ireland and northern Britain by fostering the foundation of new monasteries, one, called Rechra, in the territory of the southern Uí Néill and the other, in 635, on the island of Lindisfarne, in the territory of the Anglo-Saxon Bernician King Oswald, who zealously supported the Columban holiness represented by Lindisfarne's founder, Aidan. Extension of the Columban federation into southern Uí Néill territory in Ireland began the royal patronage that would, in the early ninth century, establish the monastery at Kells and continue to support and promote it for centuries afterward. Lindisfarne's foundation represented growth of important political connections as well, but even more significantly the presence of a large, successful Columban monastery in Northumbria assured the spread of Iona's Christianity throughout the northern Anglo-Saxon kingdom.[42] The situation in Northumbria came to a head nearly fifteen years after Ségéne's death, when the rigidly conservative nature of the Columban tradition began to clash with an increasing awareness of Roman liturgical practices and the broader cultural and political network to which they belonged. At the Synod of Whitby in 664, Colman of Lindisfarne supported Iona's Easter calculation, but his view was defeated by Wilfrid of York, who asserted the superiority of St Peter over Columba.

During the early period of the Columban federation, Pope Gregory the Great had, in 596, initiated his Roman mission to the Anglo-Saxons, a loose affiliation of germanic tribes from the north coasts of the Continent who had established kingdoms in Britain during the fifth century. While the mission was pastoral in its aims, Gregory, himself a monk and zealous supporter of monasticism, chose his monastery's prefect, Augustine, to lead the mission of forty brothers. Gregory's choice of the monk Augustine indicates the importance he placed on administrative and spiritual allegiances: the monks vowed obedience to Augustine, their abbot, and in turn to Gregory in Rome.[43] Arriving in Kent, Augustine and his monks founded sees at Canterbury, London, and Rochester, and directed conversion efforts at the peak of the Anglo-Saxon political and social hierarchy. The central contact point of an ecclesiastical and cultural network between the Anglo-Saxons and Rome had been set in place, putting Kentish Christianity directly in touch with, among other things, Mediterranean book art. The late sixth-century Cambridge 'Gospels of Augustine' (Corpus Christi College, MS 286)[44] almost certainly was brought from the Mediterranean to Kent early in the seventh century, if not with Augustine's mission. Written per cola et commata in uncial script, it was illustrated with at least the one surviving page of small narrative scenes and full-page, naturalistic evangelist portraits, at least one of which, namely the surviving portrait of Luke, incorporated panels of narrative scenes into the picture's architectural frame. It contrasts with Usserianus Primus and speaks of the opulent contemporary book culture brought with the mission from Rome.

Despite setbacks, Augustine's practice of nurturing aristocratic conversion eventually proved effective. The Roman Church in Kent began to attract the attention of Northumbrian nobles, two of whom, Benedict Biscop and Wilfrid of York, became extremely important in determining the nature of Christian culture in Anglo-Saxon England.[45]

Benedict Biscop and Wilfrid started their religious lives at Lindisfarne but were drawn to Canterbury, with its international connections. In 653, the pair set out from Kent for Rome. Although they travelled a good part of the way together, each absorbed different aspects of Mediterranean Christian culture.[46] Wilfrid, a gifted speaker and dyed-in-the-wool churchman, became expert in litigation and ecclesiastic rules, while Biscop, who had spent his early adult life as a secular nobleman, immersed himself in the material and intellectual culture of monasticism.

Upon returning to Northumbria, Wilfrid so impressed the Deiran under-king Alchfrith, son of King Oswy, with his expertise in Roman doctrine that Alchfrith, urged by political rivalry and ambition, pressured his father, a supporter of Ionan traditions, to hold a debate on the Roman and Columban calculation of the date of Easter. The actual issue was the degree of authority permitted variant traditions against Catholic doctrine and practice. Wilfrid's victory at the Synod of Whitby, which he won by citing the authority given by Christ to Peter, resulted in the departure of Bishop Colmán and the Columban community from Lindisfarne.[47] Wilfrid became bishop of York and, from beginnings at Ripon and Hexham, founded his own powerful monastic network observing the Benedictine rule, the monastic rule of Benedict of Nursia, imported from Italy, which would later become the standard. Moreover, Wilfrid's activities reached as well into Ireland through his personal contact with the Anglo-Saxon community at Rath Melsigi. The implications of Wilfrid's Irish involvement for manuscript art, recognized and explored only recently by Ó Cróinín, could point to the first steps clarifying the possible origins of some of the disputed early decorated manuscripts, such as the Echternach Gospels.[48]

Benedict Biscop, also with royal patronage, founded the twin monasteries of Wearmouth (674) and Jarrow (681–82), basing the rule governing their spiritual practice upon the Rule of Benedict of Nursia. Attentive to the visual culture of Christianity and versed in aristocratic embellishment of churches as practised in Italy, he brought artisans from the Continent to build Wearmouth's church of stone, and he bedecked his monasteries with liturgical objects and books collected on his several Roman pilgrimages. He and his successor, Ceolfrid, assembled an exceptional library and scriptorium to support an advanced program of bible study.[49] The scriptorium's most splendid surviving product is the Codex Amiatinus, a colossal pandect of the Bible written in uncial and illustrated with illusionistic frontispieces imitating Late Antique paintings. This context of Mediterranean learnedness, moreover, shaped the intellect and agenda of Jarrow's leading scholar, Bede, who spent his life within it. While the contemplative ideal prominent in the Rule of Benedict may sometimes colour modern views of Biscop's twin monasteries as inward-looking, Wearmouth-Jarrow deeply influenced Northumbrian monasticism and pastoral activity, probably serving as training centres for ecclesiastic and monastic leaders and exerting pressure for romanisation upon other important centres such as Lindisfarne.[50]

In 669 romanisation escalated in Britain with the arrival, in Benedict Biscop's care, of the newly consecrated archbishop of Canterbury, Theodore of Tarsus. A Greek-speaking easterner from Cilicia and one of the most learned theologians of his time, Theodore instituted a school at Canterbury for the study of Greek as well as Latin texts.[51] Moreover, he restructured British and Anglo-Saxon dioceses so that bishoprics were consistently subordinated to Canterbury. As a result, the ecclesiastical network connecting the Anglo-Saxon Church with Rome and the Mediterranean became increasingly efficient in its cultural transformation of Britain, broadening the stream of influences from Italy and the East Mediterranean. The Lindisfarne Gospels were created in this late seventh- and early eighth-century environment of powerful ecclesiastic and artistic influences flowing from the Mediterranean via Canterbury, Wearmouth-Jarrow, and Wilfrid's foundations.[52]

From early in the seventh century, the Irish were aware of Rome's mission. The Roman Church's presence nearby intensified their need to place themselves within the Christian world and its history. Modern discussion may appear to present the attitude of the Columban community as representative of seventh-century Irish Christianity in general, but in fact it was provincial and conservative within the context of Ireland and stood in opposition to vigorous seventh-century Irish reformers, the Romani. As early as 631 the southern Irish Synod of Mágh Léine sent a fact-finding delegation to Rome to confirm data on Easter calculation. Their pilgrimage predated the journeys of Biscop and Wilfrid by thirty years and indicated the southern Irish recognition of papal authority.[53] Cummian, a southern Irish cleric, wrote to Ségéne of Iona urging him to accept the Roman Easter, a message repeated by a papal letter to northern Irish clergy, although neither letter immediately produced the desired effect. Besides the conservative force of Columba's sanctity, papal decrees forbidding marriage between first cousins, rulings which threatened conservation of property within aristocratic families, also encouraged a backlash of adherence to old traditions in the North and elsewhere. The controversies fuelled seventh-century Irish literary production. An outpouring of computistics, law tracts, exegesis, hagiography, and cosmological studies engaged a dialogue to establish the pre-Christian and Christian Irish élite within the new spiritual geography and the history of God's presence on earth.[54]

Máire Herbert has portrayed the late seventh-century abbot of Iona, Adomnán (679–704), as an innovator who envisioned the Columban community's participation in the universal Church.[55] Herbert has also pointed out Adomnán's direct relationship to the royal branch of the Cenél Conaill, suggesting that his *Vita Columbae* promoted a view placing Uí Néill claims to kingship of Ireland under divine approval.[56] Adomnán's broad perspective and royal ties, even more than his visits to Northumbria, might well account for his ability to support the Roman Easter and his attempts to convince Iona to conform to it. Herbert connects his concern for Iona's relationship with secular power and his royal point of view with a Columban drive for primacy in the Irish Church, to which Armagh responded with a promotion of the primacy of St Patrick.[57] Adomnán was unsuccessful in his lifetime in convincing Iona to adopt the Roman calculation of Easter, but he built the intellectual and political bridges needed for the community to join the rest of Christianity while maintaining its founding saint's status and the essence of his traditions.[58]

The Irish world view was expanding. An important role in this expansion was held by the ascetic, spiritual exiles sent out of Ireland as missionaries to the Continent, which brought them directly in touch with the older Churches of Gaul, Spain, and Italy, as well as with the papacy. Having at least the influence exerted by contact with the international Christian culture flooding in next door, Irish missions to the Continent intensified effects at home of exposure to the early medieval world. Starting with Columbanus's mission to Gaul around 590, Irish monasticism, developed for a non-urban social context, had begun to exert a deep influence upon Christianisation north of the Alps.[59] Furthermore, Anglo-Saxon and Irish missionaries returned to Ireland, bringing with them ideas and liturgical objects. The seventh century held the flowering of a rich new context, in which Irish and Anglo-Saxon interaction was easily accomplished because of the presence of Anglo-Saxons in monastic communities in Ireland and in Irish communities on the Continent, as well as the presence of the Irish in Northumbria and Southumbria. The concept of holy exile, or *peregrinatio*, was a powerful one, motivating the spread and interchange of variant forms of monasticism and liturgical practice. The Benedictine ideal of monastic spiritual kinship seems to have overridden to a partial extent conservative ties of natural kinship, the cement of indigenous aristocratic power networks.[60] Irish and Anglo-Saxon missionary activity on the Continent contributed to the eventual triumph of the centralized, universal Church. Moreover, the missions made accessible to the Irish the latest theology, liturgical forms, and Christian doctrine being articulated in Gaul, Spain, and Italy.[61]

The direct cultural and papal contact which the missions opened up to the Irish must also have played an important part in the artistic expression of Insular Christianity as it negotiated its place in the new world of early medieval Europe. Insular manuscript art was developing in kingdoms being shaken loose from their conservative traditions and brought into the collective effort to Christianise the world. The recent studies by Ó Cróinín and Netzer[62] on the broad influence of Irish and Anglo-Saxon missionary links with the Continent have successfully undermined any simplistic picture of seventh- and eighth-century Insular art production as occurring solely in isolated centres, such as Lindisfarne, with narrow links of influence from Rome. By the time the Book of Kells was made Ireland's participation in the universal Church was established and the concept of *peregrinatio* articulated within Irish society. The spirituality of Columbanus represented the world as a pilgrimage, the body as a temporary tent wandering through it. Such belief did not necessarily demand the literal practice of exile. It also allowed small-scale responses more compatible with pastoral needs, such as local pilgrimage or temporary exile.[63] Even more compellingly, however, it evoked an understanding of the world as spiritual time and space.

Christianity spread throughout Irish and Anglo-Saxon society in the eighth century, although the process continued through the early Middle Ages, negotiating Christian and native social ideals.[64] The new religion had become established in Ireland and the Anglo-Saxon kingdoms by a continuing alliance with aristocracy, and then additionally under the cultivating and shaping authority of Rome. The process resulted in the Church's political and economic involvement in both places with magnates, aristocracy, and royalty, who had supported conversion and establishment of monasteries and churches. By the end of the eighth century, interests and identity of ecclesiastics and aristocracy had long been merged. Furthermore, the centralized model of the universal Church had given a new dimension to native competition.

For Irish centres with royal connections, such as Armagh, Rome's most immediate importance was its provision of a model of centralized authority to be imposed upon the diverse and independent Irish Churches. Armagh's purpose in emulating Rome was to establish itself as the head of the Irish Church.[65] Herbert has pointed out that this may well have represented a response to Iona's similar move.[66] The situation in the eighth century then remained one of competition between Churches, indeed on a larger scale because of competition for primacy. But the overlay of centralized control being developed by the powerful ecclesiastic centres did little to simplify the picture. Evolving concepts of episcopacy and the relationship of bishops to monastic centres in control of physical resources took place in the Irish context of independent churches functioning within a patchwork of affiliations and interconnections.[67] Furthermore, strategists at Iona and Armagh linked their drive for primacy with competing branches of the Uí Néill, the political innovators who had been developing a dynastic, territorial hierarchy of kingship since the mid-seventh century. In Ireland, over-king and patriarchal saint intertwined in mutual dependency, intensifying the rivalry.[68]

Christianisation of society had been largely achieved but not without the proliferation of exceedingly wealthy monasteries directly involved in native, secular power. On the other hand, ideals emanating from Rome, and to an extent those resident in Insular Christianity, promoted the concept of spiritual kinship upon which is formed a universal community of the Church, with its hierarchy of clergy, religious, and lay. The Benedictine model of sanctity follows the Roman template of spiritual kinship, fortifying it with monastic ideals of humility, poverty, and chastity. Similar ideals seem to have been expressed by the 'Romani' reformers in Ireland, whose advocacy of the Roman Easter in the seventh century was only one aspect of their promotion of the universal Church centred at Rome. In Anglo-Saxon England and in Ireland, ideals obviously conflicted with actual practice, and supporters of orthodox ideals, whose model dictated intolerance of variant practices as well as Christian universality, advocated reform.

Bede's criticism of aristocratic family monasteries is well known. His criticism and eighth-century calls for reform in documents such as the canons of the Council of Clofesho of 747 may be seen as manifestations of the tension between the centralized ecclesiastical network undergoing development since Theodore's time and the royal and aristocratic monasteries which responded to the expedients of pastoral care on a local level as well as serving the native power structure. While the diocesan network and the monasteries supporting it such as Wearmouth-Jarrow were effective in their promotion of the universal Church, availability of resources and needs for social and political adjustment made the centralization process a lengthy one, with laity in many areas of Britain probably struggling to deal with inadequate pastoral care.[69] The issue of reform concerned authority and the process of imposing, with limited resources, a centralized Christianity upon local, native power structures with which it was still necessary to negotiate in order to continue the process of conversion. In Ireland, the issue of reform was similar in these respects.

Reform in eighth-century Ireland was inevitably complex because of the intertwined pattern of its secularized ecclesiastical structure. Great churches with far-reaching interests had emerged over the seventh century, creating vast networks of religious communities which by the late eighth and early ninth centuries were secularized and removed from practice of the contemplative religious life. Secularization and lapse of monastic contemplative, devotional practices were the deficiencies that reform texts of the eighth and ninth centuries emphatically decried.[70] A movement of religious revival arose in the last half of the eighth century in Ireland, promoting a return to the strict asceticism of seventh-century monasticism. The supporters of this movement were communities engaged in anchoritic practices who called themselves the céli dé or culdees, the 'companions of God.'[71] The céli dé were required, however, to come to terms with the changed ecclesiastic and social structure of eighth- and ninth-century Ireland. They saw that true isolation and permanent exile were no longer possible in this Christianised society where lay and monastic blended together, dependent upon each other. In late eighth- and ninth-century hagiographic and reform texts, instruction to laity and responsibilities to monastic community gained precedence over the earlier ideals of extreme asceticism practised in exile and isolation. Perhaps one of the most important solutions of the religious revival was its promotion of local pilgrimage, making a small-scale version of the holyman's exile accessible to society in general.[72] Possibly the growth of local pilgrimage combined with the zealous competition of ecclesiastic centres, especially royal centres like Iona and Armagh, contributed to the further development in the late eighth and ninth centuries of publicly conspicuous visual art, such as monumental sculpted stone crosses presenting elaborate programmes of visual images.[73] The reform seems to have been strongest in southern Ireland, although two early ninth-century monks of Iona, the abbot Diarmait and martyr Blathmac, appear to have been connected with the céli dé.[74] This may reflect enduring southern support for the general concept of the universal Church over secular interests as well as the continued involvement of Iona in the broader ecclesiastic interests of Ireland.[75] The texts associated with the céli dé suggest not only the tensions, competition, and exigencies driving late eighth- and ninth-century Irish society but also that society's dynamic blending of Christian and secular and its creativity in producing new religious forms in response to its complex, fluctuating needs.

Political rivalries and other events in eighth-century Ireland decisively affected the Ionan federation and led eventually to its founding of the monastery at Kells early in the ninth century, in the territory of the southern Uí Néill. The 'familia' of Columba exerted its strongest presence in Ireland in the eighth century, with Irish Churches becoming increasingly prominent in annalistic accounts of abbatial activities and visits of relics from Iona to the circuit of Columban communities.[76] A period of confusion appears in the textual sources for Iona's history in the first part of the eighth-century, following the death of Adomnán. Herbert and others connect the lack of clarity with the return of tension at Iona between conservatives and those favouring the Roman position on the Easter controversy.[77] The positions of Columban Churches in Ireland and Scotland on the question remain unknown because the accounts focus on Iona, but it is possible that groundwork laid by Adomnán and, decades later, the Anglo-Saxon bishop, Egbert, in Pictland and Ireland may have influenced Iona's decision in 716 to adopt the Roman Easter, made, according to Bede, because of Egbert's preaching on the topic to the community.[78] Iona continued to press its interests and those of its royal allies, the Cenél Conaill, by circulation of relics, abbatial visits, and renewal of Adomnán's Law, which protected women, children, and clerics from violence, 'a shrewd blend of social concern and self-interest' on the part of Iona.[79]

The regularity of such activities in the first half of the eighth century may have occurred in response to the increasing rivalry of the Cenél Conaill and another northern Uí Néill clan, the Cenél nEogain, but they may have represented simply a continuation of Iona's normal presence, confirming Columba's authority.[80] In any case, the political situation was volatile, with murder and other forms of violence being commonplace means of gaining kingship. Beginning in the 730s, the rival Cenél nEogain seized the kingship of Tara, or over-kingship of Ireland, from the Cenél Conaill king, Flaithbertach, whom they sent into religious life at Armagh, the Church of Patrick. The first Cenél nEogain king of Tara and new Uí Néill overlord, Aed Allán, promoted the interests of Armagh and promulgated the Law of Patrick, which superseded Adomnán's Law. The Cenél nEogain continued cultivating mutual interests with Armagh in following decades.[81]

Nevertheless, developments in southern Uí Néill territory strengthened Columban royal connections. The Clann Cholmáin king of Meath, Domnall mac Murchada, killed Aed Allán and ascended to the kingship of Tara while retaining associations with a monastery, possibly the Columban community at Durrow. He promulgated in 753 a *Lex Coluim Cille*, 'Law of Columba,' which may have answered urgent contemporary social needs but also, like the Law of Adomnán, served the interests of secular and ecclesiastic powers by requiring payment of taxes. Columba's community apparently then had obtained royal support in southern Uí Néill territory, raising Durrow to prominence among midland monasteries.[82] For most of the remainder of the century, Clann Cholmáin held the kingship of Tara and continued the promotion of Columba and his community.[83]

In 797, however, Iona's influence in Ireland diminished with the succession of another Cenél nEogain leader, Aed Oirdnide, to the kingship of Tara. Aed Oirdnide made certain the truncation of Clann Cholmáin's power by dividing Meath between the late king's sons. This extraordinary action insured the decline of Columba's influence. Aed's second name, 'Oirdnide,' refers to his unprecedented royal ordination by the Abbot of Armagh. The king's ordination, the only one recorded in the *Annals of Ulster* for the eighth or early ninth centuries, may indicate the realization by the Irish *literati* of looming political chaos and their recognition of a need to elevate Armagh's authority with visible expression.[84] In any case, a royal ordination ritual, possibly with scripturally-based anointing, would express Patrick's divine right of involvement in royal succession and moreover make tangible the maturing concept of Irish *imperator*.[85] The tensions and lessening Columban influence became more pronounced with the first Viking raids on Ireland and Britain, including a series of three attacks on Iona. Two attacks, in 802 and 806, were destructive enough to hasten the building of another monastery, at the apparently royal site of Kells in Meath in southern Uí Néill territory. The inland monastery most likely was intended to provide safekeeping for members of the Ionan community and its treasures.[86] It appears to have had only secondary importance until the late ninth or tenth centuries.[87]

Iona's relationship with Scottish leaders also changed in the late eighth and early ninth centuries, due to Iona's turn towards Ireland during this period and also to the shift of Scottish royal ecclesiastical centres to the East, to Perth and Fife, strengthening ties with Northumbria. This political rift is important to the historical background of the Book of Kells because of the striking artistic similarities of some of the manuscript's decoration with Pictish art, pointed out by Isabel Henderson.[88] In 717, the Pictish king had expelled the Columban community, but as important as this must have been politically, Columba himself and his monks were still influential in a broad sense in Scotland, the monks probably being responsible for the success of the céli dé there.[89] Also, about 849, the Scottish king, Kenneth Mac Alpin, installed the relics of Columba in his royal church, possibly Dunkeld, in Scotland when the saint's remains on Iona were divided between the abbot and king.[90] Moreover, the intensifying Viking raids had the effect of driving the community of Iona into Ireland, where their cultural roots lay, instead of strengthening their bond with the Scottish kings, which would have required extension into eastern Scotland.[91] While Columba's abbots became politically separated from the Scottish kings, the possibility of a Scottish or Pictish origin for the Book of Kells cannot be totally ruled out, especially if one accepts the art historical connections recently advanced between Columba and the manuscript's iconography.[92] Even if one were to favour a late date of origin, after the early ninth century, a Pictish origin would remain a possibility because of the presence of Columba's relics, after 849, in a Scottish royal centre and the continuing influence of his monks.[93] The manuscript's path to Kells, however, would have to be traced.[94]

Political and artistic developments in Anglo-Saxon England, during the mid-eighth to early ninth centuries, present further important elements of the broader context of the Book of Kells. Art historical scholarship has paid little attention to the connections until Michelle Brown's recent studies of the Book of Cerne and Southumbrian manuscripts.[95] As she reminds art historians and palaeographers, the Irish and British participated conspicuously in the early Church in Mercia, beginning with the first bishop of the Mercians, an Irishman named Diuma, and Chad in the last half of the seventh century. Even though romanisation affected the Mercian Church in the late seventh and early eighth centuries as it did the rest of the Anglo-Saxon Churches, ecclesiastic connections with Ireland continued throughout the eighth and early ninth centuries.[96] In addition to the artistic and ecclesiastical ties, Mercia and Ireland were experiencing similar political developments.

In both places, political events were in large part determined by attempts to impose centralized hegemony over local structures. Overlordship had been a part of the political picture of the Irish and Anglo-Saxons all along, but the situation differed from that of earlier periods in at least two ways. Firstly, the ecclesiastical model of papal primacy and, more recently, imperial political models had been influencing ideologies of rule and causing tensions between overlords, episcopacy, and local power structures. Secondly, Christianity had permeated both societies. The influence of Rome had reached through the culture, driving, among other things, an enduring artistic production incorporating Mediterranean traditions of book art and providing the context for the merging and mixing of native forms. Ideological Christian texts promoting the universal Church and expanded Christian kingship, like Adomnán's *Vita Columbae* and Bede's *Historia*, had been operating within the societies through the eighth century. Furthermore, Charlemagne was directing an impressive Christian imperial example on the Continent.

Tensions, competition, and rivalry on a large scale characterized contemporary Southumbria, where Offa of Mercia (757–796) was consistently repressing political authority of subject kingdoms, as well as attempting to control ecclesiastical administration. His actions seem directed toward funnelling economic resources to himself, but this was supported by ideological symbols of monarchy, including a royal anointing ceremony to express the concept of divine right and to obtain Canterbury's ecclesiastical approval of the perpetuation of Mercian dynastic rulership over Southumbria. He cultivated relationships with Charlemagne and the Pope, gaining from them not only influence but also expertise in imperial culture. As in Ireland, the resulting centralization was a far cry from simplified order. Offa's method involved buying the loyalty of local leadership which he had installed, superseding pre-existing royal grants, legal claims, and local authority. His policies resulted in a disordered mass of conflicting claims and intertwined dependencies.[97] Michelle Brown has related the development of impressive scripts and decoration in Mercian book art to this tension-filled, competitive society in which individuals were increasingly forced to press their interests and visual ostentation was the order of the day.[98] The Church was not excluded from Offa's expansion of power, and his attempts to subordinate Canterbury and other centres in Kent caused ecclesiastics to strengthen their ties with Rome and the Continent as a means of defending their communities and resources from the king's predatory policies. The multiple royal and ecclesiastical connections with the Continent and Rome brought a flood of Mediterranean influences which, combined with the new needs for display, decisively transformed Anglo-Saxon visual culture into a classicism exemplified by the decoration of the Barberini Gospels (Vatican, Biblioteca Apostolica Vaticana, Barb. lat. 570) and Tiberius Bede (London, British Library, Cotton MS Tiberius C.II).[99]

If the Book of Kells was made in the late eighth or early ninth century, its historical and cultural context differed in some very important respects from that of the Lindisfarne Gospels. The culture of Christianity had made conspicuous marks on the terrain, transforming both the physical landscape and the intellectual, but the changes had not been one-sided. One of the most striking indicators of the extent to which it had permeated and reacted with society may be seen in Ireland in the ascendancy of vernacular literacy in the eighth and ninth centuries. The extent of Christianisation is especially noticeable in the reshaping of Latin literary forms to vernacular traditions. This two-way process of transforming Irish society to a Christian one and making Christianity relevant to the native *gens* resulted, by the ninth century, in the vernacular assuming its place as the language of hagiography and religious instruction.[100] Moreover, the model of the universal Church and its implicit concept of political centralization had become influential in ecclesiastical and secular culture, fuelling large-scale competition and promotion of saints. It can hardly be coincidence that the papal anointing of Charlemagne's sons, Pippin and Louis, in Rome in 781, was followed in 787 by the anointing of Offa's son in Rome and by the only ordination recorded in the

Annals of Ulster, an event which also moved Armagh decidedly closer to primacy.[101] Even though ordination, albeit anointing only implied, was promoted in Adomnán's *Vita Columbae* and the *Collectio Canonum Hibernensis*, it appears that actual kingly ordination based on biblical models came to be performed only after emergent large-scale centralization had created a need for tangible expression of ecclesiastical legitimization and divine sanction of dynasty.[102] The extent of assimilation of Christianity can be seen also in Ireland where great monastic towns blurred distinctions of ecclesiastic and lay.[103] Even though monasteries and the Church in general in late seventh- and early eighth-century Northumbria undoubtedly were involved in secular political struggles and were supported by royal patronage, the picture of later eighth-century Anglo-Saxon England, Scotland, and Ireland is one of much more far-reaching Christianisation than the context of the Lindisfarne Gospels where italianate art and Christianity were still imports just beginning to be synthesized into the fabric of the culture.

Within this context of intertwined ecclesiastical and secular interests in which authority derived from historical models and in which native *gens* desired and were compelled to assimilate themselves, their ancestors, and founding holymen with universal Christian history, a need to look back to the archaic persisted and thrived. The Book of Kells participated in and reflected this world: it combined features of the manuscripts attributed to the early saints with Mediterranean features found in manuscripts like the Lindisfarne Gospels and with the latest innovations seen in contemporary manuscripts. Its art was tied directly to its functions in this context and its meaning to its audience.

Notes to Introduction

1   *See*, for example, the publications of T. J. Brown, M. B. Parkes, and J. J. G. Alexander cited in the bibliography.

2   For example, Alexander, 1978, p.75; Henderson, 1987; *also* in a study by a scholar of Old English literature, Stevick, 1994, pp.227–33.

3   Brown, 1996, pp.117–18, 122, 124–5, 167–76; Brown, 1993, p.78; Brown, 1994, exploring in detail the suggestions of Henry (1974, pp.163, 165, 214). The Barberini Gospels, although likely to have been produced in Southumbria is also linked with Northumbria; *see* discussions of Alexander, 1978, p.61; Brown in Keynes and Brown, 1991, pp.195, 205, and Brown, 1996, as cited *above*.

4   For recent summaries and bibliography of the often contentious discussion and its scholarship, *see* Nordenfalk, 1987; Campbell and Lane, 1993, pp 53–4; Nees, 1993; Meehan, 1994, pp.90–2. *Also*, Alexander, 1978, pp.30–1, 73.

5   *See*, for example, Lowe, *CLA* II, pp.xvi–xix.

6   Brown, 1972; Henry, 1974, p.216; Alexander, 1978, p.73; Henderson, 1987, p.6; Alexander, 1990, pp.288–9; Brown, 1994, p.343. For a discussion of the tenuous nature of the assumptions on which dating and place of origin are based, *see* Meehan, 1994, pp.90–2.

7   Doherty, 1991, pp.54–5; Ó Corráin, 1994, pp.15–28.

8   Sharpe, 1982; Sharpe, 1984a; *see also* C. Doherty, 1991. Other excellent studies of the Book of Armagh and the Book of Kells which nonetheless direct discussion at seventh– and early eighth-century questions and sources: Stevenson, 1990; Ó Corráin 1994.

9   *See* Wallace-Hadrill, 1988, pp.xxviii–xxix, 159–61; Smyth, 1984, 21–35, 75–6, 130–40; Mayr-Harting, 1991, pp.42–4, 117–20; Stafford, 1985, pp.97–8; Hollis, 1992, pp.15–19, 67–74, 120–30, 218–70; Bassett, 1992, pp.13–15. Bede, however, expresses admiration of Irish evangelism; *see* Wright, 1993, pp.42–3, as well as the extended discussion of Goffart, 1988, pp.235–328.

10 On the Northumbrian bias of manuscripts scholarship, *see* Ó Cróinín, 1982; 1984; 1989. On the complexity of Northumbrian influence, *see* Netzer, 1994a; Netzer, 1993. The work of I. Henderson (1982, 1987) pointing out the close resemblance of Pictish sculpture and Insular manuscript art has also served as an important counter to the Irish-Northumbrian dichotomy.

11 Ó Corráin, Breatnach, and Breen, 1984; Ó Corráin, 1986, 1987, 1994; Carney, 1969, 1976; Bischoff, 1976; Lapidge and Sharpe, 1985; Carey, 1989; for summaries of scholarship *see* Patterson, 1992, pp.3–61, McCone, 1990, pp.1–28; and Ó Cróinín, 1995, pp.8–13.

12 Witness the well-known studies of manuscripts terminating at AD 800: Lowe, *CLA*; McGurk, 1961; Nordenfalk, 1977b; Henderson, 1987. Some recent exceptions have been Alexander, 1978; Dodwell, 1982; Ryan, 1987; Youngs, 1989; Webster and Backhouse, 1991; Spearman and Higgitt, 1993. *See* the recent arguments of Netzer (1994a, pp.60–1, 81–3; 1994b) against Friend's 1939 assertion of a Carolingian model for beast canon tables. Another important exception in historical study is Herbert, 1988.

13 *See* recent discussions and bibliography in O'Sullivan, 1994a; O'Sullivan, 1985, pp.353–4; Brown, 1989; Ó Cróinín, 1989; Ó Cróinín, 1987; Ó Cróinín, 1984; Ó Cróinín, 1982; Netzer, 1989; Bruce-Mitford, 1989; Henderson, 1987, pp.54–5, 91–7.

14 G. Henderson (1987, pp.179–98) has written on its possible political context of Ireland and Iona, c.750–800.

15 T. J. Brown, 1982, 1984. *See also* Bischoff, 1990, pp.83–90.

16 Stevenson, 1989, 1990; Harvey, 1987

17 Mytum, 1992, pp.22–52.

18 *Chronicon*, §1307, cited in Dumville, 1984, pp.16–7; *see also* Bourke, 1993, p.4.

19 Ó Cróinín, 1995, pp.23–7; de Paor, 1993, 14–25, 38–45, 88–95; Bourke, 1993, pp.7–8; Sharpe, 1984a, pp.71–2; Thompson, 1980, pp.12–27.

20 Brown, 1980, p.9; Brown, 1982, pp.102–5; Brown, 1984, pp.311–16.

21 1980; 1982; 1984. *See also* the discussion and examples in Brown, 1990, pp.28–9, 48–57. For alternative opinions, *see* Bischoff's comments on the origins of Irish scripts, 1990, pp.83–8; and O'Sullivan, 1994b.

22 T. J. Brown, 1984, p.326; Vezin, 1987, p.54; Verey, 1980, p.17.

23 Parkes, 1993, pp.23–6; Parkes 1987, pp.16–23; Irvine, 1986, pp.19, 25–7, 38; Irvine, 1994, 280–8.

24 Parkes, 1993, p.25; *see also* Parkes, 1993, pp.23–6, 175; Parkes, 1987, p.23; McGurk, 1961b. Parkes, 1993, p.25, also explains how the scribes of the 'Cathach' of St Columba (Dublin, Royal Irish Academy, s.n.) 'exploited the decorative potential of the [7-shaped] mark,' and the ways in which 'the Irish feeling for punctuation dominated their decorative principles.'

25 Farr, 1994, pp.437–8, and Pl. 67; and the discussions in Chapter 2, pp.80–2, and Chapter 3, pp.122–31, 132 and Appendix 2.

26 Alexander, 1978, No. 1, Ill. 1.

27 The Valerianus Gospels (Munich, Bayerische Staatsbibliothek CLM 6224), the small copy of the Gospel of John from Chartres (Paris, Bibliothèque nationale lat. 10439), and the Bologna Lactantius from North Africa (Bologna, Biblioteca Universitaria 701); *see* T. J. Brown, 1984, pp.311–12; Nordenfalk 1947; Nordenfalk 1970, pp.63–5; McGurk, 1961, No. 60; Alexander 1978, p.27; Bischoff 1990, p.24.

28 Alexander, 1978, p.27; Bischoff, 1967, pp.286–8, also points out cross forms on early book covers.

29 *See* Chapters 2, pp.80–6, and 3, pp.119–32; *also* Farr, 1994, 440–3; de Bruyne, 1914, pp.506, 513.

30 Stevenson, 1990, pp.19–20.

31 Clancy and Markus, 1995, pp.22–5; Openshaw, 1993.

32 *See* Herbert, 1988, for detailed study of Columba and Iona. *Also*, Smyth, 1984, pp.84–115.

33 Clancy and Markus, 1995, pp.4–5.

34 MacNiocaill, 1990, p.27.

35 Smyth, 1984, pp.92–100.

36 Sharpe, 1992, pp.101–9.

37 Herbert, 1988; Clancy and Markus, 1995, pp.10–11.

38 On Ségéne, *see* Herbert, 1988, pp.40–3.

39 Herbert, 1988, pp.18–19, 24–5, 134–5.

40 Herbert, 1988, pp.136–50; edition in *Adamnán's Life of Columba*, ed. A. O. and M. O. Anderson.

41 Walsh and Ó Cróinín, 1988.

42 Herbert, 1988, pp.42–5, 68–108.

43 Mayr-Harting, 1991, pp.59–61; Amos, 1987, pp.169–70.

44 Lowe, *CLA* II, p.4, no. 126; G. Henderson, 1982; Brown, 'Appendix,' in G. Henderson, 1982, pp.33–45. For illustrations, *see* Weitzmann, 1977, PLATES 41, 42.

45 The following on Wilfrid and Biscop is based on Mayr-Harting, 1991, pp.103–59; Bede, *Historia Ecclesiastica*, III.25, V.19, ed. Plummer, 1896, pp.181–9, 321–30, tr. L. Sherley-Price, 1968, pp.185–92, 305–12, and *Lives of the Abbots*, I–IV, tr. D. H. Farmer, 1983, pp.185–200.

46 Ó Carragáin, 1994a, pp.1–27.

47 *See also* Herbert 1988 pp.44–6, on the effects of the Whitby decision on Iona, and Mayr-Harting's updated comments on Alchfrith, Wilfrid, and Whitby (1991) pp.7–9.

48 Ó Cróinín, 1984, pp.21–6; Ó Cróinín, 1987, pp.40–1.

49 Parkes, 1982.

50 Thacker, 1992, pp.140–2, 153.

51 Webster and Backhouse, 1991, pp.71–7; Lapidge, 1986; Lapidge, 1988.

52 Brown, 1982, p.108; Parkes, 1987, p.25; Henderson, 1987, pp.119–20.

53 Ó Carragáin, 1994a, pp.1–2; Sharpe, 1984a, pp.65–8.

54 Ó Corráin, 1994, pp.16–21; *see also* the important works of Ó Cróinín and Walsh, and the literary studies of Carney, Carey, and McCone, although these focus on later vernacular literature.

55 Herbert, 1988, pp.47–56.

56 *See also* Enright, 1985a, pp.5–78; Enright, 1985b.

57 Herbert, 1988, pp.53–4; Sharpe, 1992, 1984a; Doherty, 1991.

58 Herbert, 1988, p.55. *See also* Smyth, 1984, pp.116–26, 129–40, on Adomnán.

59 James, 1988, pp.129–37.

60 *See* Mayr-Harting, 1976, on Bede's expression of this ideal and its tension with Anglo-Saxon society.

61 Ó Corráin, 1994, pp.15–16; Hughes, 1966, 91–102; Mytum, 1992, pp.77–9.

62 *See* Netzer (1989, 1993, 1994a) on Insular manuscript production on the Continent, Ó Cróinín (1984, 1987, 1989) on historic context.

63 Hughes, 1966, pp.91–2; *see also* Bitel, 1990, pp.222–34, on the social context and development of concepts and practice of exile and pilgrimage, 6th to 9th centuries.

64 *See*, for example, Ó Corráin, 1981; Hollis, 1992.

65 Sharpe, 1992, 1984a; Doherty, 1991.

66 Herbert, 1988, pp.53–4.

67 Sharpe, 1984a, 68–72; Sharpe, 1992; Etchingham, 1991, 1993, 1994.

68 Henderson, 1987, pp.180–3; Enright, 1985a, pp.48–51.

69 Thacker, 1992, pp.151–2, 164–5; Foot, 1992, pp.220–5; Thacker, 1983. For a concise summary of conflicts of ecclesiastic and aristocratic landholding in the Anglo-Saxon period, *see* Bailey, 1988, pp.112–13.

70 Sharpe, 1992, p.107. Sharpe cites the texts associated with the Máel Rúain of Tallaght.

71 O'Dwyer, 1981.

72 Bitel, 1990, pp.115–44, 228–34; Mac Niocaill, 1990, pp.29–31; Hughes, 1966, pp.173–7.

73 *See also*, however, Edwards, 1990, pp.114, 118, 121, on isolated sites associated with the céli dé. The reformers were reacting against the opulence of contemporary monasteries. On the other hand, these sites were often near large monastic centres, were visited by pilgrims, and had monumental stone sculpture. For example, Monaincha, an important pilgrimage site, began as a seventh-century hermitage, but in the late eighth century became associated with the reform. By the twelfth century, it was 'one of the four great places of pilgrimage in medieval Ireland' (Harbison, 1991, pp.132–3). For early monuments at Irish pilgrimage sites, *see* Herity, 1989.

74 Clancy and Márkus, 1995, p.17; O'Dwyer, 1981, 50–4; Hughes, 1966, p.182.

75 Stevenson, 1989, p.163, has commented on the possibility of a more comfortably merged Christianity and secular culture in the South due to a history of contact with Rome since the late sixth century and Christianisation possibly as early as 400, whereas the Uí Néill probably were Christianised in the sixth century.

76 Herbert, 1988, pp.57–63.

77 Herbert, 1988, pp.57–9.

78 Smyth, 1984, pp.138–9.

79 Herbert, 1988, pp.50–1; Bannerman, 1993, pp.18–20, 24; Doherty, 1984, pp.96–7.

80 Herbert, 1988, pp.61–2, argues the latter.

81 Herbert, 1988, pp.63–4; Henderson, 1987, pp.183–4.

82 Herbert, 1988, pp.65–6.

83 Henderson, 1987, p.184, suggests that Columban asceticism 'may have been the central theme' of the

Synod of Tara in 780 and points out Donnchad's alleged dishonouring of Patrick's relics, recorded in the *Annals of Ulster*, 789.

84 The ordination may have taken place in either 797, the date of his succession to Uí Néill overlordship, or in 804, as Binchy (1958, p.119) suggested, at the Synod of Armagh.

85 Enright, 1985, pp.9, 34–5, 48–51, 62–73; Charles-Edwards, 1994, pp.117–19; Herbert, 1988, pp.67, 71–2; G. Henderson, 1987, p.209, note 54.

86 Herbert, 1988, pp.66–7.

87 Herbert, 1988, pp.72–87.

88 Henderson, 1993, p.216; 1987; 1982; Henry (1974, 216–18) had brought up this point, also, in support of her attribution of the Book of Kells to Iona and Kells.

89 Clancy and Márkus, 1995, p.17.

90 Herbert, 1988, p.72; Bannerman, 1993, pp.29–47.

91 Smyth, 1984, pp.185–8.

92 O'Reilly, 1994, 345–58; Meyvaert, 1989; Henderson, 1987, pp.131–94. Brown (1972) first suggested an origin in Scotland or Pictland.

93 As late as 865 an abbot of Iona died in Pictland (Herbert, 1988, p.73).

94 A few possibilities exist, most supposing arrival via Iona. One would be that it was among the 'precious objects' or minna of Columba brought to Kells from Iona in 878 (Mac Niocaill, 1990, p.31), an event which marked Kells's rise to preeminence among Columban monasteries. This would imply that the Book of Kells was made at Iona but does not rule out production elsewhere in Scotland or even Northumbria. G. Henderson (1987, pp.32, 55, 185–94) attributes the Book of Durrow to 'the Columban Church in England,' suggesting its route to Durrow via Iona, with arrival in Ireland in 878 in the company of Columba's shrine and the Book of Kells, which he attributes to Iona, under royal patronage, and associates with the shrine.

95 Brown, 1996, pp.114–18, 120–1; 147–55, 176; 1986, pp.133–4; 1994; 1993, especially pp.77–8. Her interesting suggestions of similarities between themes of the prayers in the Book of Cerne and iconography presented by illustrations in the Book of Kells seem completely convincing, although I see no reason why fol. 202v, Book of Kells, can not depict the Lucan version instead of or as well as the 'Temptation passage from Matthew' (*see* Brown, 1996, p.114). The thematic connections made are further strengthened by the specific reverberations of text and images in the two manuscripts, such as the Cerne prayer 'Protege me d(omi)ne scuto veritatis tuae …' (Kuypers, 1902, p.223) and the significance of the Temptation of Christ image, interpreted in a Lenten context, as I propose for the Book of Kells.

96 Brown, 1994, p.342; Brown, 1996, p.118.

97 Brooks, 1984, pp.111–42; Keynes and Brown, 1991, 193–4.

98 Brown, 1986, pp.133–4; Brown, 1994.

99 Brown, 1996, pp.16–18.

100 Sharpe, 1991, pp.21–2.

101 Herbert, 1988, pp.67, 71.

102 Enright, 1985, pp.9–10; *see also* Charles-Edwards, 1994, especially his discussion pp.107–11, 117–19. The *Collectio Canonum Hibernensis* is dated *c.*700–725; *see* Lapidge and Sharpe, 1985, pp.156–7, for bibliography.

103 Ó Corráin, 1994, 28–32; Ó Corráin, 1987; Sharpe, 1992; Doherty, 1985.

THE PLATES

PLATE I Book of Kells, fol. 202v, Temptation of Christ

PLATE II Book of Kells, fol. 203r, Luke 4.1

PLATE III Book of Kells, fol. 114r, Passion of Christ

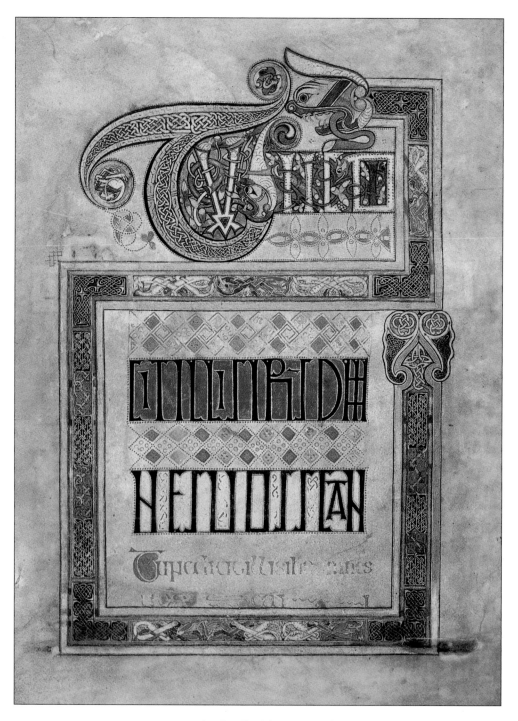

PLATE IV Book of Kells, fol. 114v, Matthew 26.31

PLATE V Book of Kells, fol. 7v, Virgin and Child with Angels

PLATE VI Book of Kells, fol. 32v, Enthroned Christ

PLATE VII Book of Kells, fol. 124r, Matthew 27.38

PLATE VIII Book of Kells, fol. 292r, Incipit, the Gospel of John

CHAPTER ONE

————◄○►————

Gospel Manuscripts and Early Medieval Liturgies

Liturgical Functions of Gospel Manuscripts

READING passages, or pericopes, from the Gospels has formed part of the liturgy of the mass since perhaps as early as the middle of the second century.[1] The pericope for each day was selected to reflect the themes of the season or feast day on which it was read. The reading from the Gospel, also called the Gospel lection, was preceded by a reading from the Epistles or Acts of the Apostles. In very early liturgies, an Old Testament lection preceded both. The lections were followed by a sermon or homily, interpreting the scriptural themes for the audience, whether lay, monastic, or inclusive of both. Gospel lections were less prominent in the liturgy of the office, or daily round of prayer observed in monasteries. The opening phrase of the day's Gospel lection, however, was sometimes recited before the reading of a sermon on the Gospel pericope, usually taken from the writings of one of the Church fathers, such as Augustine, Bede, or Jerome.[2] In the early Middle Ages, the cycle of lections was not standardised. Lection systems of different regions, even different Churches, varied widely. The patristic and scriptural readings for the office, in particular, were variable, chosen by the abbot of each monastery.[3]

Gospel books had at least two important uses directly connected with their function as textual objects which could be read.[4] They were objects of contemplation and study, their text ruminated upon (the practice of *ruminatio*) to reveal many levels of hidden meaning and connections with other biblical texts. This contemplation formed part of the daily study of monks and nuns, the *lectio divina*.[5] Also they had a public dimension. Gospel books were visible, tangible, liturgical objects signifying the authority of the Gospels as the word of God. The Gospel book's presence in the liturgy and the status of the deacon as its caretaker are clear from discussions of its handling during the mass and exegesis on the spiritual significance of the deacon's duties.[6] The book held a prominent place not only in the liturgy of the mass but also in the liturgy of baptism, the importance of its visibility being absolutely clear in early descriptions of rituals.[7]

While reading, especially reading for the liturgy, can leave its mark upon a page in many different ways, there were two ways of indicating liturgical lections and their feasts in a Gospel manuscript. The method that became most frequently used after the ninth century, although it existed much earlier, was to list the feast days of the year and their pericopes. Such lists, called *capitulare evangeliorum* or capitularies, were usually placed with the prefatory material at the beginning of the Gospel book. The most well-organised capitularies refer to the Eusebian sections or other sets of chapter numbers indicated in the margins of the pages of Gospel text. Often, however, the lists are ambiguous in some way, such as the lists in the Lindisfarne Gospels without indication of incipits (beginnings) of lections, so that their actual use in the reading of the book cannot be established beyond doubt.[8] The method used in most early Gospel manuscripts was marginal notation of the feast day beside the lection's incipit.[9] The relationship of these markings to the actual reading of the text is often unclear. Sometimes notation of feast day was not considered necessary, for whatever reason, and the lection's incipit was marked with a cross, often a 'skeletal' cross of five points. Some manuscripts were 'glossed' with interlinear and marginal indications of lections by indentation of the folio's surface with a stylus. Most marginally noted lection systems also display evidence of considerable alteration over long periods of time, the minimal notations presenting a challenge to the palaeographer's skill in dating them.[10] In another method, Gospel pericopes read in the mass might be written out in a separate book and arranged according to the liturgical year, creating the type of book called a lectionary, evangeliary, or evangelistary, but such books seem to have been rare in the Insular period. Only a few surviving fragments provide evidence of their existence.[11]

Modern scholars sometimes assert that large-scale luxury Gospel books like the Book of Kells would not have been read from during the liturgy.[12] The actual function of such books as a class, whether purely for display or for reading, in fact remains unproven either way. Careful study and examination of early medieval Gospel manuscripts suggests that opulently decorated as well as plain books were used for liturgical reading. At least one early illustrated Gospel book from the East, the Rabula Gospels, was made at a monastery expressly for reading in the liturgy, and two Insular luxury Gospels from the late eighth century, the Barberini and St Petersburg Gospels, have marginal notations for liturgical lections.[13] Furthermore, Alcuin wrote prefatory poems for ninth-century Carolingian bibles that tell of the luxurious manuscripts' purposes as ornaments of the Church and for reading aloud to the Church's community.[14] One may also ask why a luxury book like the Lindisfarne Gospels was given a capitulary list. Even if the book was not used publicly in the liturgy, is it possible that somehow the list expresses the Gospels' connections with a public context?

Decorated books often present overlays of subsequent markings to adapt or update the manuscript for liturgical reading. For example, in the late eighth- or early ninth-century Breton Gospels of St Gatien (Paris, Bibl. nat., nouv. acq. 1587, fol. 2v) an X was incised into the text of Mt. 1.18 to indicate the beginning of the Roman lection, which falls not at the enlarged and decorated monogram of Christ but at the next sentence, beginning 'Cum esset …'.[15] Marginal liturgical notations, dated to the early eighth century, occur in Durham A.II.17, and the text of the Baptism of Christ and the Lucan genealogy in the same manuscript were pointed, probably in the late tenth century, for chanting in the Epiphany liturgy.[16] Lections for the mass of the dead are indicated with skeletal crosses in the Stonyhurst Gospel of St John, a small 'relic' book that was placed in St Cuthbert's tomb.[17] Passion texts in the large-format Macregol Gospels were marked, probably in the tenth century, for reading by three voices (FIG. 23). Liturgy formed an ever-present frame of reference for texts, often evoked in various ways by the decoration and graphic articulation of Gospel books of all sizes, even one sealed away from human view like the Stonyhurst Gospel in Cuthbert's tomb. This small copy of the Gospel of St John may have been read from for the funerary liturgy, possibly even that of St Cuthbert, but the liturgical markings may equally have been believed to have a significance within Cuthbert's tomb. Gospel manuscripts of all types frequently display an accretion of markings, corrections, and glosses tracking their use for liturgical reading as well as for study and contemplation.

Moreover, the status of nearly any book could change. Book shrines were made for aging 'pocket Gospels', changing their status from working book to relic. They were made as well for venerable, large luxury books, as known from King Flann's enshrining of the Book of Durrow as a relic of Columba and the actual example of the Lough Kinnale shrine, recently discovered in the surprising context of a crannog.[18] Very few early Gospel books seem to embody the concept of the pristine, absolutely correct text, used only in a single, originally-intended way.

The Book of Kells and its Full-Page Images

The Book of Kells presents a modified Vulgate text of the Gospels, with prefatory material, in an unusually large format.[19] The manuscript is heavily embellished with decoration so detailed and extraordinary that, in spite of its apparently unfinished state, the book stands among the most magnificent western manuscripts ever produced. Its cycle of images and ornament includes nearly every type of decoration of text and page known in Insular manuscripts: elaborate beast canon tables, a carpet page, evangelist portraits, four-symbols pages, Chi-rho monogram, interlinear decoration and decorated letters within the text.[20] An unusually large number of folios present full-page images: one carpet page, three four-symbols pages, twelve folios presenting decorated full-page incipits or short sections, and six full-page images of human figures. Two of the latter represent the manuscript's surviving evangelist portraits. Four others depict Christ.

Of these full-page depictions of Christ, only two can be called true illustrations: the Temptation of Christ, on fol. 202v, (PLATE I) and the so-called 'Arrest of Christ', on fol. 114r (PLATE III, 'Passion of Christ'). The other two (the Virgin and Child, fol. 7v, PLATE V, and the Christ Enthroned, fol. 32v, PLATE VI) may be more accurately termed 'portraits'.[21] The differing relation of portraits and illustrations to the text of the manuscript is perhaps most tellingly reflected by the different ways in which the folios carrying them are bound into the codex, which is known to have been rebound several times.

The two portraits are presented on stubs or single folios, the backs of which are blank.[22] Even though probably originally conceived with a defined significance and purpose, they cannot be associated readily with any part of the Gospel text or prefatory material. Thus, their original positions within the manuscript remain unknown and their intended purposes can only be guessed.[23] In this respect, they resemble the carpet page, also on a stub, one side of which is blank. The carpet page and the Christ Enthroned are now paired facing each other at fols 33r and 32v, at the text of the genealogy according to Matthew.[24] The miniature depicting the Virgin and Child, fol. 7v, now faces the beginning of the *breves causae* of Matthew, preceding the Gospel text.[25] Although a later binder may have placed the picture at this point because of the incipit 'Nativitas' of the chapter summaries, the illustration represents the Virgin and Child enthroned with angels and not the Nativity or Adoration of the Magi, the events which begin the facing *breves causae*.[26]

Unlike the portraits, the two illustrations are carried on original bifolia having no blank sides.[27] The depiction of the Temptation of Christ, fol. 202v, faces a full-page, decorated incipit on fol. 203r (PLATES I, II), beginning Luke's narrative of the Temptation. The recto of fol. 202 carries the end of the genealogy according to Luke 3.36–8, which is terminated by a panel of ornament topped with the bust of a bearded human figure. The other illustration, the so-called 'Arrest' at fol. 114r, presents at its top one sentence of the Gospel text from the Passion according to Matthew 26.30, while the folio's verso carries the incipit of the following verse enlarged to full-page, elaborately bordered and decorated (PLATES III, IV). The two illustrations unquestionably remain in their originally intended positions within the Gospel text.

More full-page illustrations seem to have been planned because of the occurrence of completely and partially blank folios at important points within the Gospel text.[28] The blank fol. 123v, opposite the beginning of the Crucifixion narrative in Matthew (PLATE VII), strongly suggests that the book's makers planned a full-page depiction of the Crucifixion to illustrate the text. The existence of other Insular full-page illustrations depicting the Crucifixion supports this suggestion.[29] Moreover, the border surrounding the full-page decorated incipit on the facing folio is ornamented with panels filled with profile faces turned toward the page opposite, possibly a deliberate reference of textual decoration to illustration.[30]

The illustrations of the Temptation and 'Arrest' represent the earliest known western illustrations inserted into the Gospel text.[31] Sometimes they are pointed out as early examples of narrative Gospel illustrations.[32] However, while the two images were certainly intended to accompany a specific Gospel text, each presents elements which do not illustrate the Gospel narrative into which it has been inserted. Some scholars have perceived the influence of other texts upon the iconography of the illustrations, either the influence of the text of another part of the same Gospel that is somehow related to that accompanying the illustration or the influence of a text other than the Gospel, such as an Old Testament or exegetical text.[33]

The Book of Kells as a Liturgical Gospel Manuscript

The muddled sequence of its prefatory material, the omission of numbered Eusebian sections from its text despite the presence of elaborate canon tables, and the irrelevance of its Old Latin chapter summaries to its essentially Vulgate text have all been pointed to as evidence that the Book of Kells was made for show, not for study.[34] A few notations and markings within its text may indicate liturgical design.[35] For Insular Gospel books in general, some sort of liturgical consideration, along with other influences, may have informed the selection of incipits to be given especially lavish embellishment.[36] The decoration of the text of the Book of Kells has been shown to fit decidedly into this tradition of textual structuring.

The studies of Patrick McGurk published in the 1950s and 1960s established that many of the Book of Kells's full-page illuminations and illustrations function as a part of the structuring of important parts of the text. McGurk also suggested that some may emphasise important Gospel lections.[37] During the 1980s, a few art historians made attempts to relate the iconography of its full-page illuminations and illustrations to a possible liturgical context and to patristic and Insular exegesis.[38] The first attempts were at least partially frustrated by the scarcity of published primary source material on Insular liturgies and by a lack of cross-disciplinary knowledge of other liturgical and exegetical material which could provide insights into the manuscript's iconography and its relation to the Gospel text. Since then, O'Reilly and Ó Carragáin have discussed its iconography in ways that disconnect it from actual liturgical reading. O'Reilly sees the contemplative function of its multivalent iconography within a private, monastic context as more important than presentation of text and images within a public context.[39] Ó Carragáin considers it a book that was seldom read from in public or private contexts, but he connects it as a sacred object with an environment of liturgical themes, its visual images resonating with the texts and rituals of the liturgy.[40]

The Book of Kells presents neither a surviving lection capitulary nor marginal notations positively identifiable as liturgical, and its Eusebian sections and chapter divisions are unnumbered.[41] Despite these deficiencies, the decoration of its text may be seen to have been related in some way to several systems of textual structuring, including indications of lection incipits and articulation of text, much as punctuation structures text, in ways that could have served public reading.[42] Other evidence for use in public reading may be seen in the rewritten text of Matthew 26.31, at the bottom of fol. 114v, which has been damaged by wear. The rubricated lower letters provide a more legible version of the text written above, the clarity of which is hindered by decoration and the variant forms of the display capitals.

While one must bear in mind the fact that many questions remain unanswered about the contexts in which individual luxury Gospel books were viewed and exactly who the audience would have been, questions of function and audience remain important to understanding the images and decoration they present. Without doubt luxury Gospel books assumed a role within monastic contemplative practices, but such use in itself does not answer all the questions. For example, why would such large format books be created for individual reading and viewing? Early medieval accounts exist telling of public display of Gospel books in processions, where large size would have enhanced the visual impression of the book.[43] Moreover, contemplative practices were not an end in themselves but were a step performed by the clerical elite in a continuum of prayer, learning, interpreting, and in turn passing on to the larger community the truth revealed by holy wisdom.[44]

Perhaps it would be wise not to categorise the books so rigidly, as either exclusively for study or for use in the liturgy. Even if the Book of Kells was never read from at all, it is still possible that for some reason its decoration and full-page images were influenced by the processes and significance of public presentation of the word of God.

Gospel Manuscripts and the Liturgical Context: Meaning and Audience

Although it brings up additional, probably unanswerable questions, placing the full-page illustrations in the context of liturgy and public reading may resolve some questions. The modern viewer is tempted to view the decorated pages of the Book of Kells as a kind of 'open' text, its shifting and ambiguous images leading the viewer on to an endless chain of hermeneutics.[45] As John Higgitt has pointed out and O'Reilly has shown, a kind of open-ended reading may have been practised in the context of Insular monastic culture.[46] Higgitt has raised some important objections, however. As O'Reilly's work implies, Christian exegetical methods would have imposed limitations upon the informed viewer, preventing truly free reading. Furthermore, Higgitt argues, questions still remain about how this audience, however privileged, would have had access to such a book allowing them the necessary time to descend into a never-ending maze of interpretative connections. Difficulties of knowing the limitations on Insular readers' creation of meaning from the pages and the context of their access to the manuscript may be partially alleviated by considering the use of the book in liturgical contexts or at least considering the possibility that public presentation of the Gospel text had some bearing on its decoration. A liturgical context would bring together ensembles of texts. It would provide specific physical and visual contexts of viewing and hearing. It would provide spoken, verbal interpretation in the form of sermons. The power of the text in the Middle Ages was not static, simply resident within the text itself, but rather was brought to life in its mediation in dynamic, public presentation of interpretative prayers, rituals, and visual images.[47] In addition, the liturgical cycle itself represents a multi-layered, interpretative structuring of time, in which past, present, and future, literal and mystical, physical and spiritual exist simultaneously. The communal, public context of liturgical presentation of text and image would not only put the two in tangible relationship to each other but would also take into account the possibility of diverse audiences. Even members of monastic communities attained literacy at different levels, and large Insular monasteries included lay communities with access to reading and interpretation of Scripture, as provided by monks and clergy.[48] Placing the Book of Kells within a liturgical context could suggest limits as well as preserve the possibilities for openness of its text to interpretations by diverse audiences, and it may have the further advantage of connecting the manuscript more definitely with its historic context.[49]

The unanswered questions of contemplative context are especially crucial for the Book of Kells. Why was such an elaborate articulation desirable if the monks were given what may be called an 'open text' to ruminate using the digestive system installed in their minds by monastic learning and spirituality?[50] It is true that extensive articulation of text does not prevent rumination. It is also important to remember that early Irish and Anglo-Saxon graphic articulation and 'grammar of legibility' were developed in response to particular attitudes towards Latin text that separated it, as a foreign, written language, from the spoken word and to the requirements of the new possibility of silent reading, which was developing in the sixth and seventh centuries.[51] It should be kept in mind, however, that public presentation of Latin texts by native speakers of languages other than Latin remained a concern alongside these developments. Much of the problem was due to the array of graphic marks operating in punctuation systems in use by the last half of the eighth century. These caused much scribal confusion and served the reader in unsatisfactory ways. In addition to the variety and confusion of punctuation forms, problems arose from their mixed service to silent and public reading. 'Hyper-characterization', as explained by Parkes, threatened effective determination of textual meaning by graphic means.[52]

During the period in which the Book of Kells was probably made, this problem was being dealt with systematically in Carolingian scriptoria, with the help of an Anglo-Saxon scholar, Alcuin. The Carolingian project had a double focus, of developing clear graphic articulation systems for texts for study and for liturgical texts. Alcuin wrote a treatise on orthography in which he particularly recognized the need for careful scribal punctuation of liturgical texts to ensure their proper public presentation. The Insular background of Carolingian developments may be seen through comparison of systems in use in both places.[53]

Perhaps it would be helpful to see the Book of Kells as a participant in these late eighth- and early ninth-century developments, although perhaps only indirectly connected with them and probably not as a passive recipient of Carolingian influences. Parkes has pointed out that liturgical manuscripts written after the early seventh century tend to be more heavily punctuated than other kinds of texts.[54] He has also written about the highly visual and decorative nature of Irish systems, which seem in many ways to have lessened the clarity of relationship between text, graphic articulation, and decoration.[55]

Possibly the Book of Kells, with its massive textual articulation, fits into this picture of confused graphic forms and an accompanying concern for correct liturgical reading. As will be seen in the following chapters, its decoration articulates several systems of division (chapter divisions, Eusebian sections) as well as providing cues for reading strategies (for example, the zoomorphic and figural run-over marks). Throughout the manuscript, the different systems seem in competition with one another. For example, interlinear figures sometimes attempt to override the elaborate decorative articulation of chapter divisions and Eusebian sections in an effort to unify sections of text that should be read as one. An extremely concrete example of this appears near the top of fol. 255v, at Luke 17.2–3, where the serif of the **m** of 'unum' forms an equestrian monk's tonsure as his horse's hooves clatter over the last words, 'pecaverit in', of the line below.[56] Thus the monk 'overrides' the splendid acrobat letter A's articulation of the Eusebian section beginning the line below. The horseback monk probably cues the reader to continue. While the monk could work well for the private reader, he may have been especially effective for a reader performing the text aloud. With his original green cloak, now self-destructed because of the unstable pigment, and patterning of white, brown, and black, he would have been visually prominent on the folio, even at a distance of one or two metres. The monk on the page may have provided the necessary immediately intelligible cue to the real monk reading aloud to his community. The powerful visual impact of the manuscript's decoration perhaps contributed to its function as a liturgical manuscript as well as to its luxury and expression of high status. It will be shown in Chapter 2 that the decoration of the text of the Lucan story of

Christ's Temptation could serve as cues to facilitate public reading. Chapter 3 will show that the point in the text of Matthew 26 into which the illustration on fol. 114r is placed probably had liturgical significance, as well as being an important point of textual division. Moreover, the iconography of the two full-page illustrations may be shown to present relationships to liturgical ritual and public interpreting (preaching).

The public dimension of the Book of Kells is an important possibility to consider because of the book's likely historic context in late eighth- to early ninth-century Iona, Scotland, and Ireland. This setting would have been shaped by the growing pressures from the volatile political situation and by Viking raiders. The contemporary political climate in Ulster led to creation of the Book of Armagh, a decorated manuscript presenting a collection of biblical and seventh-century hagiographical texts meant as a statement of Armagh's spiritual authority. By that time, the Irish missions to the Continent were well established, and the reform movement of the eighth-century had spread across Ireland. This was a period of maturity of Church establishment, when the landscape itself had become Christianised in a complex network of administration and resource management, usually the realm of monasteries, and spiritual authority, held by bishops. Their administrative and spiritual interconnections arranged in complex webs instead of a single hierarchy, monasteries were interwoven by political and jurisdictional interests and by blood relationships with the politically powerful figures of Ireland.[57] In such a context of intense competition and promotion, it seems quite possible that creation of a large scale, extremely opulent Gospel manuscript may have been motivated by more than the contemplative exercises of monks. The political connections which may be implicit in production of extremely high quality visual objects could have had important bearing on meaning created when the Book of Kells was viewed and read.

Notes to Chapter One

1 Martimort, 1992, pp.15–20.

2 Martimort, 1992; Gneuss, 1985, pp.105–10, 120–5; Hughes, 1982; Salmon, 1959a, pp.144–5.

3 Martimort, 1992, pp.71–96; Klauser, 1972, xi–xxxv; Salmon, 1959a, pp.140–9.

4 As sacred, iconic, and commemorative objects, they had taken on further important functions and identities, often similar to those of relics.

5 O'Reilly, 1993, pp. 110–11; 1994, pp. 350–8, 395–7.

6 *See below*, pp.154–5; *also* Farr, 1991, pp.135–7.

7 Ó Carragáin, 1994b, pp.399–418.

8 Brown, in Kendrick, et al., 1956–60, p.36; Chapman, 1908, p.11; Klauser, 1972, p.xxxii.

9 Klauser, 1972; Martimort, 1992, pp.21–31.

10 For example, Chapman, 1908, pp.192–201, on Oxford, Bodleian Library, Auct. D.2.14 ('Gospels of St Augustine').

11 Gneuss, 1985, pp.106–7; Doyle, 1992.

12 Gameson, 1994.

13 Cecchelli, 1959, pp.25–6; McGurk, 1994, pp.21–2; Gameson, 1994, pp.34–5.

14 Ganz, 1994, pp.55–6.

15 The beginning of some non-Roman lections; *see* Farr, 1991, pp.129–30.

16 Verey, 1980, pp.26–8, 34; Klauser, 1972, p.xxxi; on early neumes, *see* Hiley, 1993, pp.362–3, Cattin, 1984, p.57.

17 Verey, 1980, p.32; Lowe, *CLA* 2, no. *260, p.39.

18 Kelly, 1994; Alexander, 1978, p.32; Henderson, 1987, pp.193–4. Kelly lists known examples.

19 McGurk, 1990b; Alton, in Alton and Meyer, vol. 3, 1950–1, p.22; Henry, 1974, pp.152–3. The leaves average 330 x 240 mm, but originally probably measured *c.*370 x 260 mm. A nineteenth-century binder trimmed the pages, cutting into some of the illuminations (Meehan, 1990a; Henry, 1974, p.152; Alton, in Alton and Meyer, 1950–1, p.19).

20 Meehan, 1990b; Powell's diagrammatic section, made at the manuscript's rebinding in 1953, published by Henry, 1974, Appendix 1, pp.223–5.

21 Henry, 1974, p.163.

22 Powell's diagrammatic section, Appendix 1 in Henry, 1974, p.223.

23 Henry (1974, p.154) tells of her first examination of the Book of Kells, during the late nineteen-twenties, when '22 folios at the beginning were kept loose under separate cover.'

24 Such treatment of the genealogy as a separate text is not unusual in Insular manuscripts and even occurs in some Continental ones (Henry, 1974, p.173).

25 *See* Powell, Appendix 1 in Henry, 1974, p.223.

26 Henry, 1974, p.172. Henderson (1987, pp.154–5), however, suggests that the 'Kells Virgin in her sideways pose might well be abstracted from an Adoration of the Magi.'

27 Powell, Appendix 1 in Henry, 1974, pp.223, 224.

28 Henry, 1974, p.173; Alexander, 1978, pp.72–3. Henry (1974, p.173) suggests that further illustrations were planned for the Gospel of Mark, a Crucifixion or Resurrection opposite the page of ornamental text (fol. 183r) carrying the incipit of the Crucifixion, and an Ascension on the last page of Mark, fol. 187v; for the Gospel of Luke, an Ascension or Last Judgement at the last folio (289v, now blank); for the Gospel of

John, one or two presented in the now missing folios of the Passion narrative.

29 Durham A.II.17 (Alexander, 1978, fig. 202); St Gall, Cod. 51 (Alexander, 1978, fig. 203).

30 Farr, 1989, p.4; Jennifer O'Reilly has made the same observation.

31 Alexander, 1978, pp.73–4; Henry, 1974, p.163. Other early Gospel illustrations, such as those in Durham A.II.17 and St Gall, Cod. 51, are placed at the beginnings or ends of the books of the evangelists.

32 Calkins, 1983, p.92; O'Neill, 1984, p.10.

33 Most recently O'Reilly (1994) has placed fol. 202v within the Lucan text of the baptism and genealogy of Christ through the 'sacred monogram' at Luke 4.1, on fol. 203r and connected it with patristic and Insular exegesis. Earlier studies include: Nordenfalk, 1977a, 1977b; Lewis, 1980; Henderson, 1987, pp.162–78. See also Werckmeister (1967) on the context of Northumbrian spirituality, and Henry (1974, pp.189–90; 1967, p.81) and Harbison (1985) on iconographic sources.

34 Henry, 1974, pp.153, 167, 172; See now McGurk, 1990, pp.37–61.

35 Alton (in Alton and Meyer, vol. 3, 1950–1, p.18) has pointed out that the rubricated word 'Initium' inserted into fol. 327v 'looks like a liturgical direction,' and also the configuration of red crosses marking the repeated text presented on fol. 218v may indicate liturgical reading.

36 McGurk, 1955, pp.105–7; McGurk, 1961, pp.7, 11–15, 81–2; T. J. Brown, in Kendrick, et al., vol. 2, 1956–60, pp.34, 35, 38–40.

37 McGurk, 1955, pp.105–7; McGurk, 1961, pp.7, 11–15, 81–2.

38 Lewis, 1980; Henderson, 1987, pp.153–78. Werckmeister, 1964, 1967, connected some of the decorated pages with Northumbrian monastic culture.

39 1987–88, pp.98–100; 1993; 1994, especially pp.371–4.

40 1994b, especially pp.398–400, 406–7, 434–6.

41 At least ten leaves are missing from the beginning of the book (Meehan, 1990a, pp.175–6), which could have included a lection list.

42 McGurk (1961, 1955), Lewis (1980), and Parkes (1987) were the first to explore this question. More recently: Farr, 1989, 1991, 1994; Werner, 1994.

43 Ó Carragáin, 1994b, pp.413–18.

44 Irvine, 1986; Irvine, 1994, 162–313.

45 Eco, 'Foreword', in Fox, 1990; Alexander, 1990, p.266.

46 Higgitt, 1991, pp.447, 449; see the citations of O'Reilly's articles and papers in the Bibliography.

47 Camille, 1993, pp.43–7.

48 Bitel, 1990, pp.115–28, esp. pp.126–8; Doherty, 1985, p.66; Thacker, 1992; Charles-Edwards, 1992, p.76; Foot, 1992; Sharpe, 1992.

49 I am most grateful to Jonathan Alexander for his discussion of my work in his paper delivered at the 1992 Book of Kells conference in Dublin, and for providing me with a copy of his unpublished paper.

50 See Parkes, 1993, p.18, on the lack of a need for punctuation in learned monastic contexts in sixth-century Italy.

51 Parkes, 1993, pp.19, 20–9.

52 Parkes, 1993, pp.34–6.

53 Parkes, 1993, pp.35–8.

54 Parkes, 1993, p.35

55 Parkes, 1993, pp.23–6; see also Ganz, 1987, pp.29–42.

56 Henry, 1974, PLATE 76.

57 Herbert, 1988; Sharpe, 1984a; Sharpe, 1984b; Doherty, 1985; Ó Corráin, 1994, pp.28–32; Etchingham, 1991, 1993.

CHAPTER TWO

Folio 202v, The Temptation of Christ

Images, Texts, and Exegesis
The Temple in Jerusalem, the Temptation of Christ, and Psalm 90

THE ILLUSTRATION at fol. 202v (PLATE I), placed facing the first words of Luke 4.1 on fol. 203r (PLATE II), depicts the Temptation of Christ in an unusual manner. It presents several iconographic features inconsistent with and even contradictory to the texts of the gospel story at Luke 4.1–13, Matthew 4.1–11, and Mark 1.12–13. Most scholars have interpreted the picture as the temptation on the Temple roof, the third and final episode in the story according to Luke (4.9–12), the second according to Matthew (4.5–7). As told in the Gospels, the devil takes Christ from his fasting in the desert and sets him upon the Temple in Jerusalem. There he urges Christ to fling himself down to prove that he is the Son of God. The devil quotes Psalm 90.11–12:

> Scriptum est enim quod angelis suis mandavit de te ut conservent te quia in manibus suis tollent te ne forte offendas ad lapidem pedem tuum.
> [For it is written, that *He has given his angels charge over you, that they keep you. And that in their hands they shall bear you up, lest perhaps you dash your foot against a stone*.]

Christ, in reply, quotes Deuteronomy 6.16:

> Dictum est non temptabis Dominum Deum tuum.
> [It is said, *You shall not tempt the Lord your God.*]

The illustration depicts the exchange of dialogue between Christ and Satan. Both gesture toward each other, and Christ holds what appears to be a scroll, probably representing the Torah or Pentateuch, the source of the Scripture he quotes to fend off the devil's attack.

Even though the illustration in some way depicts the temptation on the Temple roof, Christ appears atop the Temple not as the usual full-length standing figure but as a monumental head and shoulders. A pair of angels hovers in symmetrical formation above his head even though, except for the Psalm verses quoted by the devil, Luke's narrative says nothing about them. Matthew (4.11) and Mark (1.13) speak of angels who minister to Christ but only after the devil's departure. The illustration's frame shelters two more angels in its upper corners, where they present codices and share their corners with vines. Moreover, a crowd of onlookers has assembled to the right of the Temple, in contradiction to Christ's isolation implied in the gospel story. Below are more figures within the Temple, and in its doorway stands a figure who holds crossed rods terminating in flowers.

Choice of this subject is not easily explainable. Firstly, the Temptation of Christ seems theologically less important than other events in the life of Christ, such as the Baptism, which are not depicted in the Book of Kells.[1] Nor is it easily explained by considering the illustration against the background of the liturgical year, with its annual cycle of gospel readings and hierarchy of feasts. The Temptation story is almost invariably associated with the first Sunday in Lent (Quadragesima Sunday), but the version of the story almost unanimously quoted by exegetical writers and indicated as the Quadragesimal lection in western gospel books is the text of the temptation of Christ in Matthew 4.1–11.[2] The illustration in the Book of Kells is known to remain in its originally intended position at the beginning of the Temptation story in Luke because it is painted on an original bifolium that is completely secure in its place.[3] It will be shown, however, that the Lucan story (Luke 4.1–13) served as a Quadragesimal lection in some non-Roman liturgies.

In addition, the reasons for elevating this part of the text to a level equalling that of Matthew 26.30–1, the text of the other illustration (PLATE III), are not easily recovered. Even though the illustration at Matthew 26.30 also presents unusual iconographic elements, it at least stands at a crucial point in the narrative of the Passion. The Passion of Christ represents one of the most important texts of Christianity and has definite connections with the liturgy of Holy Week, the most important week of the year. The Temptation, while not insignificant, is not usually given such importance.

The Image of the Temple in Art and Literature to c.800

A central question, raised by Henderson and O'Reilly, is whether the structure in the illustration actually represents the Temple.[4] Henry and others, who have explained the building's appearance as an Insular attempt to depict a magnificent house of worship, have compared it with Irish house shrines or reliquaries, thought to resemble contemporary ecclesiastical architecture, and with early Irish architecture.[5] Nordenfalk and Mütherich have pointed out depictions in two gospel books of Otto III showing the oversized head and shoulders of Christ at the peak of the Temple's pediment.[6] Even though these Reichenau manuscripts date to c.1000, they probably depend upon earlier models and thus suggest that a depiction like that in the Book of Kells may have existed earlier. In fact, long-established visual and literary traditions of the image of the Temple already existed at the time the Book of Kells was made.

Comparing the structure in the illustration with the description of the Temple in 3 Kings, one sees that, while the picture omits many details given in the text, important similarities exist. The three horizontal divisions of the building in the picture, with the narrowest at the bottom, the broadest at the top, may correspond to those of the Temple which measured five, six and seven cubits in height (3 Kings 6.6). The two 'columns' forming part of the frame around the illustration and the two wedge-shaped, nearly blank areas on either side of the structure depicted within, which Henry referred to as 'two majestic antae and the beams of a low-reaching roof,' could represent the porticus in front of the sanctuary, flanked by the two bronze columns, Iachin and Booz in 3 Kings 7.15–22.[7]

The building depicted may also reflect a traditional image of the Temple seen through the monumental front gate. Josephus, although his account probably was not known in the Insular world, describes such a view of the building itself:

> ... for in front it had, as it were, shoulders extending twenty cubits on either side.[8]

Although the Vulgate of 3 Kings only mentions the veil of the Temple hung on golden chains, Josephus describes it:

> ... of Babylonian tapestry, with embroidery of blue and fine linen, of scarlet also and purple, wrought with marvelous skill. Nor was this mixture of materials without its mystic meaning: it typified the universe.[9]

These same colours appear in the central register of the building in the Book of Kells. The intention here is not, however, to assert the influence of Josephus's text upon the Book of Kells but rather to show that some of the details of the picture already existed in older verbal, and perhaps visual, images.

The colours are important, as Josephus indicates in explaining their cosmic symbolism. Blue, scarlet, and purple (*hyacinthus, coccum*, and *purpurus* in the Vulgate) are the colours of the hangings of another important Old Testament structure, Moses' Tabernacle described in Exodus 25–7.[10] God instructed Moses to make the hangings:

> Decem cortinas de bysso retorta, et hyacintho, ac purpura, coccoque bis tincto, variatas opere plumario facies ... Ansulas hyacinthinas in lateribus ac summitatibus facies cortinarum, ut possint invicem copulari ... Facies et quinquaginta circulos aureos quibus cortinarum vela iungenda sunt, ut unum tabernaculum fiat. (Exodus 26.1–6)
> [Make ten hangings of linen, hemmed and dyed twice with hyacinth and also with purple and scarlet, rich with featherstitch embroidery ... Make hyacinth loops along the sides and top of the hangings, so that they may be fastened one to another ... And make fifty golden rings so that the curtains of the hangings may be joined together, so that the tabernacle may form a whole.]

The structure in the illustration may present allusions to the Tabernacle. The middle register of the building in which the colours of the Tabernacle's hangings appear is edged at its top with a row of ten violet shapes forming a scallop design, like the *ansulae hyacinthinae* in the description. The minute golden T-shapes which appear in the arcs of the scallops possibly represent the ends of the columns or posts supporting the lintel upon which the curtain was hung. Moreover, the pair of angels over Christ's head may allude to the cherubim of the Ark within the Tabernacle, described in Exodus 25.18–21:

> Duos quoque cherubim aureos, et productiles facies, ex utraque parte oraculi. Cherub unus sit in latere uno, et alter in altero. Utrumque latus propitiatorii tegant expandentes alas, et operientes oraculum respiciantque se mutuo versis vultibus in propitiatorium quo operienda est arca ...
> [Make also two golden and finely wrought cherubim on each side of the ark. Let one cherub be on one side, the other on the other side. Spreading their wings, they will cover each side of the place of atonement, and covering the ark, they should look upon each other mutually with their faces toward each other into the place of atonement, by which means the ark is to be covered ... .]

The angels depicted above Christ's head lack the multiple wings of the cherubim described in Ezekiel 1.5–11 and their hands are not visible, but, like the golden cherubim of the Ark,

FIG. 1 Dura Europos, Synagogue, Torah Shrine

they face each other with wings outspread to form a canopy over the head of Christ.[11] Because of the descriptions given by biblical texts and Josephus, one may conclude that the building in the Kells illustration most probably depicts the Temple in Jerusalem multivalently, by also alluding to Moses' Tabernacle and perhaps to the Ark of the Covenant as well.

Many Jewish images of the late Antique period depict the Temple in combination with the Tabernacle and the Ark.[12] The earliest known Jewish representations of the Temple, on coins of Jerusalem made during the Bar Kochba revolt of AD 132–5, associate the Temple and Tabernacle.[13] The most famous image combining references to the two structures is probably the building depicted above the Torah shrine on the west wall of the Dura-Europos synagogue (FIG. 1), which refers symbolically to the Tabernacle, the Temple, and Jerusalem. The significance of such images relies upon an associative, historical symbolism typical of Jewish imagery. Most often the image of the Temple in Jewish art, as in literature, signifies an expression of hope for reconstruction of the Temple and for the deliverance of Jerusalem. [14]

The general shape of the Temple as depicted on the coins and at Dura, a structure enclosed within a framing arch or gabled gate, appears again in later Jewish representations. For example, a sixth-century floor mosaic from Galilee presents the Temple as a gabled structure supported by monumental columns, within which stands a smaller arched niche.[15]

FIG. 2 Codex Amiatinus, (Florence, Biblioteca Medicea-Laurenziana, MS Amiatino 1)
fols IIV–III, the Tabernacle

Also, the much later St. Petersburg Bible, dated 929, from Egypt or Palestine, presents a carpet page depicting the Temple/Tabernacle and its furnishings.[16] This is also the shape of the Temple as depicted in the Book of Kells. Known early Christian images are rare, but include an image in the Via Latina Catacomb, Rome, possibly related to the associatively symbolic Jewish images.[17]

This iconographic tradition of the ambiguously depicted Temple may have influenced Insular art during the seventh and eighth century. Probably the most important example is the diagram on fols 2v and 3r of the Codex Amiatinus (FIG. 2), believed by most scholars to have been copied from or based upon a diagram which Cassiodorus had made for his Codex Grandior and which Bede mentions having seen at Jarrow.[18] Although the diagram in the Codex Amiatinus clearly follows the description of the Tabernacle in Exodus 25–7 and Numbers 2–3, scholars are divided in their interpretations of its significance. Some believe it to be based upon a diagram of the Tabernacle which was one of two separate Cassiodoran diagrams, one representing the Tabernacle, the other the Temple.[19] Others believe that Cassiodorus describes not two diagrams, but a single diagram showing the shape of the Temple and Tabernacle together.[20] Therefore, proponents of the latter theory argue, the Codex Amiatinus diagram simultaneously represents both structures and so reflects a significance rooted in Jewish and Early Christian traditions of the associative symbolism of the Temple and Tabernacle. Kühnel and Revel-Neher, supporters of the simultaneous representation, point out the cross above the inner sanctuary's entrance to show that the Codex Amiatinus diagram transforms Moses' Tabernacle, marking it for viewing through the lens of Christological interpretation.[21] The diagram, they conclude, depicts the form of the Temple, the permanent dwelling place of God in the heavenly Church of the New Covenant, as based upon that of its predecessor, the mobile and temporary Tabernacle of the Old Covenant built during the wandering in the desert.[22] The makers of the Amiatinus diagram based it upon a tradition in which visual images were both symbolic and deliberately ambiguous.[23]

An Insular image of the Temple appears on the rear panel of the eighth-century Franks Casket (FIG. 3), in the scene identified by its inscription as Titus's sack of Jerusalem.[24] In the centre of the panel, an arch or dome rests upon a pair of monumental columns articulated into three levels. Within the central arch rests the empty container of the Ark, the stone tablets having been taken from it. Animal ornament surrounds the Ark, perhaps representing an Anglo-Saxon interpretation of the cherubim. The space flanking the arch appears to be divided into two registers of figures. The entire panel may represent the Temple and thus Jerusalem by the associative symbolism of the Temple.[25] Several studies have interpreted the scene of the rear panel Christologically, but others have rejected such interpretation.[26] The central monumental arch sheltering the Ark within, however, resembles the layout of the Kells illustration, with its monumental columns framing the smaller structure of the sanctuary.

In the Book of Armagh, the diagram of the heavenly Jerusalem at the end of Revelation (fol. 171r) depicts Christ as the Temple.[27] An oblong rectangle drawn within the plan of the city walls is labelled 'Dns noster ihs xpx,' based on Revelation 21.22–7, which states that

FIG. 3 Franks Casket, (British Museum), Sack of Jerusalem

'the Lord God and the Lamb' were both the Temple and the lamp in the city. The diagram lays out the plan of the heavenly city described in Revelation 21, with its twelve gates, each occupied by an angel ('ang' in the diagram) and inscribed with one of the names of the twelve tribes of Israel. The gates in the square city face the cardinal directions, indicated at three corners of the diagram. The names of the twelve foundation stones of the city wall and the apostles, which in the text are said to be written on the stones, also appear in the openings representing the gates, so that each gate presents names of angel, apostle, tribe, and stone. As a diagram image, it is related to the Codex Amiatinus drawing of the Tabernacle, but also it presents conceptual links to the image of the Temple in the Book of Kells in its emphasis on associative elements of sacred structures. Furthermore, the diagram in the Book of Armagh shows how the figure combining Tabernacle, Temple, and Jerusalem could be made relevant to contemporary needs through associative elements.[28] Armagh was engaged in self-promotion as the apostolic Church of Ireland, and the Book of Armagh apparently was compiled to aid Armagh's drive for primacy.[29] The diagram, with its explicit connection of Saviour, Temple, tribes, foundation stones, and apostles, could be seen as a statement of apostolic authority and of the essential role of St Patrick, the Irish inheritor of Peter, in the history of salvation.

Literary interpretations of the Temple and Tabernacle, like the visual images discussed above, demonstrate that the two structures provided multivalent figures for symbolic interpretation. Jewish interpretation emphasises a cosmic aspect, for both structures represent the dwelling of God among men and the form of the Tabernacle was revealed by God himself. As will be seen in the following discussion, Christian writers transformed the two structures, emphasising their Messianic aspects and adding elements from Christian theology. Also, Jewish and Christian writings about the Tabernacle and the Temple or events which took place in or around them tend to stress certain parts of the structures: the entrance or door, the veil, the pinnacle, the tabula or planks and the tabulata or structures formed by the planks.

Early Jewish interpretation of the Temple is reflected in the books of the Prophets. The Temple is especially important in Isaiah, Ezekiel and Zechariah, who write of the destruction of Jerusalem by the Babylonians and prophesy the rebuilding of the Holy City and the Temple.[30] Isaiah (28.16) and Zechariah (4.7) develop an eschatological imagery of the cosmic Temple and its ritual.[31] These texts took on a Messianic meaning in later Jewish interpretation and thus became especially important to Christian interpretation of the Temple as the eschatological figure of the Heavenly Jerusalem and, beginning in the late fourth century, as the figure of the Church on earth.[32]

Philo, a first-century Platonist, refers to the Temple as a figure of the cosmos existing in three dimensions, and he elaborates allegorically the cosmic significance of every detail of the Tabernacle.[33] Josephus explains the veil's material and colours as symbols of the four elements, combined in the tapestry of the veil to depict 'a panorama of the heavens'.[34] Jewish interpretation already understood the Temple and the Tabernacle to have an abstract sense carried by details of their structures.

The Temple immediately became an important figure in Christian thought and writing, for in the New Testament it is already played upon as a symbol of the Church. Its first appearance in the gospels is in the Temptation story in Matthew, where it is identified with the holy city, Jerusalem.[35] The Old Testament significance of the Temple undoubtedly affected the narrative of the Temptation story as told in the Gospel of Luke. Luke's version of the story differs from Matthew's mainly by its ordering of the episodes. By placing the Temptation on the Temple roof last, Luke emphasises the episode, with Satan exiting from the narrative *usque ad tempus* (Lk. 4.13) against the background of the Temple. For this reason, Satan's re-entry into the narrative at the beginning of the Passion, when *intravit autem Satanas in Iudam* (22.3), provides one of several links between the Temptation and the Passion.[36] These links dramatically emphasise Christ's role in the fulfilment of the New Covenant, the establishment of the New Temple or *Ecclesia*, the Church.[37]

Christ himself creates Messianic word plays using the figure of the Temple of the Old Testament and the stones of which it was constructed.[38] The figure of the New Temple, and especially the Temple as a living body of Christians, occurs frequently in the Epistles and seems to have been one of Paul's favourite images.[39] Paul also refers to the Tabernacle as the earthly reflection of the heavenly Temple/Tabernacle, in Acts 7.44–56, as does the author of Hebrews 8.1–9.10.

Early hagiography used the image of the Temple to identify the martyrs and their suffering with Christ and his temptation and passion. Paul's text on the Tabernacle in Acts 7.44–53 presents Stephen's speech contrasting the earthly Temple and Tabernacle with the heavenly Temple/Tabernacle. Stephen's final vision of Christ in the heavenly Temple instigates his own stoning, the first martyrdom, in Acts 7.54–9.[40]

Hegesippus' account of the martyrdom of James, quoted by Eusebius in his *History of the Church*, uses the Temple as its setting.[41] According to Hegesippus, the martyrdom of James occurred at Passover, when a group of 'Jews, Scribes and Pharisees' stood him upon the Temple parapet and told him to explain to the crowds gathered for the holiday that Jesus was not the Christ. When asked what was meant by 'the door of Jesus,' James replied in words echoing those of Christ (Matthew 26.64) and of Stephen, declaring that Jesus was enthroned in heaven, implying the heavenly Temple/Tabernacle, and that he would return 'on the clouds of heaven'.[42] The Scribes and Pharisees then pushed him from the pinnacle, but he survived the fall and the ensuing stoning, during which he prayed in the words of Christ, '… forgive them; they do not know what they are doing'.[43] Finally killed by a blow from a fuller's club, James was buried on the site of his martyrdom.

Hegesippus forms the story as a layer upon the existing strata of the biblical stories of the martyrdom of Stephen and the temptation and passion of Christ. James was martyred at Passover, the anniversary of the Crucifixion, and he quotes Christ's words from the cross (Luke 23.34), which Stephen also had echoed at his martyrdom (Acts 7.59). Moreover, it clearly refers to Christ's temptation on the pinnacle of the Temple, where both Christ and martyr speak of Jesus' divinity. However, those who place James upon the Temple do not tempt him as the devil tempted Christ, with an Old Testament quotation, but rather with Christ's words from John 10.9, 'I am the door'.[44] 'The door' does not refer directly to the door of the Temple, but to the heavenly door through which Christ the Good Shepherd leads his flock, which in turn alludes to the texts of Psalm 117.20, 'the door of the Lord' mentioned just before the rejected cornerstone at verse 22, and of Zechariah 11.17 and 13.7, eschatological texts on the Shepherd, one of which Jesus had quoted at the beginning of his suffering in Gethsemene, at Mt. 26.31. Hegesippus plays upon the story's setting on the Temple roof to contrast the old, material Temple with the heavenly Temple in which Jesus is seen enthroned as Christ. Furthermore, he draws a parallel between the suffering of the martyrs and the temptation and passion of Christ, thus implying that the martyrs are enthroned with Christ. These are important steps in the Christianisation of one of the central images of Judaism.

The most significant Insular writings on the Temple and Tabernacle in relation to the iconography of the Temptation scene in the Book of Kells are Bede's detailed allegorical interpretations, *De Tabernaculo* and *De Templo*.[45] Bede views the Tabernacle and the Temple as temporally distinguished figures of the Church. Book 2 of *De Tabernaculo* begins with an explanation of the two sanctuaries' present sense. Together, Bede says, they designate the 'present status of the universal Church' because part, symbolized by the Temple, now stands in heaven, but part, the Tabernacle, still exists in labour and difficulty upon the earth, each member making a pilgrimage to heaven at death only to be succeeded on earth by another. In heaven, the souls of the elect are joined together as the living stones of the Temple.[46] As he continues his discussion in *De Tabernaculo*, Bede deepens the interpretation to illuminate a sense of time past embedded in each structure:

> Item figura utriusque sanctuarii potest ita generaliter distingui. Opus tabernaculi tempus sinagogae, hoc est antiquae Dei plebis, opus vero templi ecclesiam, id est illam electorum multitudinem quae post incarnationem dominicam ad fidem.[47]
>
> [In addition, the figure of each sanctuary can be generally distinguished thus: the structure of the Tabernacle is the time of the Synagogue, that is of the ancient people of God; but the structure of the Temple is the Church, that is the multitude of the elect which has come to faith after the Lord's incarnation.]

He then advances his interpretation to indicate their future sense. 'By means of the truth of figures,' Bede says, the two buildings 'describe mystically' the entire history of the earthly Church of the present, from Adam to the last elect to be born at the end of the world, and also both 'depict miraculously' the eternal glory of the heavenly Church of the future.

The point, he says, in studying the Tabernacle is that its form and furnishings may reveal the truth and beauty of Christ as he dwells in his Church on earth and in heaven [48] Thus the forms of the two dwellings of God among men are figures for revelation. They provide objects for spiritual imitation so that those studying them may be incorporated into the 'living temple of God,' as described by Paul, and 'the Tabernacle of God with men,' appearing in John's vision.[49] As figures for revelation, Bede says, the Temple and the Tabernacle unveil the nature of the Church in their plans, their measurements and nearly every detail of material and ornament, for example:

> Tabulae ergo tabernaculi apostolos eorumque successores per quorum sermonem ecclesia per orbem dilatata est designant.[50]
>
> [The boards of the tabernacle, therefore, designate the apostles and their successors through whose word the Church has spread throughout the world.]

The boards are the apostles and their successors because they are made from brilliant white, incorruptible acacia logs and measured ten cubits in length, the number ten signifying the perfection to which the doctors strove by observing the ten commandments.[51]

This interpretation of the Tabernacle built of the boards of the saints may have influenced Bede's story of the death of St Aidan.[52] According to Bede, Aidan died in a tent attached to the west wall of a small Church, where he expired leaning against a post that served to buttress the Church's wall. The monks removed Aidan's body to Lindisfarne, but the post remained in its place, surviving unharmed three fires that destroyed the original Church and its successors. Finally, the builders, recognising the beam's powers, set it up inside the new Church, where it continued to work miracles healing diseases. Like the boards of the Tabernacle, the post inside Aidan's tent supported the present and future Churches and took on the identity of one of the successors of the apostles.

The illustration of the Temptation in the Book of Kells may present, in visual form, the same idea of a saint or an elect as a column of the Temple/Tabernacle. A figure holding a pair of rods with flower-like terminals appears to stand in the doorway, but its actual position is ambiguously depicted. Are the head and upper torso, which appear to be enclosed within the rectangle in the center of the middle register, meant to be separate from the vertical element directly below or is this vertical element the lower half of the figure? Perhaps this ambiguity is deliberate in order to express the idea that the one depicted acts as a column or post, a support of the Temple, like the boards of the Tabernacle and St Aidan's beam.

The idea of comparing apostles or saints with columns of the Church is not at all rare in the New Testament or patristic exegesis, and architectural forms themselves seem to have carried multivalent significance and resonances of meaning, especially in Irish visual culture.[53] However, the figure in the Kells illustration is remarkable in that it serves as a column in an image of the Temple which also alludes to the Tabernacle, in much the same way that Bede interpreted the two buildings as one figure.

In this regard, Bede's interpretation of the Apocalypse 3.12, *qui vicerit faciam illum columnam in templo Dei mei*, may be revealing:

> Hae columnae, id est, sancti viri, nunc sustinendo ecclesiam muniunt, tunc eminendo decorant, sicut illae duae in foribus templi Salomonis.[54]
> [These pillars, that is, holy men, at one time strengthen the Church by their support, at another adorn it by their eminence, like the two pillars at the entrance of Solomon's Temple.]

Bede equates the victor columns with saints, who both support and beautify the Temple. The *Explanatio Apocalypsis* may represent Bede's earliest commentary, dating between 703 and 709.[55] That he wrote so early of this kind of an image of the Temple, in which the elect serve as structural components, perhaps indicates that it had for some time been part of the intellectual background of Northumbria and probably of Ireland as well, particularly since the Pseudo-Isidoran *In Apocalypsin*, thought to have been one of Bede's Irish sources, gives the interpretation '*columna* sancti intelleguntur; *in templo dei* in tabernaculo'.[56] One cannot infer, therefore, that Bede's writings alone provided the inspiration for the image of the Temple in the Book of Kells.

The picture which Bede draws with words is in many respects much like the depiction of the Temple in the Book of Kells. In the illustration, the Temple is also the Tabernacle, and its lowest part is 'built' of human figures densely and uniformly packed together like the stones of a building. Moreover, the vertical columns of the frame are visually echoed in the smaller, plainer 'column' figure in the doorway. The Temple has become, visually and verbally, an abstract structure to support allegorical and typological exegesis. Its Jewish symbolism has been wholly transformed by Christian interpretation so that it is now the living Temple described by Paul in 2 Corinthians. 6.16, the dwelling place of Christ, made up of his saints. No longer a tangible building, it serves as a figure to be contemplated in search of intangible truths. Against this background of the multi-levelled symbolism of the Temple, the meaning of the Temptation as depicted in the Book of Kells will become much more understandable.

The Temptation of Christ (Luke 4.1–13), Psalm 90, and the Illustration

What is the illustration's relationship to the text in Luke? Perhaps it was placed at this point in the text because, as pointed out in the preceding section of this chapter, Luke's ordering of the narrative serves to contrast the Old Testament Temple with the heavenly Temple of the new covenant and to emphasise Christ's role as its founder. On the other hand, neither Luke's nor Matthew's text of the Temptation of Christ provides a complete explanation for all the unusual iconographic elements presented by the illustration.[57] Psalm 90 is relevant in this respect.

Psalm 90 (Vulgate):

Qui habitat in adiutorio Altissimi, In protectione Dei caeli commorabitur. (2) Dicet Domino: Susceptor meus es tu et refugium meum; Deus meus, sperabo in eum. (3) Quoniam ipse liberavit me de laqueo venantium, Et a verbo aspero. (4) Scapulis suis obumbrabit tibi, Et sub pennis eius sperabis. (5) Scuto circumdabit te veritas eius; Non timebis a timore nocturno; (6) A sagitta volante in die, A negotio perambulante in tenebris, Ab incursu, et daemonio meridiano. (7) Cadent a latere tuo mille, et decem millia a dextris tuis; Ad te autem non appropinquabit. (8) Verumtamen oculis tuis considerabis Et retributionem peccatorum videbit. (9) Quoniam tu es, Domine, spes mea; Altissimum posuisti refugium tuum. (10) Non accedet ad te malum, Et flagellum non appropinquabit tabernaculo tuo. (11) Quoniam angelis suis mandavit de te, Ut custodiant te in omnibus viis tuis. (12) In manibus portabunt te, Ne forte offendas ad lapidem pedem tuum. (13) Super aspidem et basiliscum ambulabis, Et conculcabis leonem et draconem. (14) Quoniam in me speravit, liberabo eum; Protegam eum, quoniam cognovit nomen meum. (15) Clamabit ad me, et ego exaudiam eum; Cum ipso sum in tribulatione; Eripiam eum, et glorificabo eum. (16) Longitudine dierum replebo eum, Et ostendam illi salutare meum.
[He who dwells in the shelter of the Most High, Who abides in the shadow of the Almighty, (2) Says to the Lord, 'My refuge and my fortress, My God, in whom I trust.' (3) For he will rescue me from the snare of the fowler, and from the destroying pestilence. (4) With his pinions he will cover you, And under his wings you shall take refuge; (5) He will surround you with the shield of his truth. You shall not fear the terror of the night (6) Nor the arrow that flies by day; Not the pestilence that roams in darkness Nor the devastating plague at noon. (7) Though a thousand fall at your side, ten thousand at your right side, Near you it shall not come. (8) Rather with your eyes shall you behold and see the requital of the wicked, (9) Because you, Lord, are my hope; You have placed your stronghold most high. (10) No evil shall befall you, Nor shall affliction come near your tent, (11) For to his angels he has given command about you, That they guard you in all your ways. (12) Upon their hands they shall bear you up, Lest you dash your foot against a stone. (13) You shall tread upon the asp and the viper; You shall trample down the lion and the dragon. (14) Because he clings to me, I will deliver him; I will set him on high because he acknowledges my name. (15) He shall call upon me, and I will answer him; I will be with him in distress; I will deliver him and glorify him; (16) With length of days I will gratify him, And I will show him my salvation.]

The illustration presents specific references to Psalm 90. In the first place, the episode depicted contains part of the Psalm's text: the devil is shown quoting verses eleven and twelve. Beyond this verbal reference of dialogue, the picture makes visual allusions to other verses.

The 'column' figure in the doorway probably alludes to verse 13, 'You will walk upon the

FIG. 4 High Cross, Durrow, Last Judgement

asp and the basilisk …'. This type of figure holding crossed staves or rods, in a position known to scholarship as the 'Osiris pose',[58] appears among the ornament of two additional folios of the Book of Kells and in several other Irish and Anglo-Saxon works of art.[59] Additional relief images of Christ standing upon snakes while holding crosses and foliate staves in this 'Osiris' position occur in the Last Judgement scenes on the High Cross at Durrow (FIG. 4) and the Cross of the Scriptures at Clonmacnois, as well as on an Anglo-Viking cross fragment at Burton Near Kendal. These carved Irish and Anglo-Viking examples where the figures stand upon snakes suggest that the 'Osiris pose' may have been, at least in some contexts, associated with Psalm 90.13.[60] The figure standing upon beasts or snakes represents the standard triumphal image based upon Psalm 90.13. Such figures frequently accompany the Psalm in Psalter illustrations.[61] Although the exact origins of the 'Osiris pose' as it appears in Insular art remain undetermined, similar figures occur in Mediterranean contexts where they often have an apotropaic significance offering salvation and protection from evil.[62] Some Mediterranean examples present specific associations with Psalm 90, while others depict saints or other holy personages who have 'triumphed over death', the same people whom Bede envisioned as the boards and stones of the Temple and the Tabernacle.[63] Because the figure trampling beasts as inspired by Psalm 90.13 and the 'Osiris pose' are associated with protection from evil and triumph over it, the two images may have become equivalent, as further suggested by their conflation on the Irish and Anglo-Viking crosses. Like these images of Christ and the Mediterranean images of saints, the column figure in the Kells illustration represents *qui viceret* and probably refers symbolically to the triumphal image expressed in verse 13, which follows the verses quoted by the devil to tempt Christ. Straightforward depiction of basilisks, asps, lions, or other evil creatures under the feet of the column figure becomes superfluous in the Temptation picture where (1) the triumphal verse is literally implicit, in the devil's quotation of the Psalm verses which precede it, (2) the devil himself is depicted as subject to the triumph of Christ and his Body, and (3) the column figure is within the triumphant Body and Head.[64] This is not a literal or straightforward image, but a multivalent one.

The picture presents further references to Psalm 90. One of the figures to the left of the temple's gable holds a red disk next to the pair of animal heads at the end of the top angle of the Temple roof, just behind the juncture of Christ's body with the building. This red disk represents a shield as can be seen from the lighter coloured circle in its centre, representing a central boss, and the four very small circles on either side of the boss, which represent the nails or rivets attaching the handle on the other side. Further support for the red disk's identification as a shield can be found in comparison of it with the shields held by the spear-bearing warriors depicted on fols 4r and 200r. The warriors hold their shields in exactly the same manner as the figure on fol. 202v, and all shields are nearly the same in size relative to the figures as the disk in question. Moreover, bosses have been indicated in the centres of all the warrior's shields. Possibly the detail of rivets or nail heads was added to the shield on fol. 202v to make certain its identity, which might otherwise be in doubt because of its depiction outside the literal context of warrior and weapon. The purpose of the shield in the Temptation illustration is to call to mind the image presented in verse 5 of Psalm 90: 'He will surround you with the shield of his truth'.

Finally, the bust of Christ atop the crowd-filled temple creates a visual image of the Lord's protection much like the verbal one expressed throughout the Psalm. The Psalm itself suggests the general idea of the architectural imagery and specifically much of the imagery of protection seen in the illustration.

The protective imagery of Psalm 90 appears in a variety of contexts and probably was well-known to Insular Christians. For instance, Irish and Anglo-Saxon prayers recorded in eighth- and ninth-century manuscripts associate the words of the Psalm with protection, especially protection from evil. A fragment of a prayer inserted into a litany in an Anglo-Saxon prayerbook of the eighth or ninth century, B.L., Harley 7653, uses the words of verses 5 and 6: [65]

> Si quis hanc scripturam secum habuerit non timebit a timore nocturno sive meridiano.[66]
> [If anyone will hold onto this writing, he will have nothing to fear from the nocturnal or noon-day terror.]

Hughes thought that 'secum habuerit' indicated that the English 'must have carried prayers around with them for protection',[67] but the words might also have been used in a more abstract sense to mean a figurative wearing of the Lord's truth or occupation of his shelter, as expressed in the Psalm and perhaps also in the illustration in the Book of Kells. Another use of Psalm 90's imagery may be seen in the first of two short prayers presenting Irish connections which appear at the end of a fragment of a pericope list preserved in an early ninth-century Carolingian manuscript fragment.[68] The prayer calls upon divine protection as expressed in verses 11 and 12:

> Manus domini sit sup[er] nos
> mittat angelum suum
> custodem qui custodiat
> nos in omnibus viis nostri[s].[69]
> [May the hand of the Lord be over us:
> let him send his angel
> as a guard who may watch over us
> in all our ways.]

Here the hands of the angels of verse 12 have become the sheltering hand of the Lord, who is called upon, with the words of verse 11, to send an angel to guard the believer from evil. A final example, a phrase appearing twice in prayers of the Book of Cerne and also in another Anglo-Saxon prayerbook in the British Library (B.L., Royal 2.A.xx) evokes an image similar in some respects to the illustration of the Temptation in the Book of Kells: [70]

> Protege me dne scuto veritatis tuae ac fidei tuae ut me diabolica ignita iacula non pen[e]trent.
> [Protect me, O Lord, with the shield of your truth and your faith, so that the diabolical fiery darts may not pierce me.]

By speaking of 'fiery diabolical darts', the prayer evokes protection from the devil's temptation, which may approach the believer in a variety of forms, as described in Psalm 90.

In view of Insular use of Psalm 90's verbal imagery and considering the visual allusions presented to it in the illustration, one may conclude that the Psalm's protective imagery could by itself have inspired the peculiar depiction of the Temptation of Christ in the Book of Kells. However, exegeses of the Temptation and Psalm 90 open a much wider door onto a still deeper understanding of the illustration.

Exegesis of The Temptation of Christ and of Psalm 90

Bede, writing in *De Templo*, begins his interpretation of the structures covering the temple roof (*tabulata*, meaning approximately 'breastworks' or 'boardwalks')[71] by reminding his readers that the tabulata are mentioned in the gospel when Christ is tempted by the devil on the pinnacle of the temple, and that his brother James also was lifted up to the pinnacle of the temple to address the Passover crowds.[72] Bede repeats an idea found in Irish interpretations:[73]

> Utrum autem moris fuerit doctoribus ut in his sedentes tabulatis ad circumstantem inferius turbam fecerint sermonem nusquam in scripturis invenimus.[74]
> [Whether it was the practice of teachers to deliver their lectures to the people standing around below them while they sat on these breastworks is something we find nowhere in the Scriptures.]

However, Bede turns from this theory on the function of the *tabulata* as a pulpit to an interpretation of them as the three grades of the holy who are united with Christ.[75] The meaning of the tabulata as a part of the living temple, Bede implies, outweighs the significance of their function. Did the figure of the living temple exert any influence on exegeses specifically concerning the Temptation of Christ? Could such interpretations connect somehow with the idea of preaching or teaching the truth of the Scriptures, as seen in the stories of James and Stephen and as suggested by Bede's juxtaposition of them? Furthermore, do interpretations on the Temptation provide more precise verbal imagery which may explain even more completely the iconography of the illustration in the Book of Kells? Did Insular exegetes know of such interpretations? In Bede's writings other hints appear that the Temptation of Christ was interpreted in terms of the living body of the temple and that this tradition was known and drawn upon at least in Northumbria.

The tradition which Bede seems to have known appears in patristic and Insular commentaries on the Temptation of Christ as told in the Gospels but also, and in some ways more importantly, in exegeses of Psalm 90, the Quadragesimal Psalm. The figure of the living body of the Church seems to have become influential in the late fourth century in western exegesis, although due to its biblical origins, traces of it appear, for example, in the fragments of Origen's commentary on Matthew and in Eusebius' Commentary on Psalm 90.[76] Nevertheless, the writer who made the figure of 'Christ, the head, and his body, the Church' one of the standard tools of western exegesis was a late fourth-century North African Donatist named Tyconius. Tyconius wrote a handbook for exegetes, the *Liber Regularum*, seven rules for interpreting any passage in Scripture, no matter how unpromising the passage may seem for Christian interpretation.[77] Rules 1 and 2, entitled 'The Lord and his Body' and 'The Lord and his Two-Part Body', present the most important figure. All Scripture, Tyconius says, speaks either of this blessed body or of that other evil body, the Devil and his followers, described in Rule 7.[78]

The brilliance of Tyconius's rules rests in large part upon their simplicity and broadness. The figure of 'Christ and his Body' combines visual metaphors of architecture, like those which Bede used later in his interpretations of the Temple and Tabernacle, with metaphors of the body (head, limbs, feet, right and left sides), along with all the implications of those words, many of which are already played upon in the Bible. Moreover, the figure of Christ the head and his body the Church proved especially effective for Western interpretation because it presented a clearly defined and tangible metaphoric figure. Using Tyconius's first rule, a writer can construct a clear image in the mind of the reader, an image that is bold in its outline, but which can receive within its contours an infinite amount of detailed allegorical embellishment.[79] This visual image, which functions almost as a diagram, can be the parent of verbal or visual interpretation, and it can unite them.

The figure can express simultaneously the Incarnation of Christ and the existence of the Church through time:

> Corpus itaque in capite suo filius est Dei, et Deus in corpore suo filius est hominis, qui cotidie nascendo venit et *crescit in templum sanctum Dei*. Templum enim bipertitum est, cuius pars altera quamuis lapidibus magnis extruatur destruitur, neque in eo *lapis super lapidem relinquitur*. Istius nobis iugis adventus cavendus est, *donec de medio* eius discedat Ecclesia.[80]
> [And thus the body is the son of God in its head, and God in his body is the Son of Man, who daily comes after being born and *grows into the holy temple of God* [cf. Eph. 2.21]. The Temple is two part, the other part of which is destroyed even through it may be built from great stones, nor in which *will be left a stone upon a stone* [Mt. 24.2]. The advent of this should be watched for continually by us *until from his midst* [cf. 2 The. 2.7] the Church will part asunder.]

Like a living body, the body of the Church grows by increment. Other passages, Tyconius says, also tell of the future tearing apart of the good from the bad, all of which now dwell in the earthly Church.

Although he quotes no gospel text of the Temptation as an example for interpretation, he cites Psalm 90 in a way that became influential in Temptation exegesis. In his first rule, Tyconius explains how Scripture can either speak about the Lord or his body, sometimes shifting without warning from one to the other, or it can speak of the two together as one. He then poses Psalm 90.11–16 as an exercise for the reader, prefacing it with the comment, 'it is written about the Lord and his body – what pertains to it is to be discerned by [spiritual] reason'.[81] Following his quotation of the Psalm, he asks rhetorically if God would command his angels concerning Christ but not show his salvation to his body,[82] meaning that the Psalm speaks of Christ and the Church as one.

He follows this with scriptural quotations on the bride and bridegroom:

> Unum corpus dixit utriusque sexus sponsi et sponsae, sed quid in dominum quid in Ecclesiam conveniat ratione cognoscitur. Et idem Dominus dicit in Apocalypsi: *Ego sum sponsus et sponsa*.[83]
> [He said one body of both sexes, of bridegroom and of bride, but it is known by reason what pertains to the Lord, what to the Church. And the Lord says the same in the Apocalypse: *I am the bridegroom and the bride* [Ap. 22.16–17].]

67

Psalm 90.11–16 and the bride and bridegroom texts, he says, speak about two parts of a single thing, as head and body are related to one another in their literal sense. This portion of Tyconius's first rule, along with a few passages from other parts of his book, appears to have influenced exegeses of Psalm 90 and the Temptation which reached Ireland and Northumbria.

Such interpretations may have provided the verbal image upon which the Temptation illustration in the Book of Kells was based. The influence of such an image would not simply be that an artist depicted it in the manuscript because the image does not function just on the level of illustration of event or interpretation of the event. It is an interpretative figure, used for teaching interpretation. It provides a way of ensuring orthodox reading of text. As Tyconius says at the beginning of the *Liber Regularum*:

> Clausa quaeque patefient et obscura dilucidabuntur, ut quis prophetiae inmensam silvam perambulans his regulis quodam modo lucis tramitibus deductus ab errore defendatur.[84]
> [Whatever things are closed will be opened and things that are dark will be illuminated, so that he who walks through the immense forest of prophecy may be defended from error by these rules, in the manner of light along the footpaths.]

The universal Christological value of the figure of head and body becomes clear in patristic writings, especially Augustine's.

In his *enarrationes* or commentaries on the Psalms, Augustine interprets Psalm 90 in terms of the Temptation of Christ using Tyconius's first rule. He derives much of his commentary from Tyconius's passage on Psalm 90 and the bride and bridegroom. Augustine's knowledge of the *Liber Regularum* is documented by his summary of it, accompanied by a discussion of Tyconius's Donatism, in *De Doctrina Christiana*.[85] Also, in his commentary on Psalm 90, Augustine summarises the first rule, although without referring to its author.[86]

The *Enarratio in Psalmum XC* comprises two sermons, delivered on consecutive days.[87] Augustine begins the first sermon by marking the Psalm as the one 'from which the devil dared to tempt our Lord Jesus'.[88] Christ became a man and allowed himself to be tempted, Augustine says, in order to present a model for human imitation in overcoming evil and achieving salvation.[89] By imitating Christ, 'we enter through the door …, enter by Christ who himself said, `I am the door".[90] If a direct relationship exists between Augustine's interpretation and the illustration in the Book of Kells, the image of the door as the entrance for those who follow Christ's lesson may have influenced the placement of the 'Osiris' column figure in the center of the two lowest registers of the temple and may have provided part of the reason for the depictions of crowds to Christ's right and within the temple. The figure of triumph over evil and death, the holy man who has imitated Christ and so has become a column within his body, stands in the door of the Temple, while the crowd of onlookers by the Temple roof observes the lesson being given by Christ. The figures in the Temple are those who imitate Christ and dwell under his defence as stones or planks in the body of the Church. The illustration could be seen as a depiction of the temptation of Christ and his entire body of believers, an idea Augustine elaborates further in his explanation of how '… Christ was tempted so that the Christian would not be overcome by the tempter'.[91]

Augustine first evokes Tyconius's rule to explain the beginning of verse 7, *cadent a latere tuo mille; et decem millia a dextris tuis*, as an image of the elect sitting in innumerable multitude with Christ at the Last Judgement. The words speak of Christ and the heavenly Church of saints appearing as one judge, as inseparable head and body.[92] Furthermore, he says, the rest of the verse, *ad te autem non appropinquabit*, is addressed to the body of martyrs, saints and believers, all who 'dwell in the protection of the most high'.[93] Those who trust in the Lord will be victors over the devil and his torments. In his conclusion to the first sermon, Augustine calls upon Tyconius's first rule to provide a unifying figure whereby he may interpret all of Psalm 90 in terms of Christ's temptation, the passion of the martyrs, the torment of believers and also the final cosmic temptation of the body of Christ, which is to culminate in the Last Judgement. The Book of Kells illustration, the lower section of which resembles some Irish representations of the Last Judgement, may present a visualisation of such a multi-levelled interpretation of the Temptation, and also a diagram of the means by which these hidden truths are known: the interpretative figure of the head and body, itself pronouncing the truth against the devil's false interpretations.[94]

Augustine makes use of the rule throughout Sermo II to interpret the part of the Psalm cited by Tyconius as a lesson in the use of the first rule. His introduction to the second sermon presents a detailed description of this figure, first describing Christ, the head, as he appeared on earth and is to appear in heaven.[95] He then describes the Church, the body, as the community of all believers of all times and all places, the city toward which the faithful toiling on earth make a pilgrimage:

> Corpus huius capitis ecclesia est, non quae hoc loco est, sed et quae hoc loco et per totum orbem terrarum; nec illa quae hoc tempore, sed ab ipso Abel usque ad eos qui nascituri sunt usque in finem et credituri in Christum, totus populus sanctorum ad unam civitatem pertinentium; quae civitas corpus est Christi, cui caput est Christus. Ibi sunt et angeli cives nostri; sed quia nos peregrinamur, laboramus; illi autem in civitate exspectant adventum nostrum.[96]
> [The body of this head is the Church; not the Church of this locale only, but of the whole world as well; not of this age only, but from Abel himself down to those who will to the end be born and believe in Christ, the whole assembly of the saints belonging to one city; which city is Christ's body, of which Christ is the head. There too dwell the angels who are our fellow-citizens; but we toil, because we are as yet pilgrims; while they within that city are awaiting our arrival.]

Thus, the image, Augustine says, simultaneously depicts Christ and the entire Church:

> Talem ergo scientes Christum totum atque universum simul cum ecclesia ... Ipse est caput nostrum ... Hunc intuentes, sic audiamus Psalmum ...[97]
> [We understand, therefore, such a thing to be the whole Christ and also at the same time together with the entire Church ... He himself is our head, he is God ... Looking upon him, thus let us hear the Psalm.]

This introduction is remarkable in several ways. Its all-inclusive definition of place and time for the Church and its description of those on earth as pilgrims or wanderers guided by Christ echo Tyconius, whose rules speak of the Church of the past, present and future. Moreover, this temporal sense and description of the earthly Church of pilgrims also looks forward to Bede, whose writings on the Temple and the Tabernacle describe in similar ways the two Old Testament structures as temporally distinct types of *Ecclesia*. Furthermore, Augustine exhorts his listeners to 'look upon him' as they hear the Psalm, as if they were to look in their minds at the verbal picture he has just finished painting, the image of Christ the Head with his Body the Church. Augustine follows this exhortation with his summary of Tyconius's first rule.[98] This evocation of an image, executed verbally with careful detail, seems to serve the same purpose as the creation of a multivalent visual image, such as the Kells illustration in which the interpretative figure itself is prominent.

With verse 9, Augustine tells his listeners, the Church begins a prayer to its head. The Church speaks of its hope for resurrection granted by Christ's resurrection and ascension:

> Praecessit in capite quod membra sperent … Dicat corpus capiti suo: *Quoniam tu es, Domine, spes mea; altissimum posuisti refugium tuum*, id est, ideo resurrexisti a mortuis, et in caelum adscendisti, ut altum poneres refugium tuum adscendens, et fieres spes mea, qui in terra desperabam, et me resurrecturum esse non credebam; modo iam credo, quia adscendit in caelum caput meum; quo caput praecessit, et membra secuta sunt … Vox enim est ecclesiae ad Dominum suum, vox est corporis ad caput suum.[99]
>
> [He went before at the head that the limbs may hope … Let the body say to its head: *Because you are, Lord, my hope; you have put your refuge very high*, that is, therefore, you have resurrected from the dead, and you have ascended into heaven, so that you the ascending one might place your refuge high, and that you might become my hope, I who used to despair on earth and did not believe that I was going to be resurrected; only now I believe, because my head has ascended into heaven; where the head has gone before, the limbs also are to follow … It is the voice of the Church to its Lord, it is the voice of the body to its head.]

Augustine's verbal picture of the Church at prayer expressing its hope for salvation may reflect the recitation in reality of Psalm 90 at mass on Quadragesima Sunday and during the office throughout Lent. This liturgical context undoubtedly influenced the composition of Psalm titles quoting phrases from the passage cited above and others from this section on verses 9 through 12, to be discussed below.

Augustine, like Tyconius, does not refer directly to the Temple but rather to the civitas, the holy city or community. In this section, however, he speaks at length about the 'tabernacle of God' in his interpretation of verse 10, … *et flagellum non appropinquabit tabernaculo tuo*. Like Bede, Augustine views the Tabernacle as an earthly dwelling of God, but specifically as the flesh inhabited by the Word. [100] In his tabernacle of the flesh, Augustine says, 'Christ the Emperor' battled the devil in the open so that humans could see him and learn from him.

From this point, Augustine develops further the idea of the earthly and heavenly Churches:

> Hoc autem tabernaculum eius sensit flagella in terra; manifestum est quia flagellatus est dominus. Numquid in caelo sentit flagella? Nequaquam. Quare? Quia altissimum posuit refugium suum, ut esset spes nostra, et non ad eum accedent mala, nec flagellum propinquabit tabernaculo eius. Longe est super omnes caelos, sed pedes habet in terra; caput in caelo est, corpus in terra.[101]
>
> [Nevertheless, this tabernacle of his felt the scourge on earth; as it is well known because the Lord was scourged. Does he feel the scourge in heaven? Not at all. Why? Because he has put his refuge very high, so that he may be our hope, and no evils will come near him, nor will the

scourge approach his tent. He is far away above the heavens, but he has feet on the earth; the head is in heaven, the body on earth.]

This image could be compared with that given by Bede describing the simultaneous existence of earthly and heavenly Churches. The Temple and the Tabernacle at the same time designate the Church on earth, protected by Christ through the example of his temptation and through the victory achieved by his passion, and designate also the Church in heaven, the dwelling place of Christ. They are two parts of one thing, one body with a heavenly head but with limbs and feet on earth. The germ contained in Tyconius' first rule has been cultivated by Augustine, and perhaps also by Bede, into an elaborate allegorical figure.

Augustine returns to the theme of the 'head in heaven, feet on earth' in explaining verses 10 and 11, those quoted by the devil:

Si caput in caelo pedes in terra, quid est pedes Domini in terra, nisi sancti Domini in terra? Qui sunt pedes Domini? Apostoli missi per totum orbem terrarum. Qui sunt pedes Domini? Omnes evangelistae, in quibus peragrat dominus universas gentes. Metuendum erat ne evangelistae offenderent in lapidem: illo enim in caelo posito capite, pedes qui in terra laborabant, possent offendere in lapidem. In quem lapidem? In legem in tabulis lapideis datam.[102]
[If the head is in heaven, the feet on earth, what are the Lord's feet on earth if not the Lord's saints on earth? What are the Lord's feet? The apostles sent through all the lands of the earth. What are the Lord's feet? All the preachers in whom the Lord travels through all nations. It was to be feared that the evangelists would strike against a stone: with that head now put in heaven, the feet which were toiling on earth might strike against a stone. On what stone? On the law given on stone tablets.]

Augustine's image of Christ ascending to heaven in the hands of angels in order that the feet of his body would not strike against the stone of the Law may find visual expression in the Kells illustration, where angels hover at Christ's head, their hands concealed behind his halo. Perhaps they are present not only as a reference to the guardian cherubim of the Ark of the (Old) Covenant but also to the angels of the New Covenant who played a part in freeing the earthly Church from the law when Christ ascended into heaven. The angels depicted at Christ's head in the illustration could have some connection with those seen in Ascension iconography where they may in some instances visually suggest the cherubim paired face to face over the Ark.[103] If so, the reason for their inclusion in a depiction of the Temptation of Christ can only be explained by an interpretation such as Augustine's which pulls together many texts from Scriptures into a multi-levelled exegesis. Like Augustine's exegesis, the picture in the Book of Kells multivalently cites past and future events and, in so doing, depicts the collective temptation of the Church and its collective victory, guided by Christ its head who 'went before' it. The figure of head and body, an interpretative figure that is both verbal and visual, provides the means of the images created by Augustine and in the Book of Kells.

Placing Augustine's *Enarratio* and the Kells illustration side by side reveals important similarities between the two. The image of 'Christ the Head and his Body the Church' provides the general structure of both. Both expand meaning by making references to texts and events extending beyond the time and place of the text interpreted or the event illus-trated. Moreover, they are parallel in their particular details and references. Augustine inter-prets Psalm 90 in terms of the Temptation of Christ. The illustration depicts the Tempta-tion with allusions to the protective imagery of Psalm 90: the shield, the shelter of Christ's shoulders, the supporting angels, the triumphal 'Osiris' figure. Augustine embellishes the figure of Head and Body with imagery of the Door, the Last Judgement, the Tabernacle and the Ascension, all of which seem to appear in the illustration. In both verbal interpre-tation and visual illustration, the Temptation of Christ becomes the multi-levelled figure of the temptation of the Church: the Church in heaven and the Church on earth, the passion of Christ and the passion of the martyrs, the future temptation of all creation and the present temptation of the faithful.

The Figure of the Head and Body:
Historic Context in Insular Exegesis and Liturgical Texts

What influence did Tyconius's rules and Augustine's *Enarrationes in Psalmos* have on Insular interpretations of the Temptation of Christ and Psalm 90? What types of interpretation make use of the Rule? Did Augustine's interpretation of Psalm 90 influence some types of interpretation? Do the Insular interpretations using the figure of the Head and Body sug-gest a liturgical context in which a luxury gospel book might have served for public reading and/or display? Furthermore, assuming momentarily that the connection between text and image could be proved beyond doubt, could the manuscript's possible place or places of origin be narrowed down to centres or areas in which Tyconius's *Liber Regularum* or Augus-tine's *Enarrationes in Psalmos* was known?

Augustine's interpretations of the Psalms were known in Northumbria during the eighth century,[104] and so were Tyconius's rules, although probably indirectly from Augustine's *De Doctrina Christiana* or Isidore's *Sententiarum.*[105] The Irish knew of the *Enarrationes* as early as the seventh century.[106] Exactly how well the Irish were acquainted with Tyconius's *Liber Regularum* is more difficult to determine, but the following discussion will show that the interpretive figure of head and body was known in eighth-century Ireland.[107] The ques-tion of localising the Book of Kells by means of a perceived connection between either of the two texts and the illustration can be answered immediately and negatively. The *Liber Regularum* and the *Enarrationes in Psalmos* were so widely known and influential that a cen-tre's knowledge of one or the other or both sheds no light on the origin of the Book of Kells.

Bede inserted into his interpretations of the Temptation of Christ a few passages men-tioning the figure of the head and body. For example, Bede interprets the forty days and nights of Christ's fast in terms of the collective temptation of the Church on earth:

> Quadraginta autem dies et noctes quibus eum temptat, totum huius saeculi tempus insinuant quibus membra eius, videlicet sanctam ecclesiam temptare numquam desistit, quia nimirum quadripertitus est mundus in quo domino famulamur decem vero praecepta per quorum observantiam Domino famulantes contra hostis indefessi malitiam, certamus, decem autem quater

ducta, quadraginta faciunt ideoque totum militiae nostrae tempus apte quadragenario dierum ac noctium numero comprehenditur.[108]

[Now the forty days and nights, in which he tempts him, intimate the whole time of this age during which he never ceases to try his [Christ's] members, namely, the holy Church. For indeed the world in which we serve the Lord is fourfold, and there are ten commandments by the observation of which we, in serving the Lord, battle against the evil of the indefatigable enemy. Four times ten makes forty, and so the whole time of our military duty is appropriately understood by the number forty days and nights.]

When reading this interpretation, one should keep in mind that the number forty also equates with the forty days of Lent. Thus Christ's fast and the Lenten fast of those who heard the story read from the Gospel were seen as types of the collective temptation of the Church during its earthly pilgrimage. Bede's interpretation bears similarities with an anonymous eighth-century commentary on Luke, possibly from an Irish milieu in the region of Salzburg.[109] According to the anonymous Irish writer, Christ 'heals the square world through a square fast' (*quadratum mundum per quadrata ieiunia sanat*). The forty days of fasting signify the whole time during which the devil assaults the Church on earth, which time of tribulation will end with Judgement day when Christ arrives, appearing as the paschal lamb.[110]

In another example, a passage of Bede's *In Lucam* presents a brief quotation from Gregory the Great's Quadragesima homily:

Certe iniquorum omnium diabolus caput est et huius capitis membra sunt omnes iniqui. Quid ergo mirum si se permisit ab illo in montem duci qui se pertulit etiam a membris illius crucifigi?[111]
[Certainly the devil is the head of all the evil ones and all the evil ones are the limbs of this head. What is extraordinary if he permitted himself to be led by that one [the head of evil] onto the mountain who submitted himself to be crucified by the limbs?]

This passage clearly bears some relation to Tyconius's seventh rule, 'The Devil and his Body'. Bede, however, left out Gregory's sentences which bridged the gap between the two he copied. Gregory had asked his listeners if Pilate, the Jews who persecuted Christ, and the soldiers who crucified him were not the limbs of the devil.[112] This last point is of interest because interpretations similar to Gregory's appear in Irish exegeses of the Temptation of Christ.

One such interpretation is found in the late seventh-century[113] Pseudo-Hieronymian *Expositio Quatuor Evangeliorum*:

In sancta civitate, id est, Jerusalem; *super pinnam templi*, id est, super murum arcae maceriae, elationem significant: non est, ut a capite se tentare dimisit, qui per membrum a Pilato crucifigi permisit.[114]
[*In the holy city*, that is, Jerusalem; *on the pinnacle of the Temple*, that is, above the wall of the enclosure of the ark, they signify pride: it is not as if he forbade himself to be tempted by the head who allowed [himself] to be crucified through the limb by Pilate.]

Bede probably knew of and used as a source the *Expositio* or another Irish work including much of the same material.[115] The most important point, however, is that the figure was a fairly familiar one in Insular as well as patristic exegesis, familiar enough that Bede could leave out the details of connecting thought and still expect to be understood.

Besides the Temptation exegeses, a second category of Insular exegetical writings, Psalm titles or headings, provides examples of Anglo-Saxon and Irish knowledge of the interpretative figure of the head and body.[116] Psalm titles are brief inscriptions for individual Psalms composed to help direct prayer and to facilitate Christian interpretation. They also reflect the important role of the Psalms in the liturgy and sometimes indicate a specific liturgical context.[117]

Moreover, the prominence of Psalm titles in Insular texts indicates their didactic importance in the monastic schools in which the ecclesiastic élite were trained.[118] The didactic function of Psalm titles is explained in an Old Irish treatise on the Psalter, probably composed before 850. The treatise compares the Psalter with a building full of treasure houses (the Psalms), each of which has a key, its title, which opens riches of knowledge to the reader.[119] The image resembles Quintilian's mnemonic house of rooms opened with key words, a memory device used in medieval education.[120]

Several series of Psalm titles are known to exist in Psalters, Breviaries and Bibles dating from the seventh to fourteenth centuries, where they may be found distributed one by one following the biblical title of each Psalm, written in the margin or grouped, either at the end, in a wholly separate section or, according to the Insular tradition, at the head of the Psalter. The oldest texts of the titles date to the fourth and fifth century.[121] Irish and Anglo-Saxon exegetes and scribes appear to have made a significant contribution to the preservation, development, and spread of Psalm titles.[122]

The most straightforward use of the figure of the head and body in connection with the Temptation of Christ appears in the heading for Psalm 90 in the Pseudo-Hieronymian *Breviarium in Psalmos*:

> Iste Psalmus non habet titulum, eo quod de capite, vel membris cantatur. Caput in coelo: membra in terra. Et proprie intelligitur de jejunio, et illa tentatio [sic] eremi. Praevidebat propheta, quod venturus erat Christum in carne, ut tentaretur a diabolo.[123]
> [This Psalm does not have a title, because it is sung about the head or else the limbs. The head [is] in heaven, the limbs on earth. And in particular it is to be understood [to be] about the fast and that temptation in the desert. The prophet foresaw that Christ was going to come in the flesh so that he might be tempted by the devil.]

The heading not only says that the Psalm is about the head and the body, but it also repeats nearly verbatim Augustine's phrase 'caput in caelo est, corpus in terra', and places the figure of head and body in the context of Christ's temptation in the flesh. The *Breviarium in Psalmos* presents a complex collection of exegetical material compiled in Ireland as early as the seventh century, possibly as the result of a long development depending ultimately upon a late fifth- or sixth-century commentary of undetermined origin.[124] Whatever the origin of the individual title, it clearly shows the use in an Insular context of the interpretative figure of head and body to connect Psalm 90 multivalently with the temptation and the liturgy, indicating, as does Tyconius's first rule, that the Psalm speaks simultaneously of the Lord and his body.

Martin McNamara considers some of the headings of the *Breviarium in Psalmos* to be 'close to the exegesis implicit in the St Columba series',[125] appearing in the Cathach of St

Columba and the Codex Amiatinus.[126] The 'St Columba' title for Psalm 90 condenses a phrase used by Augustine in his commentary on the Psalm:

> Vox Ecclesiae ad Christum. Legendus ad evangelium Marci ubi temptatur Christus.[127]
> [Voice of the Church to Christ. To be read with respect to the Gospel of Mark where Christ is tempted.]

The first sentence closely resembles Augustine's words on verse 9, 'Vox enim est ecclesiae ad Dominum suum …'.[128] The phrase appears again in the title presented in the eighth-century Pseudo-Bedan *De Titulis Psalmorum*:[129]

> Pro victoria Ezechiae de Assyriis cantatur. Aliter legendum ad evangelium Marci, ubi tentatur Christus. Vox Ecclesiae ad Dominum.[130]
> [It is sung on behalf of the victory of Hezechiah over the Assyrians. In another manner, it is to be read with respect to the Gospel of Mark, where Christ is tempted. The voice of the Church to the Lord.]

The *Glossa in Psalmos* in Vatican, Biblioteca Apostolica, Codex Palatinus Latinus 68, also presents the phrase, 'Vox aeclesiae ad Dominum', within a lengthy heading of multiple historic references to Old Testament voices of Moses, Hezechiah, and David.[131]

While phrases such as 'Vox ecclesiae ad Dominum' belong to a relatively common literary form of Psalm titles,[132] the occurrence of this phrase in Augustine's commentary and in the Columban, Pseudo-Bedan, and the Vatican Codex Palatinus Latinus 68 *Glossa in Psalmos* headings is significant. The phrase is important in Augustine's multivalent exegesis of the Psalm because it unifies the temporal locations of his interpretation, enabling them to be understood as mystically simultaneous. In his animated verbal picture, the earthly Church chants a prayer of hope to the ascended Christ, who is in heaven but is nonetheless the head of the body of the Church and who has suffered in the flesh as the earthly Church suffers. In the discussion following, it will be seen that such imagery was directly connected with the context of Lent. Possibly the image of the Church praying with the words of Psalm 90 would have served well as a spiritual orientation for the season of fasting and to teach the meaning of Lent to those in training to be clergy.[133]

Having surveyed Insular exegeses of Psalm 90 and the gospel story of the Temptation of Christ, one can say that Insular writers refer relatively often to the figure of the head and body. When viewed in the light of Insular exegesis and its probable sources, a depiction of the Temptation of Christ showing Christ as the Head of the Temple, which is also his Body, and placed at the beginning of the text of Luke 4 in a luxury gospel manuscript begins to make perfect sense.

The illustration's iconography becomes understandable when viewed against a background of exegeses of the Temptation and Psalm 90. In order to understand fully the reasons for depicting the Temptation in this way and to begin to understand how the illustration would have been perceived by those who created and used it, one may look to what was possibly its main context of viewing. This context may have been the season and liturgy of Lent.

The Illustration and The Liturgy

The illustration of the Temptation of Christ in the Book of Kells exhibits possible ties with liturgy by its placing within the gospel text, by its allusions to Psalm 90, and by its subject's associations with Lent in exegetical writings. What follows is an attempt to reconstruct the liturgical context and the meaning of Lent, in particular of Quadragesima Sunday, in eighth- and ninth-century Ireland and Northumbria in order to understand how the illustration may fit into that context.

Luke 4.1–13 as a Lection: the Evidence

The passage nearly always read from the gospel on the first Sunday in Lent is the Temptation story as told in the Gospel of Matthew 4.1–11.[134] For some reason, the makers of the Book of Kells attached a greater importance to the Temptation story as told in Luke 4.1–13 than the nearly identical one told by Matthew.[135] Because of the illustration's specific references to Psalm 90 and the overall significance of the Temptation in respect to the duration, purpose and practices of Lent, one may still suspect, in spite of the illustration's peculiar placing, that the reason for this emphasis was tied to the manuscript's possible liturgical function. For instance, it may have been the book from which gospel lections were read at mass, perhaps only on special occasions, or it may have served to display a gospel incipit at the divine office. Beyond these possibilities of direct use in the liturgy, it may have had other connections with the public presentation of the gospels in the liturgy.

Was Luke 4.1–13 ever read as a gospel lection? Could Northumbrian or Irish liturgies contemporaneous with the Book of Kells have included it as a lection for Quadragesima Sunday? The questions can be at least partly answered by studies of 1) early gospel lections and 2) decoration of the incipit and text of the story of the Temptation of Christ in gospel manuscripts, dating up to the early ninth century.

Early Gospel Lections

Four gospel manuscripts dating before the ninth century are known to indicate Luke 4.1–13 as a lection. Three of the manuscripts indicate it as one of two lections for a single day (See Appendix 1). In all four manuscripts, marginal notations, not lists, indicate liturgical lection of Luke 4.1–13.[136]

The Rabula Gospels and the Codex Forojuliensis (Appendix 1, Numbers 2, 3) note both versions of the Temptation story as lections for Quadragesima Sunday. Some, although not all, of the notations of the Rabula Gospels may date from the sixth century.[137] Those of the Codex Forojuliensis may date as early as the seventh.[138]

The eastern liturgy represented by the Rabula Gospels may have shared influences with the Aquileian or North Italian liturgy represented by the Codex Forojuliensis,[139] but the two probably were not closely related. Indeed this argument does not intend at all to connect the liturgy of the Rabula Gospels directly with Insular ones. The important point to be realized here is that the indication of Luke 4.1–13 as a lection for Quadragesima in the Rabula Gospels, as well as in some Latin Gospel books, demonstrates the possible early, widespread existence of this Lenten lection. Such a widespread tradition could in turn have been at play in the formation of possible early Insular systems in which Luke 4.1–13 may have been read as the Quadragesimal lection. A comparison of the lections from a group of gospel manuscripts considered Aquileian with those of the Rabula Gospels shows only scant similarity between them, most notably in their inclusion of Luke 4.1 as a Quadragesimal lection and in a unique set of lections for Holy Thursday (Matthew 26.17, Mark 14.12, and John 13.1).[140]

The two manuscripts' notations also share status as representatives of very old liturgies developed independently of Roman authority. The ancient Aquileian liturgy was shaped by its participation in a region at crossroads between Alexandria and other African regions, from Arles and Milan, from Ravenna and the Byzantine East. Not until well into the ninth century was Aquileia pressed into the uniformity the Roman Church pursued during the Carolingian period.[141]

The third manuscript, the Codex Valerianus (Appendix 1, Number 5), has lost part of its text of Matthew, from 3.15 through 4.23,[142] so that one cannot know whether a marginal notation marked Matthew 4.1–11 as yet another lection for Quadragesima Sunday. Even so, two notations mark lections for Quadragesima Sunday, one the Temptation story in Luke and the other the very unusual lection from Matthew, *Intrate per angustam portam*.[143] Morin and White believed that most of the notations in the Codex Valerianus represent a liturgy from South-eastern Europe, probably the Danubian area.[144] Others see an overall agreement in its notes with northern Italian, especially Aquileian, liturgy.[145] Palaeographers and liturgical specialists have dated the notes variously, to the seventh, eighth, and ninth centuries.[146]

The so-called St Kilian gospels (Appendix 1, Number 10) indicate Luke 4.1–13 as a lection for the second rogation day.[147] This is interesting because the rogation days were three days of fasting, a sort of abbreviated Lent, preceding the feast of the Ascension. The rogation days, therefore, have liturgical themes in common with Lent. Adopted in Rome by Leo III (795–816), the rogation days originated as a traditional custom of the British and Gallican Churches in which clergy and laity fasted until the ninth hour (none of the daily office) and engaged in the singing of litanies in processions displaying crosses and relics.[148] The rogation days were, by the time of this notation, celebrated in the Little Hours (terce, sext, and none) of the daily office and concluded with a mass.[149] The pericope notes in the St Kilian Gospels represent a pre-Carolingian Gallican liturgy, perhaps related to that of the Luxeuil Lectionary, although attribution is difficult.[150] The notes are written in Tironian shorthand, suggesting that they may represent working notations used for planning liturgical lections.[151] The monk who authored the liturgical notes also annotated the text to follow other modified Vulgate and pre-Vulgate versions. The text of Luke 4.1–13 is annotated in seven different places, perhaps an indication that its liturgical reading was from a venerable manuscript containing a pre-Vulgate copy of the Gospels.[152] The Kilian Gospels, like the previous three manuscripts, provide evidence that the story of the Temptation of Christ according to Luke had a place in an early, non-Roman liturgy and also that the passage served as an office reading for a day of ascetic practices to which were assigned special multiple lections.

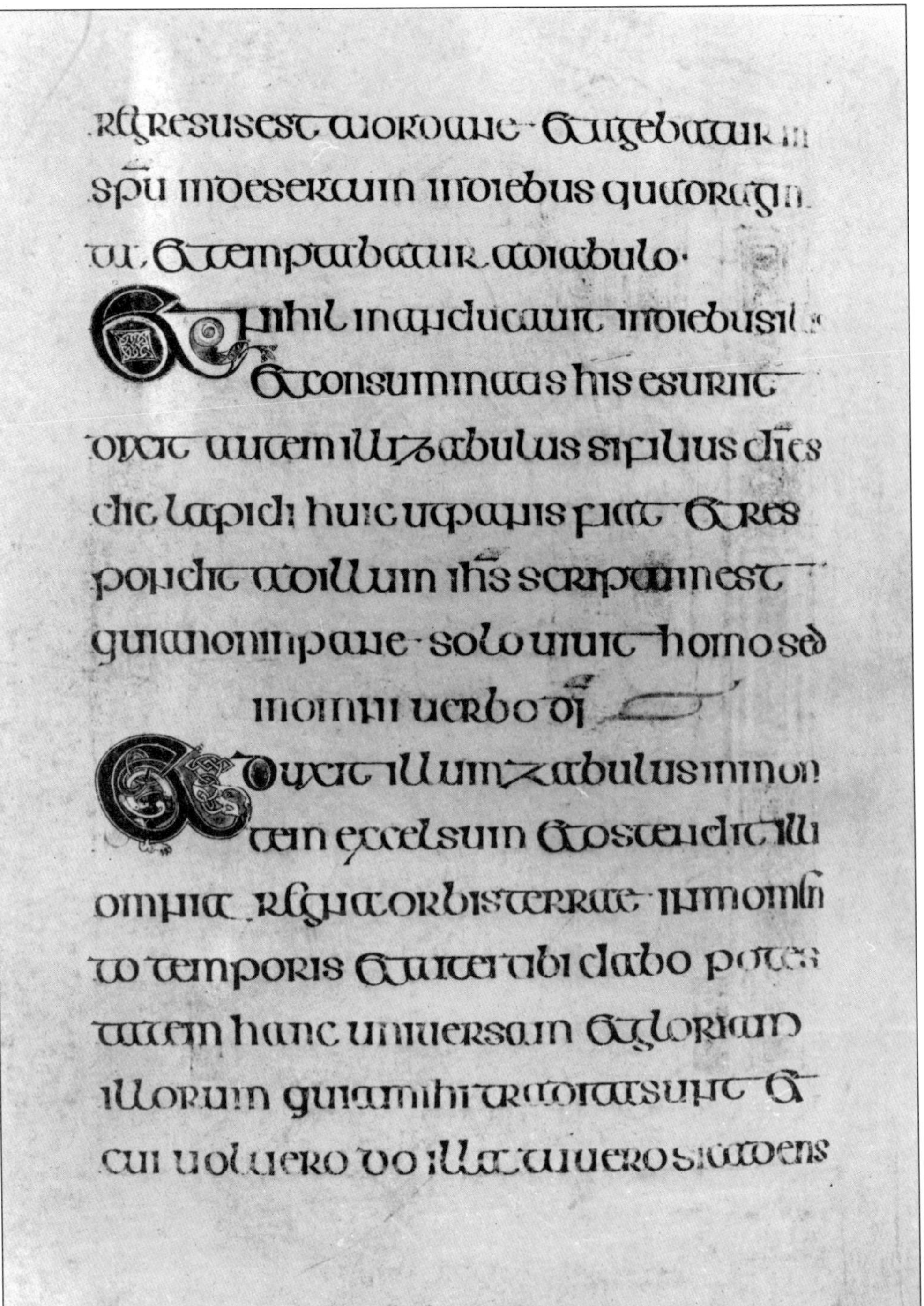

.REGRESUSEST AIOROANE · GAGEBATUR in
spu indesercum indiebus quadragin
ta · Ettemptabatur adiabulo ·
Et nihil induducauit indiebusil
lis Etconsummatis his esuriit
dixit autem illizabulus sifilius dies
dic lapidi huic utpanis fiat Etres
pondit adillum ihs scriptumest
quianoninpane · solo uiuit homosed
inomni uerbodi
Et duxit illum zabulus inmon
tem excelsum Etostendit illi
omnia regnaorbisterrae inmomen
to temporis Etaitei tibi dabo potes
tatem hanc uniuersam Etgloriam
illorum quiamihitradditasunt Et
cui uoluero do illa tuuerosiadoras

FIG. 5 Book of Kells, fol. 203v, Luke 4.1–7

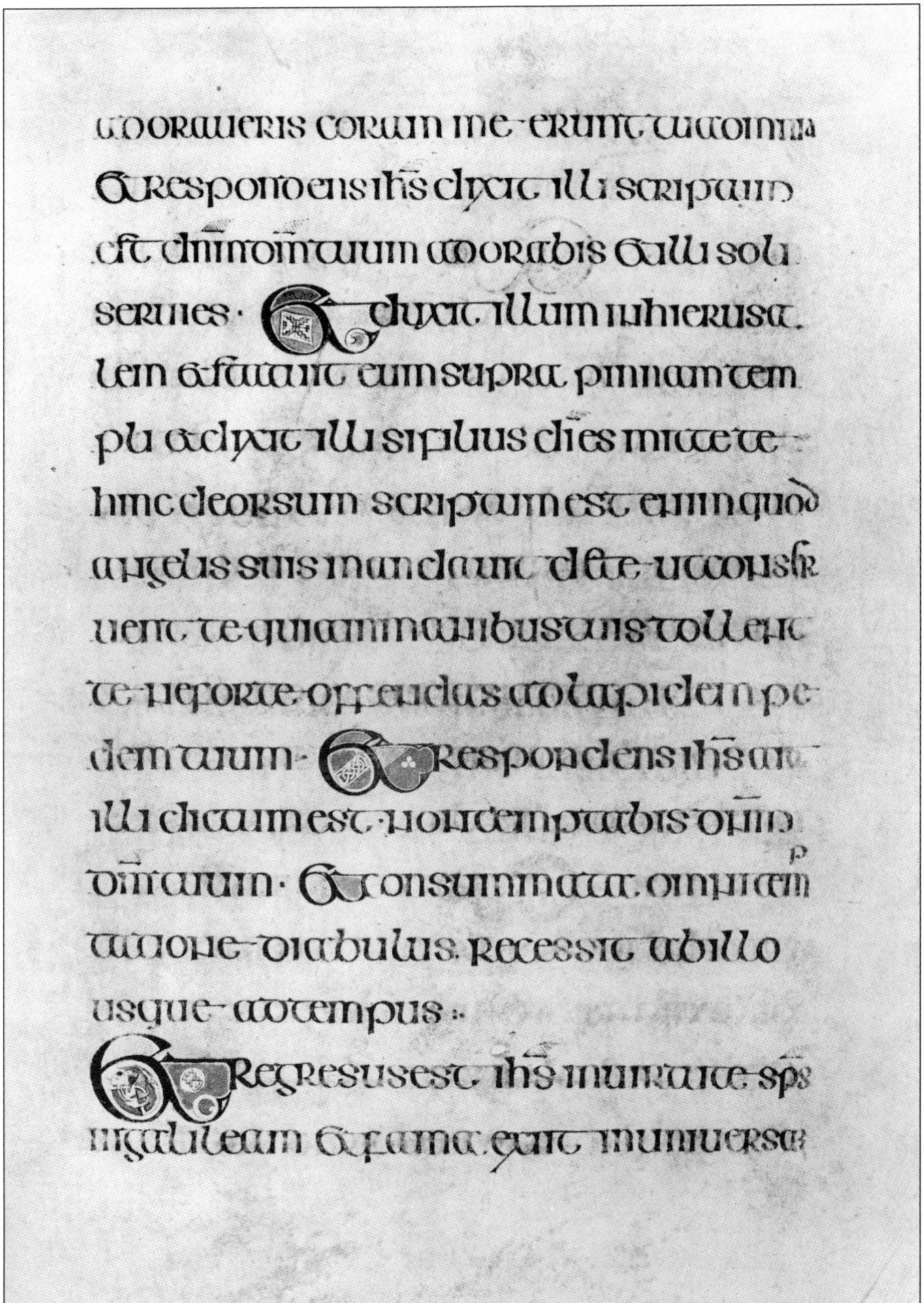

adoraueris coram me·erunt tua omnia
Et respondens ihs dixit illi scriptum
est dominum tuum adorabis et illi soli
seruies· Et duxit illum inhierusa-
lem et statuit eum supra pinnam tem-
plu et dixit illi siplius dies mitte te·
hinc deorsum scriptum est enim quod
angelis suis mandauit de te· ut conser-
uent te quia in manibus tuis tollent
te neforte offendas ad lapidem pedem tuum· Et respondens ihs ait
illi dictum est· non temptabis dnm
deum tuum· Et consummata· omni tem-
ptatione·diabulus·recessit abillo
usque adtempus ··
Regresus est ihs in uirtute sps
in galileam et fama exiit inuniuersae

FIG. 6 Book of Kells, fol. 204r, Luke 4.7–14

As a group, the four gospel manuscripts are characterised by their non-Roman pericopes and by the double lections for Quadragesima Sunday given in three of them. Morin and de Bruyne attempted to explain the double lections in Forojuliensis and Valerianus by asserting that one from each set must have been meant for the Monday following Quadragesima Sunday.[153] However, if one studies Lenten lection notations, the purpose of the notes in Forojuliensis and Valerianus becomes clear: both manuscripts indicate two lections for Quadragesima Sunday.

As de Bruyne himself points out, the marginal note of the Codex Valerianus specifically designates text beginning at Lk. 4.1 for Sunday ('Domineca …'), while the Forojuliensis note indicates the same passage 'In caput Quadragisime'.[154] Lections for Quadragesima Sunday are not always specified with the word dominica. For example, 'in quadragesima',[155] 'in caput Quadragesimae',[156] and 'quadragesima'[157] designate in different manuscripts the conventional gospel or epistle lections. The original liturgical use of the term 'quadragesima' was for the first Sunday in Lent, and it was not until the ninth century that its use extended to Ash Wednesday, which, in such cases, was still designated 'feria iv initium quadragesimae'.[158] In the seventh or eighth century, the Monday following the first Sunday in Lent would certainly have been noted 'feria ii'. Because of the ambiguity of many notations for Quadragesima Sunday, liturgical scholars hesitate to attribute more than one lection to it.

Pericope lists and notations offer firm evidence that the story of Christ's Temptation as told in the Gospel of Luke served as a gospel lection for Quadragesima Sunday in liturgies of the Monastery of St John at Zagba where the Rabula Gospels were read, of monasteries in the region surrounding Aquileia, and possibly in Danubian monasteries founded from Aquileia. The discussion in Chapter 3 will further underscore the importance of non-Roman liturgical lections for the placing and iconography of the two illustrations in the Book of Kells.

Decorative Structure of Luke 4.1–13 in Insular Manuscripts

Another important source of information on possible public reading of texts lies in the articulation of Insular Gospel manuscripts, that is, the structuring of the gospel text by means of decoration.

Patrick McGurk has studied the Insular tradition of major enlarged gospel incipits, including the incipit of Luke 4.1, some of which are consistent throughout the luxury decorated manuscripts.[159] Julian Brown wrote briefly about the initial of Luke 4.1 of the Lindisfarne Gospels, but suggested that its emphasis was for decorative effect rather than having any articulating function within the text.[160] The line of thinking followed by McGurk, Brown, and Alexander is that for some decorative and structural reason this text and others were emphasised according to an Insular tradition. From this tradition developed full-page illustrations, such as the Book of Kells's depiction of the Temptation scene.[161]

Until recently the enlarged incipits have been viewed mainly as beginnings of text. Considering, however, the Insular tradition of decorative division within blocks of text using hierarchies of script, it is important to analyse the graphic and decorative articulation

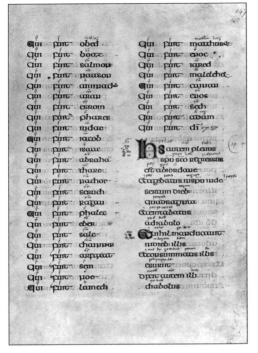
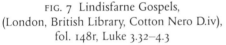

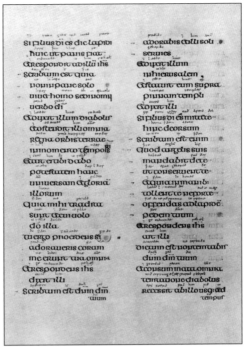

FIG. 7 Lindisfarne Gospels,
(London, British Library, Cotton Nero D.iv),
fol. 148r, Luke 3.32–4.3

FIG. 8 Lindisfarne Gospels,
(London, British Library, Cotton Nero D.iv),
fol. 148v, Luke 4.3–13

of longer passages in an effort to discover the circumstances of reading the text and to see if some sort of interpretative overlayer has been placed upon it to facilitate public reading. Within the Insular block layout of text, of which the Book of Kells provides an example, the double-sided, dividing, as opposed to incipit, function of enlarged and decorated letters must be recognized, as will be seen in the discussions following and in Chapter 3.

Tables 1.a and 1.b in Appendix 2 compare the articulation of the text in the Book of Kells with that in nine other manuscripts, all of them Insular except for the Oxford St Augustine Gospels (Bodleian Library, Auct. D.2.14), a sixth-century gospel book from Italy which was brought to England by the eighth century.

Table 1.a compares the Book of Kells's text with manuscripts written *per cola et commata* (*see also* PLATE II *and* FIGS 5 through 10). *Per cola et commata* is a system of punctuating sentences by means of layout. It originated in Mediterranean manuscripts of Roman authors and was adopted by St Jerome in his Vulgate edition of the Bible. Each rhetorical or sense unit is set out on a new line. Thus line length indicates the position of pauses and clarifies the meaning of a sentence, much as commas and semicolons do in modern punctuation.[162] The meticulousness and consistency of the articulation of the Lindisfarne Gospels (FIGS 7, 8), Royal 1.B.vii (FIGS 10, 11), and the Oxford St Augustine Gospels is evident in the number of lines and the consistency of line beginnings. They are nearly the same in all three manuscripts. This is true also of the beginning of the text in the Book of Durrow, which articulates *per cola et commata* until the end of the first page, changing to a block of text layout on the next.

Comparison of textual articulation reveals similarities between these manuscripts and the Book of Kells, in that all the letters or words emphasised in Kells are also line beginnings in the other manuscripts. Furthermore, points emphasised with decoration and colour applied to more than one letter are shared by Kells, Lindisfarne, and Durrow, as though a layer of hieratic decorative emphasis has been placed upon the methodical structure of the Italian uncial manuscript. The Oxford St. Augustine Gospels use colour and enlarged script minimally, allowing emphasis only at the chapter beginning, at *Ihs autem*, but denying it even to the lone Eusebian section in the pericope, at *et nihil manuducavit*. The scribes of the Lindisfarne Gospels and the Book of Kells seem to have been aware of and to have combined two traditions of textual articulation, the Mediterranean *per cola et commata* and the Insular hieratic decorative emphasis which was rooted in the block format of early Irish manuscripts, undecorated examples of which can be still seen in eighth- and ninth-century 'pocket' gospels, such as British Library, Additional MS 40618 (FIG. 9).[163] Both are ways of 'disambiguating' text, facilitating reading but also ensuring correct sense, as reading itself is an act of interpretation.[164] Interpretation may be more important in the hieratic system, in that the narrative or linear structure of the text can be more clearly indicated and, also, selected points of division valuated. Where *per cola et commata* expresses a precise, absolutely correct reading of text, Insular decorative articulation can give a sense of the text's overall structure and emphasise, subjectively or even arbitrarily, certain points within it.

Table 1.b, comparing the Book of Kells (FIGS 5, 6) with five other Insular manuscripts presenting text in block format, indicates this different kind of structure in which decoration divides sections of text. The subjectivity of structuring can be seen in the variation of exact positions of emphasis. Still, the manuscripts share an approximate structuring of the story episode by episode, and only the Barberini Gospels (FIG. 16) adds a unique point of emphasis, at the beginning of the story (*regressus est*). The Book of Kells's adherence to older forms can be seen in the correspondences of points of emphasis with Durham A.II.17. These points of emphasis are shared also with a gospel manuscript dated late seventh to early eighth century, Oxford, Bodleian Library, Rawlinson G.167 (FIGS 12 and 13), and to a degree with the Hereford Gospels, dated to the late eighth century and associated by later ownership with western England and Wales.[165] In Kells, Durham A.II.17, and Rawlinson G.167, the third episode receives the heaviest articulation of any part of the story's text. The capricious decorative articulation of the otherwise grand-scale Macregol (FIGS 14, 15) and Barberini Gospels (FIG. 16) may relate to changing uses of hierarchies of script in the last half of the eighth century, pointed out by Michelle Brown in her studies of Southumbrian manuscripts, in which decoration and letter forms also serve impressive effect rather than primarily to articulate the text's meaning.[166]

Some of the features of textual articulation and decoration of the manuscripts suggest that the text of Luke 4.1–13 or part of it may have been read publicly or in the liturgy. First of all, the structure of the story is clearly articulated in the text of the Book of Kells, with

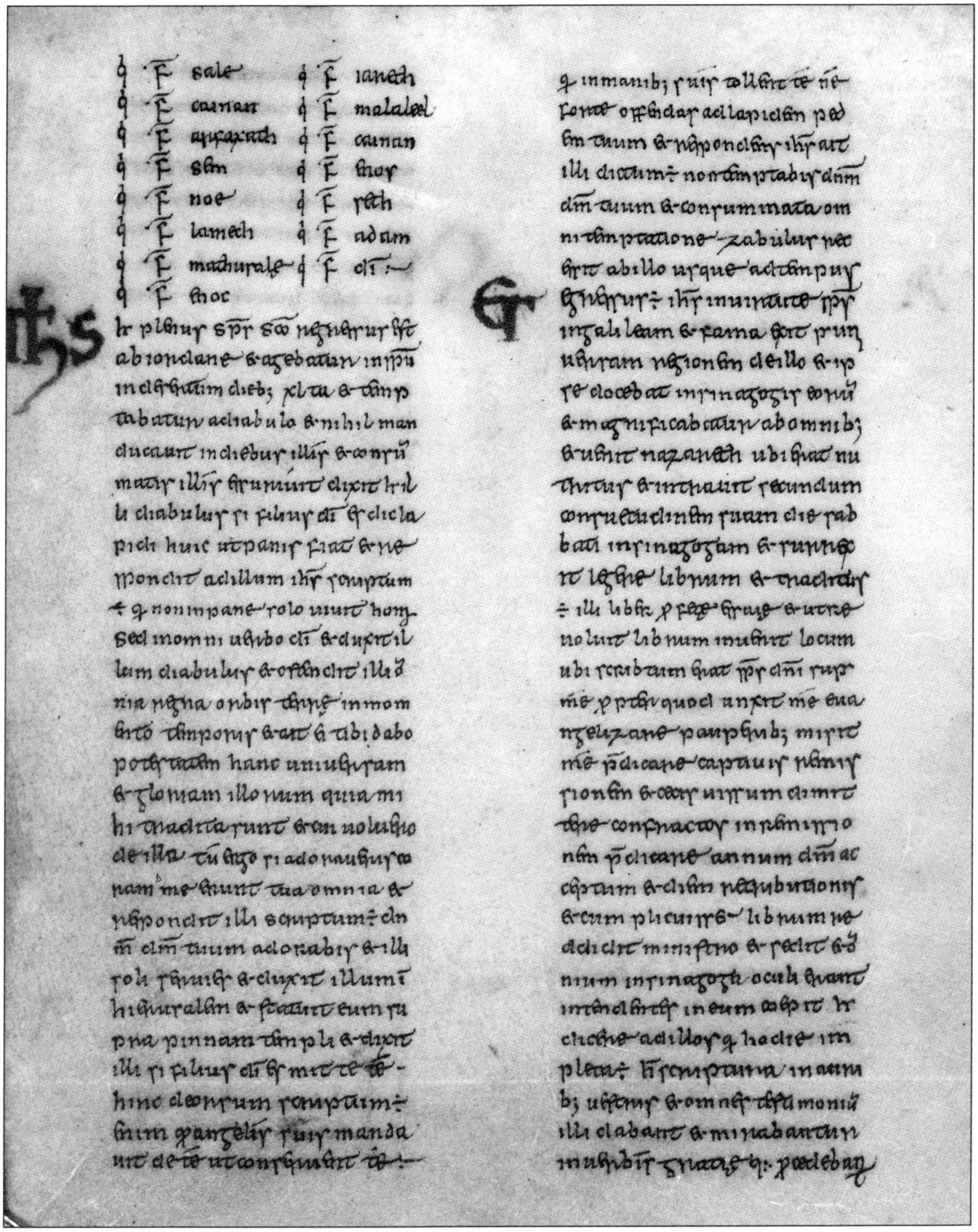

FIG. 9 London, British Library, Additional MS 40618, fol. 26v, Luke 3.35–4.22

an unusual number of decorated letters in the text block, compared with following folios in the manuscript. Moreover, in Durham A.II.17 and Rawlinson G.167, incipits of dialogue are sometimes emphasised, a feature seen also in the Lindisfarne Gospels. Even in Royal 1.B.vii medial points are placed before beginnings of dialogue in mid-line in the final episode of the Temptation story. Meticulous *per cola et commata* articulation like that in the Royal Gospels usually eliminates the need for punctuation, but the dialogue in this narrative was

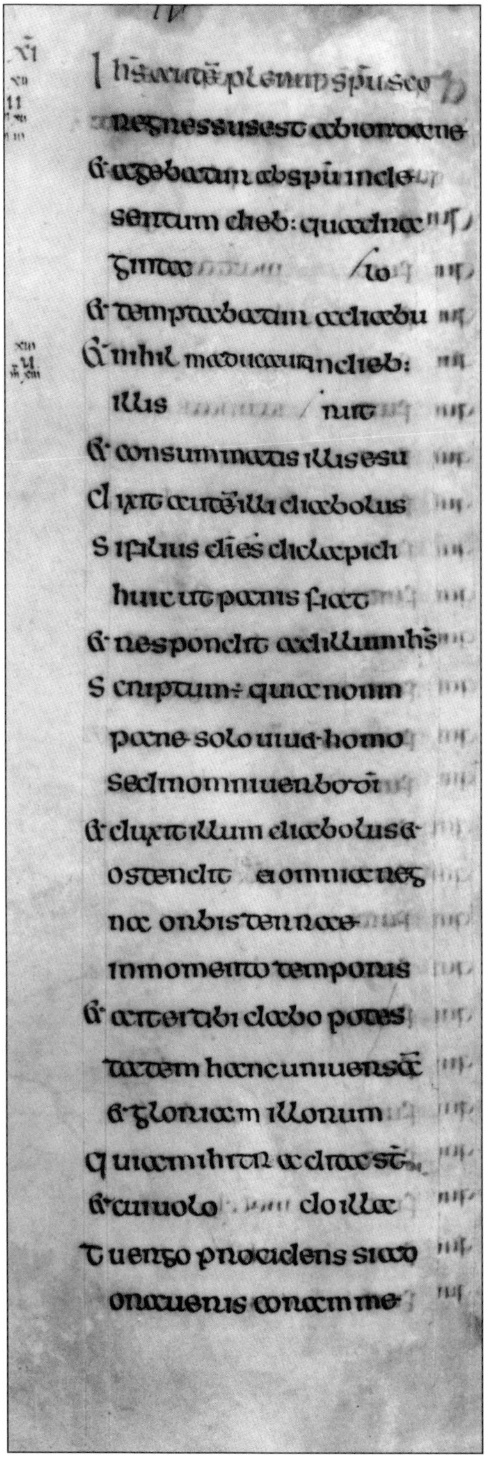

FIG. 10 London, British Library,
Royal I.B.vii, fol. 90v, Luke 3.34–4.7

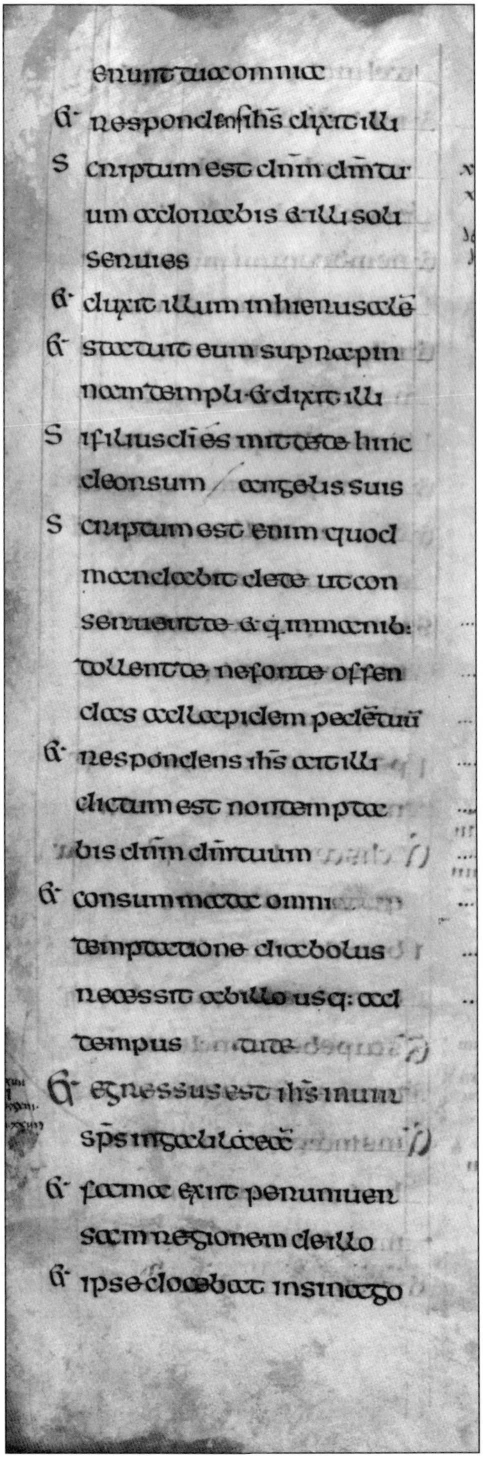

FIG. 11 London, British Library,
Royal I.B.vii, fol. 91r, Luke 4.7–21

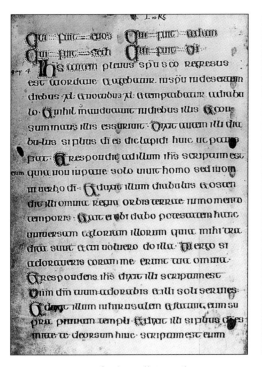

FIG. 12 Oxford, Bodleian Library,
Rawlinson G.167, fol. 10v, Luke 3.38–4.10

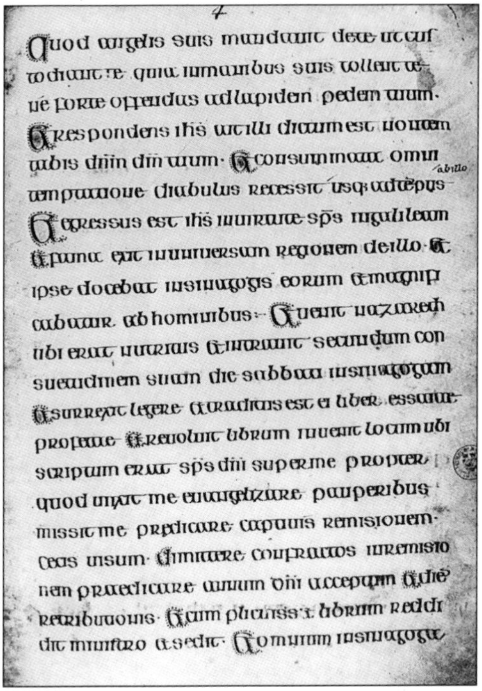

FIG. 13 Oxford, Bodleian Library,
Rawlinson G.167, fol. 11r, Luke 4.10–20

punctuated. Conveying the sense of this text effectively in public or liturgical reading would depend upon the reader's ability to distinguish for the audience the dialogue from the narrative and to articulate the step-by-step structure of the story, either by pauses or by changes in tone or level of voice. Palaeographers have remarked upon the general tendency of liturgical manuscripts produced after about AD 600 to be more heavily punctuated than other types of manuscripts.[167] The articulation of episodes and dialogue in the text of Luke 4.1–13 in Insular manuscripts give some support to the theory that it was read as a liturgical lection. Moreover, the practice of liturgical reading may still have influenced articulation of the text in a gospel manuscript, even if the manuscript was not actually read publicly.

Two of the manuscripts, Durham A.II.17 and the Oxford St Augustine Gospels, present clear evidence that the text of Luke 4.1 was read or sung liturgically from the manuscript, probably as part of the lection for Epiphany. In both manuscripts, the genealogy of Christ is marked with neumes. The neumes begin in the Oxford St Augustine Gospels at Luke 3.21 (*Factum est autem cum baptizaretur* …) and continue into 4.1, at *regressus est a Iordane*. In Durham A.II.17 they begin at the same point and continue through the opening of the genealogy, but the incipit of Luke 4 has been cut out of the page, leaving only a stub of vellum at the gutter of the manuscript. The neumes in Durham A.II.17 probably date from the tenth century.[168] Those in the Oxford St Augustine Gospels are not known to have been dated, but probably they are no earlier since the earliest neumes date from the ninth century.[169] The Lucan genealogy in the Oxford St Augustine Gospels is also marked for liturgical reading

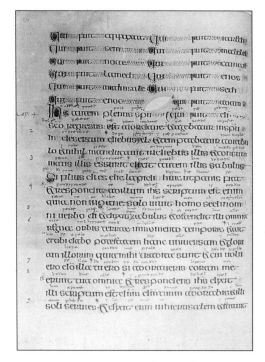

FIG. 14 Macregol Gospels,
(Oxford, Bodleian Library, Auct. D.2.19),
fol. 93v, Luke 3.36–4.9

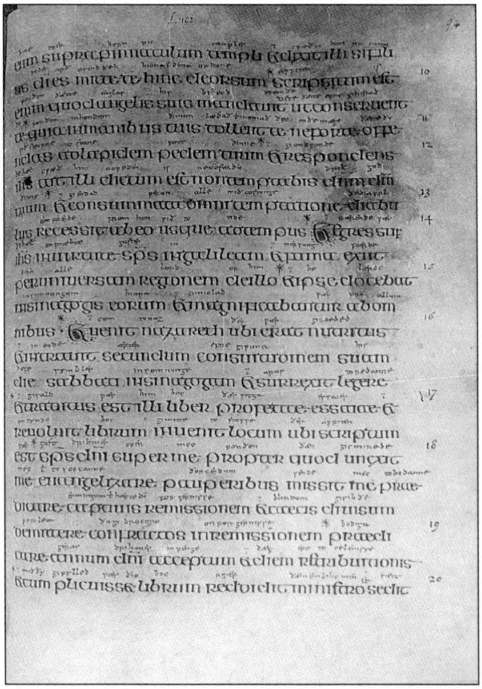

FIG. 15 Macregol Gospels,
(Oxford, Bodleian Library, Auct. D.2.19),
fol. 94r, Luke 4.9–20

with letters l and t alternating by each line of the text, probably indicating antiphonal reading in two voices. Moreover, in the margin of the Oxford manuscript, at the beginning of the genealogy on fol. 78v, a faint, only partially legible notation reads 'epi ora t hic [-] scri[–],' which could originally have indicated a lection for Epiphany. Chapman seems to include this inscription among those he dates to the seventh and eighth centuries, and its script resembles that of the notations to which he assigns this dating. He does not include it in his list of tenth-century notations, although he does not discuss it directly.[170] The Lucan genealogy is known to have been sung in later liturgies as a special reading in the secular office of nocturns before the Te Deum on Epiphany.[171] Copies of the Matthean and Lucan genealogies are among the earliest surviving notated texts, neumed in the ninth century.[172] For this reason, a seventh or eighth century date for the Oxford St Augustine notation seems plausible.

George Henderson and Jennifer O'Reilly have suggested detailed exegetical connections linking the Temptation illustration to the Baptism and genealogy of Christ through the phrase, *Ihs autem plenus spiritus sancto*.[173] The illustration would thus follow or stand in the middle of, rather than preceding, the text to which it is connected. In view of the possibility that the closing words of the Baptism, the genealogy and the verse on the holy spirit filling Jesus were recited as an Epiphany lection, their suggestions seem cogent. But it also means that the picture in the Book of Kells may well have had a public function and

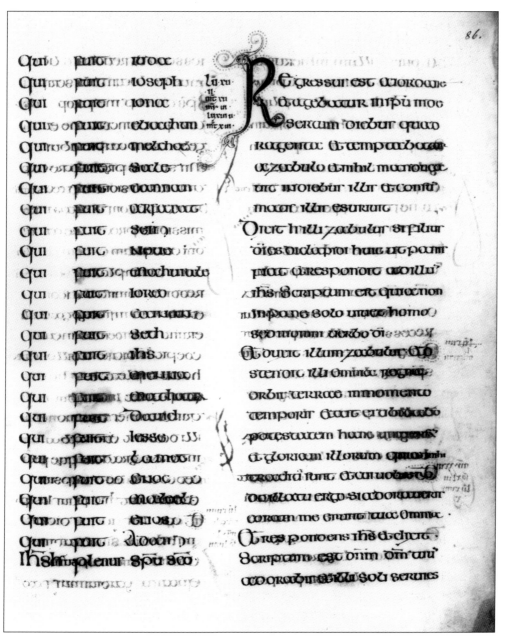

FIG. 16 Barberini Gospels (Vatican, Biblioteca Apostolica, Barb. Lat. 570),
fol. 86r, Luke 3.30–4.8

have had something to do with reading and interpreting the gospels in the liturgy.

Furthermore, as Henderson suggests, the picture may stand in the middle of an important section of text. This idea also makes much sense because of the nature of Insular decorative articulation within block-format text. As will be seen in discussion of the picture on fol. 114r, division markings within a block of text can easily be double-sided, being seen as both the end of one section and the beginning of another. When a division falls within an important lection, this double-sided function becomes prominent. Possibly the full-page illustration showing Christ atop the Temple in Jerusalem was placed in the Book of Kells because two important lections included the text at Luke 4.1, a reading for Epiphany and one for Quadragesima. The two feasts and their readings are linked as well in the symbolic structure of the liturgical year, the Baptism of Christ having taken place on the anniversary of the Epiphany and also being the event before the forty-day fast in the desert, which is expressed in the liturgy as Lent.

Luke 4.1–13 as a Lection: Conclusion
That Luke 4.1–13 was read as a gospel lection in some non-Roman liturgies has been established beyond a doubt. Besides this, there is some hint that a liturgical tradition may have influenced the decoration of Insular manuscripts. The elaborate articulation of the text in the Book of Kells seems to suggest that it could have served public reading.

Among the texts associated with the illustration, Psalm 90 has especially powerful associations that reach into several areas of liturgy, including the liturgy of Church dedication.[174] The Psalm is recited during the dedication as part of the purification ceremony. This aspect, however, must be set aside at this point in order to continue consideration of connections between the illustration and the liturgy of Quadragesima.

The Liturgy of Quadragesima Sunday and the Illustration
If the illustration of the Temptation of Christ was created to be viewed during the liturgy of Quadragesima Sunday, then a necessary step toward understanding the illustration's meaning and purpose would be to reconstruct the ritual which may have surrounded the picture when it was displayed. However, sparseness of sources allows only a generalised recreation of the Quadragesimal liturgy, limited mostly to assembling the probable lections. On the other hand, even though nothing can be said of uniquely Insular rituals enacted on Quadragesima Sunday, the illustration can be related to the character and meaning of Lent in general. Some idea of the illustration's liturgical context may be compiled from scraps of information gleaned from hagiography, Bede's *Historia Ecclesiastica*, exegetical writings, and the few surviving liturgical texts.

One can probably assume that throughout Ireland and Northumbria the gospel lection for Quadragesima Sunday was the story of the Temptation of Christ, whether from Matthew or Luke, that the Epistle lection was 2 Corinthians 6.2–10, and that Psalm 90 was recited as a tract (in its entirety) during mass and the divine office, its verses also providing antiphons and responses. These assumptions are based mainly upon the consistency with which notations and capitula indicate the Temptation of Christ from Matthew or Luke as the gospel lection and Paul's enunciation of the 'weapons of righteousness' in his second letter to the Corinthians as the Epistle.[175]

Besides the textual connections of Psalm 90 with the Temptation story, it has known associations with Lent from very early times.[176] Its presence in Northumbrian and Irish

Quadragesimal liturgies is supported by (1) the Insular Psalm titles and (2) by the antiphons in Alcuin's *De Laude Dei*.[177] Three titles for Psalm 90, from the *Breviarium in Psalmos*, the Pseudo-Bedan series, and the St Columba series, connect the Psalm with the Temptation of Christ, although with the brief account in the Gospel of Mark, which is unknown as a lection in any surviving systems.[178] The *De Laude Dei* is Alcuin's earliest florilegium, or collection of writings on loosely related themes.[179] In the section *De Antiphonario* of this work, a group of verses identifiable as taken from canticles, antiphons, and responsories of the Lenten liturgy presents short texts derived from Psalms 90.2–3 and 21.1:

> Dicam Deo: Susceptor meus es, Deus meus–Sperabo in eum quoniam ipse liberabit me de laqueo venantium et a verbo aspero.
> Deus meus, in auxilium meum respice.[180]

Psalm 21 is most obviously associated with Good Friday, but it also appears alongside Psalm 90 and verses from the Matthean story of the Temptation of Christ in a collection of antiphons for Quadragesima in the eighth- or ninth-century manuscript in Paris, Bibliothèque nationale, nouv. acq. lat. 1628, which is written in an Insular script although attributed to a centre in France.[181] Bullough believes that the *De Laude Dei*, especially its section *De Antiphonario*, documents the liturgical usage of eighth-century York.[182] Certainly it, and the Paris antiphon collection, document the presence of Psalm 90 texts in eighth- and ninth-century Quadragesimal liturgies on the Continent where Insular influence was present.

While the picture in the Book of Kells appears to make no direct references to 2 Corinthians 6.2–10, this Epistle text is nonetheless also relevant to the illustration. In this pericope, Paul describes the upcoming spiritual battle which must be waged in preparation for the day of redemption.[183] Moreover, the Roman office lection for matins extends the reading to verse 16, which speaks of the 'temple of the living God', the dwelling of God among men, which must separate itself from the false and the idolatrous.[184] This collective spiritual battle between the Church and the devil, waged by Christ and his body with weapons of truth and righteousness, has already been suggested as the probable theme expressed by the illustration. It also represents the theme of Lent. The usual epistle lection, therefore, presents a message so appropriate to the gospel lection and Psalm 90 that it is completely consistent with the illustration. The picture unifies the texts of Quadragesima Sunday's liturgy, presenting a visual exegesis of their themes. Because it is so closely tied to the texts of the liturgy, the illustration is incomplete without the context of the liturgy. Furthermore, because Quadragesima Sunday begins Lent, the full meaning of the picture cannot be known unless it is considered against the background of the season of spiritual contest into which the medieval viewer would have been about to enter.

For the Irish and Northumbrians, as for all Christians, Lent was the season of self-denial and purification, of spiritual strengthening in preparation for Easter and the three holy days preceding it.[185] Lent probably included the baptismal scrutinies and other events known to western liturgies in general.[186] Like patristic writers, Insular authors equate the forty-day fast with the fasts of Moses, Elias and Christ and with other forty-day or forty-year periods from Scripture. Some Insular writers interpret it in terms of the figure of the present Church, whose struggle against the devil on earth will end with the Second Coming and Last Judgement.

The earliest known Insular interpretation mentioning Lent directly, the seventh-century Irish *Expositio IV Evangelia*, refers to Lent only briefly by repeating the commonplace explanation, known from patristic literature, that the number of days of Lent represents one tenth of the year, a tithe offered out of the lives of the faithful.[187] The patristic writings from which this explanation derives present the idea of the tithe of Lent as part of the fulfilment of Old Testament law as stated in Exodus 22 and Leviticus 27.[188] The Irish gospel commentary interprets the forty days of Christ's fast and temptation almost exclusively as fulfilment of Old Testament law and prophecy. Thus, Christ performed his fast not only upon the authority of the fasts of Moses and Elias but also in fulfilment of the forty days of the flood because, like the floodwaters which cleansed the world of wrongdoers, his fast signalled the eradication of the sin of Adam.[189] Only a few phrases in the commentary connect the temptation with New Testament events, such as the Crucifixion, or relate it to the life of the reader, as in the abbreviated explanation of Lent as a tithe, itself a reference to Old Testament law. In spite of the commentary's scrambled arrangement of passages collected from different sources,[190] it may reveal to some extent an Irish view of Lent as a present-day fulfilment of Old Testament prophecy as Christ had fulfilled it in the New Testament.

In his commentary on Luke, Bede writes of Lent and Christ's forty-day fast with considerably less emphasis on Old Testament authority. Discussing the meaning of the forty days of Christ's fast, he mentions only the fasts of Moses and Elias, all three of which fasts provide the scriptural authority for Lent:

Quadragesima ieiuniorum habet auctoritatem et in veteribus libris ex ieiunio Moysi et Heliae et ex evangelio quia totidem diebus dominus ieiunavit demonstrans evangelium non dissentire a lege et prophetis. In persona quippe Moysi lex in persona Heliae prophetae accipiuntur inter quos in monte gloriosus apparuit ut evidentius emineret quod de illo dicit apostolus: *Testimonium habens a lege et prophetis*. In qua autem parte anni congruentius observatio quadragesimae constitueretur nisi confinis atque contigua dominicae passionis quia in ea significatur haec vita laboriosa cui opus est continentia ut ab ipsius mundi amicitia ieiunetur.[191]
[The forty-day period of fasting has authority both in the books of the Old Testament from the fasting of Moses and Elias and from the Gospel because the Lord fasted the same number of days as they, demonstrating that the Gospel does not dissent from the law and prophets. Indeed, in the person of Moses is understood the law, in the person of Elias, the prophets. Between them he appeared glorified on the mountain, that it might emerge more clearly what the apostle said about him: [he] 'having the witness of the law and prophets' (Rom. 3.21). Moreover, in what part of the year would the observance of Lent be more fitting than coterminal and contiguous with the Lord's passion, because in it is signified this laborious life for which there is an effort at continence, that there may be abstention from the fondness of the world.]

Bede brings the Old and New Testament texts into focus on the present purpose of Lent and expands its meaning into a metaphor of the struggle of the present life, lived in a world which must be denied to attain the eternal life promised by Christ in his resurrection. On another level, Bede continues, Christ enacted an antetype of his fast when he returned for forty days after his resurrection, eating and drinking with his disciples,[192] an event mentioned but not interpreted by the Irish author. As Christ's fast set the example of abstinence, his feasting after his resurrection signifies the hope with which the believer should live, 'simultaneously rejoicing with hope, and suffering with tribulation' (Rom. 12.12).[193] The number forty, he explains, is a sign of the present age in which those called to Christ from the four parts of the world battle in the forefront of the combat in fulfilment of the ten precepts of the Law. Four times ten equals forty. The forty-day fast signifies the time of the Church on earth as it struggles against the assault of the devil. In his later works, such as the commentaries on Mark and on the Temple,[194] Bede delineates in detail the figure of the Church of the present in the number forty, even giving a hint of Tyconian influence upon his description of the struggle of the Church of the present. In the writings of Bede, one finds multi-levelled interpretations of the forty-day fast which encompass Old Testament precedent as well as a present and an eschatological significance.

It seems less likely that Bede himself synthesised this coherent interpretation from different sources than that he simply articulated with increasing clarity an interpretation of the forty days of Lent already known to the Irish and Northumbrians. A pre-existing Insular tradition may be evidenced by the mention, in the Irish gospel commentary, of Christ's post-Resurrection feast and by the Insular Psalm titles which interpret Psalm 90 in terms of the Church.[195] The existence of a complex interpretation in an oral tradition is possible but remains out of the reach of proof.[196] On the other hand, Bede seems to have developed further his interpretation between the time he wrote his commentary on Luke and his later one on Mark, in which he succinctly explains the forty days as the temptation of Christ's body which is 'the holy Church'.[197] He may have encountered either Insular or patristic interpretations, such as those of Augustine, presenting the figure of the body of the Church in connection with Christ's fast.

On this account, perhaps it is worth noting that Tyconius presents in his fifth rule an interpretation of 'numbers containing four' that resembles in some respects the interpretations written by Bede and the Irish exegete.[198] Tyconius writes of the forty days of the flood as the key to the meaning of forty days or years of fasting and hardship, of feasting and peace: all are symbols of the time of the Church of the present as it simultaneously suffers and hopes, but which will stand, as Christ, triumphant over the devil at the end of the world. The forty days of fasting and forty years of hardship provide the scriptural model for the Church's fast 'in the desert', presumably a reference to Lent. Although certainly neither the first nor the only to do so, Tyconius includes in his interpretation the same forty day periods of fasting and feasting as the Irish gospel commentary.[199] But also, like Bede, Tyconius explains the idea of simultaneous suffering and rejoicing to be ended with the Second Coming, expressed by the image of 'the one ruling the earth … beneath the feet of the Church, the Son of Man.' It appears that a Tyconian interpretation of the forty-day fast may have influenced Bede.

In later Insular exegeses, similarities with Bede's interpretations of the forty days of Christ's fast often appear.[200] The late eighth-century Irish commentary on Luke attributed to the circle of Virgilius of Salzburg, combines the Old Testament preoccupations of the seventh-century commentary on the Gospels together with the eschatological interpretations found in Bede's exegesis. It fails to repeat only the theme of Christ's feasting with the apostles after his resurrection. It mentions Lent once directly, interpreting the meaning of its time in terms of an Old Testament figure and the time of the Church:

> Sciendum est nobis, si in consummatione ieiunii diabulus Iesum an per spatia totius quadragensimae. Per totum tempus ieiunii diabulus illum temptavit. Quid in Goliat figuratum est, qui Israheliticum populum in valle positum per dies quadraginta expugnavit, qui diabulum per tota tempora mundi istius ecclesiam expugnantem significat usque ad sollemnitatem diei iudicii. Cum autem verus David, id est, Iesus Christus, advenerit quasi pascha consumit labores quadragensimi. Et quasi libertas consumit temptationi, Israhel per David [liberatur]. Sic iudicium consumabit labores sanctorum.[201]
>
> [It should be understood by us whether the devil tempted Jesus at the end of the fast or through the period of all forty days. The devil tempted him through the whole time of the fast. This is prefigured in Goliath, who assaulted the Israelites positioned in a valley for forty days, [and) who signifies the devil who through all the time of this world assaults the Church until the celebration of the day of judgement. When David, that is Jesus Christ, arrives just as Easter, the labours of the forty days are finished. And just as freedom finishes temptation, Israel [is freed) through David. Thus the judgement will finish the labours of the saints.]

Once again an Old Testament figure presents a multi-levelled historic semiosis. Goliath's temptation signifies simultaneously the time of Christ's fast, of Lent, and of the time of the Church of the present. The advents of David and Christ, whose victories ended the time of struggle, are compared with the arrival of Easter, ending the spiritual trials of Lent. The ultimate arrival and end to all tribulations of the faithful will come about on Judgement Day. Furthermore, the commentary explains the meaning of the devil's departure at the end of the forty days:

> *Usque ad tempus:* Id, crucis usque ad bellum antichristi in fine mundi ...[202]
> ['Until the time': That is, of the cross until the war of the antichrist at the end of the world ...]

Thus it links the Temptation and, therefore, Lent in a narrative, or syntagmatic, sense as well as symbolically, or paradigmatically, to the Passion and to the time of the Church on earth.

The Irish Lucan commentary expands the significance of the forty-day fast based upon existing Irish traditions and upon Bede's interpretations. Although at this point in his commentary the Irish author does not use the Tyconian figure of the body of the Church, he does apply the first rule of Tyconius to the Temptation of Christ. He describes it as a battle between the 'head of idolatry' and the 'head of truth' and with the Tyconian figure of Jacob and Esau, the worse of whom tormented the better while in the womb, an interpretation following much the same 'logic' also as Tyconius' exegesis of the rising and falling of the floodwaters.[203]

Considering the multivalent significance of Lent as presented in Insular exegesis and the probable influence of Tyconian interpretation upon its expression, it is possible that this significance affected the depiction of the Temptation of Christ in the Book of Kells. The illustration, as has been shown, may depict the collective temptation of the Church based upon a multi-levelled exegesis influenced by the rules of Tyconius, such as Augustine's commentary on Psalm 90. If the illustration marked the lection for Quadragesima Sunday, then it presents a symbolism not confined to texts of the liturgy but a significance expanded to include the community which viewed it, who would have considered themselves part of the Church of the present as depicted in the illustration. As did homilies and other exegeses, the picture made its audience aware of their place within the struggle against the devil, reminding them of the scriptural precedents of the Lenten battle about to begin and showing them the promise of the future victory, when Christ will triumph over death and the Church will stand upon the body of the devil.

However, precisely because most of the literary material on Lent considered so far belongs to the category of exegesis, one may question how well such explanations were known and understood by viewers outside the élite, such as monks who may have been literate only at a low level. A remote possibility exists that a section of Augustine's commentary on Psalm 90 might have served as the patristic lection for nocturns or matins of Quadragesima Sunday in the monastery which kept the Book of Kells, thus placing the illustration, the gospel lection from Luke 4.1–13, and the commentary into a closely related liturgical ensemble. However, no specific evidence is known to support such a suggestion. Little precise evidence exists to build a picture of the actual Insular experience of Lent or whether monks and laity understood it in terms of a symbolism as complex as that presented by Bede.[204] Only a few direct references to Lent occur in Insular hagiography and monastic rules. In addition to combing through the few and brief early references, one can, although less satisfactorily, turn to later literature which depends upon earlier accounts of saints' lives. One account belonging to this class, the *Voyage of St Brendan,* depicts Lent as a kind of *peregrinatio* within a *peregrinatio.*[205] Apparently, some sort of self-imposed exile or retreat was practised during the season of Lent.

Early medieval writings from the Insular and Frankish worlds create a picture of Lent as a season of spiritual battle set apart from the rest of the year, a time of struggle rigorously endured by monks and bishops. Bede tells of the monks of Lindisfarne seeking Bishop Eadberht in his retreat to show him the incorrupt vestments of St Cuthbert which they had discovered along with the saint's incorrupt body upon opening his coffin in preparation for translation of the relics on the anniversary of burial, March 20. Eadberht customarily passed Lent and the forty days before Christmas 'in prayer and severe fasting, shedding tears of devotion' alone on a patch of ground which became an island at high tide, one of Cuthbert's sites of 'solitary battle for the Lord'.[206] The story appears to present the Lenten retreat as a special element of the Lindisfarne community's spiritual identity with Cuthbert, because Eadberht not only spent his retreat as Cuthbert had, but also, upon seeing the relics and spontaneously composing a hymn about the miracle of their preservation, he fell ill with a 'long and wearing illness', died and was laid to rest in Cuthbert's tomb beneath the saint's coffin,[207] thus becoming further assimilated to the identity of Cuthbert.

A retreat similar to Eadberht's was practised in the Gallican and Spanish Churches during Lent and the Gallican 'Lent of St Martin', the period between the feast of St Martin and the Nativity.[208] In their sermons, Maximus of Turin and the Spanish Priscillianist urged their listeners to imitate Christ's fast by performing a solitary forty-day retreat in the 'desert', meaning confined to a monastery, in an enclosed cell or on an island. [209] Gregory of Tours tells of the Lenten retreats of Eparchius, a bishop of Clermont-Ferrand who isolated himself in a monastery atop Mont Chantoin, and Palladius, Bishop of Saintes who went 'off to pray on an island in the sea'. Both returned to their Churches on Holy Thursday, Eparchius accompanied by the singing of Psalms and a procession of clergy and townspeople, but Palladius, in a much simpler way, awaited by his congregation at the cathedral, where he would celebrate 'the Lord's Supper, according to custom'.[210] The reality of a 'desert' fast enduring temptation and the meaning of such an experience must have been accessible to all members of Insular monastic communities.

A liturgical context for the illustration's viewing actually allows reception by an illiterate or marginally literate audience.[211] At the very least, any monk or possibly any lay person with fairly close connections with the Church viewing the illustration on Quadragesima Sunday would have recognised it as a depiction of the spiritual battle performed by the Church on earth in imitation of the temptation of Christ and under the protection of his example. As he anticipated the season of hardship and looked forward to its end at Easter, the viewer would have heard the Psalm's promise of protection and salvation, listened to the galvanizing words of Paul's Epistle to the Corinthians and heard of Christ's triumph over the devil, as told in the Gospel of Luke. Perhaps he would have also recognised in the illustration an expression of this promise of triumph, to be fulfilled symbolically by the events commemorated during Holy Week. The illustration was probably created exactly for this purpose: to make clear the deeper meaning of Quadragesima in the context of its liturgy.

Notes to Chapter Two

1 Nordenfalk, 1977a, p.275; O'Reilly, 1994, pp.345–54, 366–70, 376–91.

2 Klauser, 1972, pp.19, 65, 107, 146, 175; Beissel, 1907, pp.31, 36, 62, 79, 85, 92, 98, 112, 133, 151; Godu, 'Evangiles', 1922.

3 Powell, Appendix 1, in Henry, 1974, p.224.

4 Henderson, 1987, pp.168–73; O'Reilly, 1994, 370–97.

5 Henry, 1974, p.204; Hovey, 1928, p.116; Nordenfalk, 1977b, p.123; Henderson, 1987, pp.168–70; Nordenfalk, 1977a, p.277; Lewis, 1980, p.156, fn. 71; Karkov, 1991, pp.33–4.

6 Munich, Bayerische Staatsbibliothek, Clm 4453, fol. 32v; Aachen, Cathedral Treasury, Gospels of Otto II/III, page 52. Clm 4453, fol. 32v, in Dessler et al., 1977–78, vol. 1, fol. 32v; Nordenfalk, 1977a, p.277; Nordenfalk, 1977b, p.123; Mütherich, 1977–78, p.98. *See also* Goldschmidt, 1928, pp.4, 5, 29, PLATES 2, 27; Boeckler, 1949, p.8; Weis, 1971, pp.311–62.

7 Henry, 1974, p.190; Farr, 1989, p.34.

8 *The Jewish War*, V.(4), p.263.

9 *The Jewish War*, V.(4), p.265.

10 Classical and late Antique writers used *hyacinthus* ambiguously to describe colours ranging from deep blue to a violet, probably like the colour of an amethyst. André, 1949, pp.197–8 on *hyacinthinus*, pp.90–4 on *purpura*, p.116 on coccum. *Also* Stancliffe, 1982, pp.28–36, on Irish interpretation of colours, and Brown, 1996, pp.122–3, on Bede's interpretations.

11 I am most grateful to John Higgitt for this thought, expressed in a personal communication, September 8, 1987. Philo envisioned the two cherubim with faces together as the angels are depicted in the Kells illustration. Philo's reasoning was allegorical, that the two cherubim were one, like husband and wife together (Goodenough, vol. 4 (1954), p.130, and for illustrations of Jewish amulets depicting the cherubim over the ark, vol. 3 (1953), figs. 1068–70). While Philo's works probably were unknown to eighth- and ninth-century Ireland, the resemblance of his literary images to patristic interpretation, discussed *below*, and the existence of visual images of the cherubim over the ark from this period are of interest to show the Late Antique and early medieval background of the theme.

12 *See* the examples given by Kühnel, 1987, p.160; 1986–87, FIGS 1–3, pp.147–50; Revel-Neher, 1982, fig. 3, p.9; Roth, 1953, PLATES 8, 9, and pp.26–8.

13 Kühnel, 1986/87, p.147.

14 Kühnel, 1986/87, pp.147–8.

15 Illustrated in Grant, 1981, bottom of page 144.

16 St. Petersburg, Public Library, MS II 17, Ferber, 1976, pp.30–1, 32–3, and fig. 11; Gutmann, p.16, and fig. VII.

17 Prayon, 1986, pp.1–9; Ferber, 1976, pp.24–7; Tronzo, 1986, pp.53–8, 63, figure 4; Farr, 1989, pp.38–40.

18 Cassiodorus, *Expositio in Psalmum LXXXVI*, 1, in CCL 98, pp.789–90; and Institutiones I. V. 2, in Mynors's edition, p.23. Bede, *De Tabernaculo 2*, in CCL 119A, pp.81–2, lines 1563–70, and *De Templo 2*, in CCL 119A, pp.192–3, lines 28–40. Meyvaert suggests that Bede may have made a diagram of the Temple himself after Cassiodorus' drawing and the biblical description, but Bede augmented the diagram and description with his own calculations to include all the Temple's dimensions (1976, p.61; more recently Meyvaert, 1996).

19 Roth, 1953, pp.37–8; Meyvaert, 1979, pp.71–2, especially footnote 7; Halporn, 1980, pp.299–300; Corsano, 1987, pp.9–11; Marsden, 1995, pp.102–3, 115–19.

20 Kühnel, 1987, pp.157–9; Kühnel, 1986/87, pp.164–6; Revel-Neher, 1982, pp.6–17; Ferber, 1976, pp.27–30; Henderson, 1980, pp.5–6.

21 Revel-Neher, 1982, pp.16–17; Kühnel, 1986/87, p.166; Kühnel, 1987, p.159.

22 Kühnel, 1986/87, p.166; Kühnel, 1987, p.159.

23 In connection with this possibility, *see* Meyvaert, 1996, 844–60, and especially p.883, where he mentions the work of Fabio Troncarelli (1987, 1996) connecting the imagery of Cosmas manuscripts with an eighth-century manuscript of Cassiodorus's *Institutiones*. Meyvaert believes that this explains the presence of the Tabernacle image in the Codex Grandior. *See also* Roth (1953) on associative symbolism and interplay of allusions in Jewish art and (pp.37–8) on Cassiodorus's personal consultation with Eusebius, an Asiatic scholar. *Also*, Krinsky (1970), who points to (pp.29–30) Jewish apocryphal writings as possible sources for the inscriptions of the four cardinal directions, the first letters of which spell 'ADAM'. Augustine and Bede interpreted the name ADAM to be 'mathematically' equivalent with the time (46 years) of the construction of the Temple (Homelia II.1, 'In Quadragesima,' in *CCL* 122, pp.189–92). On patristic and Insular traditions, *see* McNally, 1959, pp.27–8; McNamara, 1975, p.26 and No. 4; Berschin, 1989, pp.99–101. I thank Walter Berschin for generously discussing this and other points with me at the St Cuthbert conference, University of Durham, 14–15 July 1987.

24 Page, 1973, pp.178–9; Beckwith, 1972, p.18, No. 1; Henderson, 1977, pp.156–8; Webster, 1982, 20–31, Wilson, 1984, pp.85–6; Neuman de Vegvar, 1987, pp.265–7.

25 Henderson (1977, p.158) sees the building's resemblance to 'the Jewish Tabernacle as it appears in early Greek bibles, with its guardian seraphim and animal offerings.'

26 *See* the bibliography given in Becker, 1973, in his discussion beginning p.63; *also* Neuman de Vegvar, 1987, pp.265–87.

27 *See* the drawing in Gwynn, 1913, p.335.

28 The image of heavenly Jerusalem described in Revelation combines Tabernacle (21.3), Temple (21.22–3), and city (21.9–11). The text also evokes many of the names of Christ used in patristic and Insular exegesis of the structures.

29 *See* Sharpe, 1984a; Doherty, 1984, 1991; and the discussion *above*, 'Introduction,' pp.21, 22–3, 24–5, 27–8.

30 Kühnel, 1987, pp.30–1, 160.

31 Danielou, 1957, pp.83–90.

32 Maiburg, 1984, pp.247–56; Sciascia, 1959, pp.23, 32–5; Kühnel, 1987, pp.30–1, 160–1; Ladner, 1942, pp.43–60.

33 Goodenough, vol. 4 (1954), pp.130–2, vol. 12 (1964), p.56; Danielou, 1957, pp.83–90; Kühnel, 1986/87, p.147; Smalley, 1983, pp.2–6.

34 Josephus, *The Jewish War* V.4, p.263.

35 Kühnel, 1987, p.49.

36 Raponi, 1983, pp.210–11, 225–7; Baltzer, 1965, pp.263–74. *Also*, the Irish Lucan commentary, *CCL* 108C p.34, lines 219–23: '*Usque ad tempus. Id, crucis usque ad bellum Antichristi in fine mundi, vel, usque ad tempus definitum prophetaturi, id, usque ad iudicium veniat.*'

37 Raponi, 1983, pp.227–36; Jeremiah, 1957, pp.57–9.

38 For example, Mt. 16.13–20, 21.42, 24.1–2; Mk. 11.15–8, 12.10, 13.1–2; Lk. 19.39–48, 20.17.

39 1 Cor. 3.16, 6.19; 2 Cor. 6.16; throughout the Epistles, he refers to the body of the Church and Christ its head. *See* Brown, 1988, pp.51–2; Martin, 1995.

40 Goodenough, vol. 12 (1965), pp.55–7.

41 Eusebius, *Ecclesiastical History*, II.23.1–19, in Lake, tr., and Schwartz, ed., vol. 1, 1926, pp.168–77.

42 Williamson, fn. 2, page 101, in Eusebius, *History of the Church*.

43 Williamson, fn. 4, page 101, in Eusebius, *History of the Church*.

44 Williamson, fn. 8, on page 100, in Eusebius, *History of the Church*.

45 *De Tabernaculo*, ed. Hurst, *CCL* 119A, pp.1–139; translation in Holder, 1994; *De Templo*, Hurst, *CCL* 119A, pp.141–234; translation in Connolly, 1995. After the fourth century, many influential Christian writings, such as Prudentius's *Psychomachia* and *Dittochaeum* and Cosmas Indicopleustes' *Christian Topography*, ad-

vanced a tradition of interpretation on the Tabernacle and Temple. *See* the summaries of scholarship and bibliographies in Kühnel, 1987; Davis-Weyer, 1986.

46 *CCL* 119A, p.42, lines 1–35; Holder, 1994, p.45–6.

47 *De Tabernaculo* 2, *CCL* 119A, pp.42–3, lines 36–40; Holder, 1994, p.46. The term *figura* can be translated only with difficulty. It refers simultaneously to the shape of the two structures and to what is signified by that shape. One should remember that Bede almost surely was thinking of the diagrams in the Old Latin pandect that Ceolfrid had brought from Rome. Holder's translation 'figure' implies both meanings. *See* Meyvaert's discussion of the diagrams in Meyvaert, 1996, pp.832–5, 844–60. I am extremely grateful to George Hardin Brown for his comments on this passage in particular.

48 *De Tabernaculo* 2.1, *CCL* 119A, p.43, lines 51–64; Holder, 1994, p.46.

49 *De Tabernaculo* 2.1, *CCL* 119A, p.43, lines 63–9; Holder, 1994, pp.46–7. The same conception may have influenced the prayer of Moucan, in B. L. Royal 2.A.xx, who describes himself in a state of sin as the temple in a state of disrepair (Hughes, 1970, pp.57–8).

50 *De Tabernaculo* 2, *CCL* 119A, pp.59–60, lines 701–3; Holder, 1994, p.66.

51 Bede, *De Tabernaculo* 2, *CCL* 119A, pp.59–60, lines 687–741.

52 *Historia Ecclesiastica* 3.17, in Plummer, pp.159–60; Farr, 1989, pp.56–7. On the relationship of *De Tabernaculo, De Templo,* and *Historia Ecclesiastica, see* Laistner, 1943, pp.70, 75; Mayr-Harting, 1976, pp.19–22, *esp.* p.21, nos. 7, 10, 12; Meyvaert, 1964, pp.1, 9–10; McClure, 1983, fn. 27, pp.80–1.

53 For example, Galatians 2.9; 1 Timothy 3.15; Apocalypse 3.12; Ambrose, *Expositio Psalmi CXVIII, CSEL* 62, 5.39, p.103; Augustine, *Epistulae, CSEL* 44, CXL 14.36, p.185; Augustine, *Enarratio in Psalmo LXXIV, CCL* 39, p.1028; Cassiodorus, *Expositio Psalmi LXXIV, CCL* 98, p.687; Gregory, *Moralia in Job* (on Job 38.6), *PL* 76, 457C–458A; Isidor*, In Exodium, PL* 83, 313 BC. *See also* Reudenbach, 1980; Deshman, 1986, pp.261–7; Deshman, 1995, pp.138–9, 152–5, 181–3; Karkov, 1991.

54 *Explanatio Apocalypsis* 1, *PL* 93, 141C–D; *also* Marshall, 1878, pp.26–7.

55 Bonner, 1966, pp.9–15; Laistner, 1943, p.25.

56 *PL Supplementum* 4, col. 1854: by 'column' the saints are understood; by 'in the temple of God,' i.e., 'in the tabernacle.' Kelly, 1982, p.404.

57 *See* O'Reilly, 1994, for a discussion of other connections complementary to those brought up here.

58 O. M. Dalton (1904) originated the misnomer 'Osiris pose', which has stuck to this type of figure giving rise to speculation, unfortunately often accepted as established fact, that such figures in Insular art depend upon Coptic models, which supposedly were transmitted directly from Egypt to England and Ireland or arrived via Gaul, even though no figures of the Insular type are known from Merovingian or Carolingian art. *See* Farr, 1989, pp.65–6.

59 In the Book of Kells, fol. 34r (Chi Rho initial), fol. 12r (initial M beginning the *argumentum* of Matthew; The Alfred Jewel; Lichfield Gospels, p.218 (portrait of Luke); Trier Gospels, fol. 5v (the 'Tetramorph'); stone cross shaft at Sandbach, Cheshire; the Tower Cross, Kells; cross at Termonfechin; Cross of Muiredach, Monasterboice; Breac Moedog; Shrine of St Patrick; and the Fuller brooch.

60 Bailey, 1981, p.119.

61 Saxl, 1943, pp.10–13.

62 For example, Goodenough, 1958, figs. 999, 1000; LeClercq, 1907, fig. 328.

63 Bonner, 1950, Pl. XVI, No. 318, illustrates an amulet from the Newell Collection, called by Bonner (p.218) 'Syro-Palestinian,' but Nees (1987, pp.207, 210) says it is Greek. The 'Osiris pose' appears on the reverse: a cross topped with a nimbed frontal figure. On either side of the figure, at the junction of the sleeves of his robe and the arms of the cross, a sceptre angles outward. One of these sceptres is clearly a cross; the other is less distinct, but it is probably a crudely formed branch with six leaves. Below the arms of the cross are the characters Alpha and Omega. The amulet's obverse depicts a nimbed rider who thrusts a spear with a cross bar near its terminal into a figure lying beneath the hooves of his galloping horse. East Mediterranean amulets of the fifth to seventh centuries often represent Psalm 90.13 with such images of triumphant riders, as evidenced by their accompanying quotations of Psalm 90 (Bonner, 1950, pp.211–21, 306–8; Numbers 319, 321, 322, 324). Even though the inscription on the Newell amulet presents a common

apotropaic formula, 'One God vanquishes Evil' (Nees, 1987, p.210) the combination of triumphal and protective should be clear. For images of saints, *see* Forrer (1891, Taf. XV, no. 6) who illustrates Coptic examples from burials at Akhmim, discussed by Dalton (1904, pp.71–7) as images of 'triumph over death'. Later examples from Italy and the East Mediterranean depicting saints are fairly numerous; *see* Garrison, 1954, vol. 4, No. 2, fig. 150; Grabar, 1972, fig. 85.

64   For further detailed discussion of this point, *see* O'Reilly, 1994, pp.377–95.

65   Harley 7653 is attributed to Mercia; *see* Brown, 1996, pp.135, 141, 142, 151, 152, 153–4, 168, 169; Gneuss, 1980, No. 443, p.29; Gneuss, 1985, p.138.

66   Hughes, 1970, footnote 3, p.53.

67   Hughes, 1970, fn. 3 on p.53.

68   Munich, Bayerische Staatsbibliothek, Clm 29164/2a, fol. 29, in Dold, 1950, pp.82, 91.

69   Dold, 1950, p.86.

70   Book of Cerne, Cambridge University Library MS Ll.1.10, fols 62, 49a, in Kuypers, 1902, as part of Prayer 25, pp.123–4, and Prayer 49, p.147, *also* pp.xvi–xvii. Royal Prayerbook, British Library, Royal 2.A.xx, in Kuypers, 1902, p.223. *See* Brown, 1996 (pp.151–5 on Royal Prayerbook); Brown, 1993; Brown in Keynes and Brown, 1991, pp.208–10; Alexander, 1978, p.84.

71   Connolly, 1995, p.34, uses these terms.

72   *De Templo* I, *CCL* 119A, pp.162–3, lines 630–4; Connolly, 1995, p.25.

73   Insular exegetes envisioned a pulpit or platform on top the Temple; *see* the discussion and works referenced in Kelly, 1982a, p.58; and *Leabhar Breac*, published in Atkinson, 1887, p.427. Cf. Henderson's idea that the illustration depicts Christ in an ambo (Henderson, 1987, pp.172–4).

74   *De Templo* I, *CCL* 119A, p.163, lines 636–41; Connolly, 1995, p.25.

75   *De Templo* I, *CCL* 119A, pp.162–3, lines 636–41; Connolly, 1995, p.25.

76   Origen, on Mt. 21.43, known to the West through a sixth-century Latin translation, in Klostermann, ed., 1935, pt. 2, pp.615–16 and p.VIII; *see also*, Sieger, 1980. Eusebius, *PG* 23, cols. 1139–66.

77   Burkitt, introduction to Tyconius, *Liber Regularum*, 1895, p.xiii.

78   *Liber Regularum* I (ed. Burkitt, pp.1–2, lines 19–3), II (p.8, lines 5–10, p.11, lines 12–28), VII (pp.70–85); *see also* Burkitt's comments in the introduction to the edition, pp.xiii–xiv; and Bonner, 1966, pp.3–5.

79   Evans, 1984, p.52.

80   Tyconius, *Liber Regularum* II, 7.24–8.3.

81   *Liber Regularum* I, ed. Burkitt, 1895, p.3, lines 12–23: Scriptum est de Domino et eius corpore – quid cui conveniat ratione discernendum …

82   *Liber Regularum* I, p.3, lines 12–23: Numquid de cuius obsequio *mandavit angelis suis* Deus eidem ostendit salutare suum, et non corpori eius.

83   Tyconius, *Liber Regularum*, I, 3.25–8.

84   Tyconius, *Liber Regularum*, p.1, lines 6–9.

85   III.92–134., *CSEL* 80, pp.104–17; translation in Robertson, 1958, pp.105–7.

86   *Enarratio in Psalmum XC*, II.1, *CCL* 39, p.1266, lines 63–9.

87   Sermo II.1, *CCL* 39, p.1265, lines 1–4.

88   *CCL* 39, p.1254, lines 1–2.

89   *CCL* 39, pp.1254–5, lines 2–50.

90   *CCL* 39, p.1254, lines 7–10.

91   Sermo II.1, *CCL* 39, p.1265, lines 8–9.

92   Sermo I.9, *CCL* 39, pp.1261–62.

93   *CCL* 39, p.1263, lines 35–46; translation in Farr, 1989, p.85.

94 For the comparison with Last Judgement scenes on Irish high crosses: Henry, 1974, p.189.

95 *Enarratio in Psalmum XC* 2.1, *CCL* 39, p.1266, lines 31–6; Farr, 1989, p.86.

96 *Enarratio in Psalmum XC* 2.1, *CCL* 39, p.1266, lines 36–44.

97 *Enarratio in Psalmum XC* 2.1, *CCL* 39, p.1266, lines 51–62.

98 *See above*, p. 68.

99 2.4, *CCL* 39, pp.1269–70, lines 11–25.

100 2.5, *CCL* 39, p.1270, lines 2–12.

101 2.5, *CCL* 39, p.1270, lines 23–9.

102 2.8, *CCL* 39, pp.1274–5, lines 44–60.

103 For example, the illustration of the Ascension in the Rabula Gospels, fol. 13v (illustrated in Weitzmann, 1977, Pl. 36), although here the angels grasp the top and sides of a mandorla so that their faces are separated.

104 Ogilvy, 1967, p.85.

105 Burkitt, 'Introduction,' in Tyconius, *Liber Regularum*, pp.xviii–xxiv.

106 McNamara, 1986, pp.53–4; Kelly, 1977, pp.143–6, 148.

107 No Insular manuscripts of *De Doctrina Christiana* are known (Gorman, 1985, p.19).

108 *In Marcum* 1, *CCL* 120, p.444, lines 291–9.

109 *Commentarius in Lucam*, *CCL* 108C, pp.1–101. The editor of the *CCL* edition (Kelly, 1976, pp.15–16) dates it *c*.780. *See also* Bischoff, 1976, pp.117, 134–6

110 *In Evangelium Lucae*, *CCL* 108C, pp.29–30, lines 33–4, 36–57, 70–8.

111 *In Lucam* 1, 3026–29, *CCL* 120, p.96.

112 Homilia XVI, *PL* 76, 1135C.

113 Lapidge and Sharpe, 1985, no. 341; Kelly, 1976, pp.12–13.

114 *PL* 30, 559A.

115 Kelly, 1982 for 1981, pp.59–60; Kelly, 1986, pp.68–9.

116 On Insular commentaries on the Psalms *see* McNamara, 1986; McNamara, 1979, 274–9; McNamara, 1973; Bischoff, 1976, p.78; Kelly, 1977, p.141; Lapidge and Sharpe, 1985, no. 1253; Walker, 1957, p.lxiv; Kenney, 1966, pp.664–6.

117 Salmon, 1959b, pp.9, 30; McNamara, 1973, pp.214–15; McNamara, 1986, pp.26–7, 35–45; Gibson, 1994.

118 McNamara, 1973; McNamara, 1986, pp.40–3, on the *Romani* mentioned in Vatican Codex Palatinus Latinus 68, *also* pp.74–5 on the possible context of the early Irish schools.

119 Meyer, 1894, pp.29–33; Bischoff, 1976, p.100.

120 Carruthers, 1990, pp.107–8, 114–21.

121 Salmon, 1959b, pp.28–33.

122 Series I, I, IV edited by Salmon (1959b) are associated with Insular manuscripts or authors. *Also*, Pseudo-Jerome, *Breviarium in Psalmos*, *PL* 26, cols. 831–1346; Pseudo-Bede, *De Titulis Psalmorum*, *PL* 93, cols. 477–1098); Vatican, Biblioteca Apostolica, Codex Palatinus Latinus 68, *Glossa in Psalmos* (McNamara, 1986). The Irish preserved the titles of Theodore of Mopsuestia (McNamara, 1973, p.216).

123 *PL* 26, col. 1162D.

124 Fischer, 1968, pp.254–6, fn. 25 on p.285; McNamara, 1973, p.225. Some earlier scholars consider it continental: Walker, 1957, p.lxiv; Morin, 1913a, p.59.

125 McNamara, 1973, p.225.

126 Salmon, 1959b, pp.47–51, on manuscript sources; edition pp.55–74.

127 Salmon, 1959b, p.67.

128 *Enarratio* in *Psalmum XC*, 2.4, *CCL* 39, p.1270, lines 25–6. Salmon (1959b, p.54) and McNamara (1973, p.216) have noticed the similarity between the St. Columba titles and Augustine's *Enarrationes* for Psalms 48, 50, 56, 60, 86, 90 and 115.

129 Fischer (1971, pp.90–110, *esp.* 93–8 on the Argumentum) believes that its basic form may be the work of Bede, an argument supported by Bailey, 1983, pp.192–3. McNamara (1973, p.217) sees relationships with Irish interpretation. *See also* Stancliffe, 1975, pp.364–5.

130 *PL* 93, 970B.

131 McNamara, 1986, p.193: Qui habitat. Heret *Et sit splendor Domini*. Vox Moisi confirmantis populum suum. Vox Ezechiae de victoria. Vox aeclesiae ad Dominum. In hoc salmo confirmat et docet beatus David unumquemque de suis socis manere in veritate et iustitia.

132 Salmon, 1959b, p.29. *See also* Scheffczyk (1983, pp.607–10) on the 'Vox Ecclesiae' formula as the basis of Augustine's figure of the Limbs of the Church in prayer to their Head.

133 *See* the discussion *above*, p. 74.

134 Callewaert, 1940b, pp.542, 559; Chavasse, 1948, pp.341, fn. 38 on p.343; Chavasse, 1952, p.99; Beissel, 1907, pp.198, 204; Klauser 1972, pp.186, 189.

135 *See also* the important exegetical reasons proposed by O'Reilly, 1994, p.359–97; *also* Henderson, 1987, pp.168–74.

136 Merk, 1912, p.203; Martimort, 1992, pp.23, 29; Klauser, 1972, pp.XXX, XXXIII, XXXV.

137 Cecchelli, 1959, pp.9, 16; Merk, 1912, pp.203–4, but his list does not seem to include those Cecchelli considers to be in a later hand. It is concluded here that the notation at Luke 4.1 is sixth-century.

138 Lowe, *CLA* 3, No. 285; Klauser, 1972, p.XXX; Gamber, 1963, p.38; Martimort, 1992, p.29. It must be pointed out that the dating of marginalia is notoriously difficult. The dates given here rely upon the authority of paleographic and liturgical scholars, but they should be taken as subject to revision, not as absolutes.

139 Huglo, 1976, pp.312, 317–18.

140 Merk, 1912, pp.213–14, compared with Godu, *DACL* 5.1, chart following col. 882, and Beissel, 1907, pp.91–7. *Also*, Farr, 1989, p.122; and Chapter 3, pp.117–9, for evidence of the existence of these particular Holy Thursday lections in Insular liturgies.

141 Huglo, 1976, pp.312–18; Cattin, 1984, pp.38–40; Martimort, 1992, pp.49–50.

142 White, 1888, p.xi.

143 Farr, 1989, p.123.

144 Morin, 1902, p.12; White, 1888, p.liii; *also* Klauser, 1972, p.XXXIII. Only two liturgical notes are contemporary with Valerianus' text: *in nativitate domini* at Mt. 2.1 and in *apparitionem Domini* at Mt. 3.13–17; G. Godu, 'Evangiles,' *DACL* 5.1, col. 882. *See* Gamber, 1975, pp.26–8, on the liturgical connections between Aquileia and Bavarian dioceses in the eighth century, as evidenced by fragments of liturgical books.

145 Martimort, 1992, p.49; Godu, 'Evangiles,' *DACL* 5.1, col. 882; Lowe, *CLA* 9, No. 1249.

146 Lowe, *CLA* 9, No. 1249; White, 1888, p.liii; Godu, 'Evangiles', *DACL* 5.1, col. 882; Klauser, 1972, p.XXXIII. Most recently Martimort, 1992, p.23: 'VII/IX siècles'.

147 Würzburg, Universitäts bibliothek MS Mp.th.q.1a, fol. 134, in Salmon, 1951, p.45.

148 Lapidge, 1991; Gatch, 1992, pp.162–7; Willis, 1968, p.232; Warren, 1987 rep. of 1881, pp.146–7.

149 Gatch, 1992, pp.164–5; Salmon, 1951, p.50, note 4.

150 Salmon, 1951, pp.38, 53; Morin, 1911, p.330; Gamber, 1963, p.40; Martimort, 1992, pp.48–9.

151 Salmon, 1951, pp.40, 53; Farr, 1989, pp.125–6; *also*, on Tironian notes, a shorthand system invented by Cicero's secretary, Tiro, in the first century BC, *see* Bischoff, 1990, pp.80–2; Ganz, 1983, pp.58–75; on liturgical planning, Bede, *Historia Ecclesiastica*, iv.18; Rankin, 1985, pp.321–2; and Fassler, 1985.

152 On the annotations, *see* Salmon, 1952, p.296; Farr, 1989, p.126.

153 Morin, 1893c, p.250; de Bruyne, 1913, p.212; *also*, Godu, *DACL* 5.1, numbers 22 and 13 in the chart following column 882.

154 de Bruyne, 1913, p.212; *see also* Appendix 1, Numbers 2 and 5.

155 Klauser, 1972, p.146, no. 73, and p.175, no. 64, lists as given in the Capitulare of Douai, Bibliothèque municipale, cod. 12; Paris, Bibliothèque nationale, Fonds latin 11957; Zürich, Zentralbibliothek, Stadtbibliothek C39; Rome, Biblioteca Apostolica Vaticana, Codex Vaticanus Latinus 8528; Paris, Bibliothèque nationale, Fonds latin 11963; for Mt. XV, or Mt. 4.1–11 in modern textual division, the notation 'In quadragesima ad Lateranis', and of Paris, Bibliothèque nationale lat. 93 and lat. 13171, for Mt. 4.1–11, 'In quadragesima ad Lateranis', in a section of the list entitled 'Incipiunt lectiones a septuagesima usque in pascha.'

156 Epistle Capitulary lists of Victor of Capua, indicating 2 Corinthians 6.2, in Beissel, 1907, p.58; *also*, Schlettstadt, MS 1093, lectionary dating to the seventh to eighth centuries, published in Morin, *Anec. Mar.* series 2, volume 1, p.449, on fol. 8: 'Incp. lictionis in caput quadrage. lictio iohel prophetae' (2.11–14). *See also* Morin, 'Lectiones ex epistolis Paulinis excerptae, quae in ecclesia Capuana saec. VI legebantur,' in *Anec. Mar.* I, 436–44.

157 The *Capitulare Evangeliorum* in the Codex Rehdigeranus (Wroclaw (Breslau), Stadtbibliothek MS R 169, now on loan to Staatsbibliothek, Berlin) on fol. 92. Edition in Morin, 1902, p.5; *see also* Martimort, 1992, p.29; Lowe, *CLA* 8, Number 1073, p.16, and Morin, 1902, p.2. Lowe describes the hand as eighth-century north Italian cursive, Morin as a Lombard hand.

158 Andrieu, 3 (1951), p.259, fn. 1, Ash Wednesday was designated 'feria iv in caput ieiunii'; Callewaert, 1940b, p.542 note 50, p.555.

159 McGurk, 1961b, pp.106–7, pp.30, 82, 119.

160 In Kendrick, et al., vol. 2, 1956–60, pp.34, 40.

161 Alexander, 1978, pp.73–4.

162 On *per cola et commata*, see Parkes, 1993, pp.15–16, and especially the examples, pp.178–9, 234–5; *also* Brown, 1990, pp.24–5; Bischoff, 1990, p.169.

163 Farr, 1994, pp.437–42; McGurk, 1987; Parkes, 1987; Parkes, 1993, 20–9.

164 Parkes, 1987, pp.14–17, 29; Parkes, 1993, p.35.

165 Alexander, 1978, pp.63–4.

166 Brown, 1996, pp.60–2.

167 Parkes, 1993, p.35. Royal 1.B.vii almost certainly was read from in the liturgy.

168 Verey, 1980, 34.

169 Hiley, 1993, pp.361–72; Cattin, 1984, 56–9.

170 Chapman, 1908, pp.191–201.

171 Hughes, 1982, p.62.

172 Verey, 1980, p.34.

173 Henderson, 1987, pp.168–74; O'Reilly, 1994, pp.345–90.

174 Farr, 1989, pp.164–91.

175 Godu, 'Epîtres,' cols. 263–320. A small cross drawn in the margin of the eighth-century Northumbrian manuscript, Cambridge, Trinity College B.10.5, fol. 13r, indicates 2 Corinthians. 6.2 as the beginning of a lection; another cross marks the end of the lection at the first word of verse 11.

176 Callewaert, 1940a, pp.484–5; Thalhofer, 1895, p.595. *Also*, a late eighth– to mid ninth-century description of the Roman offices, Ordo XII, calls for chanting of Psalm 90 at prime from Quadragesima until Good Friday, *see* Andrieu, vol. 2 (1948), pp.453–5, 463.

177 Verses based on Psalm 90 appear with a group of prayers and other Psalm verses associated with Lent in this florilegium, published by Constantinescu, 1974, no. 60 on p.46. *See also* Bullough, 1983, pp.4–11, on the antiphons and their relation to Insular and other liturgies. Bullough believes many of the antiphons

reflect the liturgy of 'the northern English Church in which Alcuin spent his adolescence and early manhood' (p.8).

178 *See also* the discussion *above*, p.74–5.

179 Bullough, 1983, pp.4–5. The work is known in two manuscripts, according to Bullough (footnote 10): the late tenth-century Bamberg, Stadtbibliothek, MS Misc. Patr. 17/B.II.10, fols 133–61v, and Escorial MS b–IV–17, fols 93–108, dated to the mid-ninth century, attributed to southern France.

180 Constantinescu, 1974, p.46, numbers 60 and 61; cf. the Vulgate text and translation of Psalm 90 *above*, 'The Temptation of Christ, Psalm 90, and the Illustration,' p.62. The Vulgate of Psalm 21.1: 'Deus, Deus meus, respice in me, quare me dereliquisti?', translating 'My God, my God, have regard for me, why have you forsaken me?' The related text: 'My God, have regard for my help'.

181 Morin, 1905, pp.329, 345–7; fols 3r–3v.

182 Bullough, 1983, pp.4–5.

183 Callewaert, 1940a, pp.482–3.

184 Callewaert, 1940a, p.483.

185 Adomnán, *Life of St. Columba*, 2.39, cited by Warren, 1987, p.146. *See also* the fragments of prayers for Lent from sacramentary fragments written in Irish and Anglo-Saxon hands, published by Gamber, 1975, pp.69, 70–1, 73–4.

186 Ó Carragáin has discussed the possible influences of the liturgy of Lent on the iconography of the Anglo-Saxon crosses at Bewcastle (1987a, pp.40–1) and Ruthwell (1986, 382–90; 1987b, 118–23). On the relation of the lections of Lent to the purposes of the season, *see* Chavasse, 1952.

187 Pseudo-Jerome, *PL* 30, 559B, and Pseudo-Gregory, *PL* 114, 870B; For patristic examples, Cassian, *De Institutis Coenobiorum* XXV, XXIX, *PL* 49, 1200B–1201A, 1208A–B; *also* Gregory, Homilia XVI, *PL* 76, 1137B–C.

188 Cassian, *De Institutis Coenobiorum* XXV, *PL* 49, 1200B–1201A; Gregory, Homilia XVI, *PL* 76, 1137C.

189 Pseudo-Jerome, *PL* 30, 558C–D, 559A, and Pseudo-Gregory, *PL* 114, 869D, 870A.

190 Bischoff, 1976, No. 11, pp.108–10; Kelly, 1986, p.68.

191 *In Lucam* I, *CCL* 120, pp.93–4, lines 2939–49.

192 *In Lucam* I, *CCL* 120, p.94, lines 2963–5: manducans autem et bibens quadraginta diebus post resurrectionem carnis velut clamabat.

193 *CCL* 120, p.94, lines 2950–76.

194 *De Templo* I, *CCL* 119A, pp.172–3, lines 1023–63.

195 Pseudo–Jerome, *PL* 30, 558C; Pseudo-Gregory, *PL* 114, 559D; *see* the discussion *above* on Psalm titles, pp.74–5.

196 Kelly, 1986, pp.67–8, 72.

197 *CCL* 120, p.444, lines 290–3; *see* text and translation *above*, p.73, 'The Figure of the Head and Body: Historic Context in Insular Exegesis and Liturgical Texts'.

198 Tyconius, *Liber Regularum*, pp.64–5.

199 For example, Hilary of Poitiers (c.315–c.367), *Commentarius in Matthaeum*, *PL* 9, 928A–929A.

200 The anonymous Irish commentary on Luke, attributed to the circle of Virgil of Salzburg, in *CCL* 108C, ed. J. Kelly, pp.29–30; and the Cracow homilies, in Cracow, Cathedral Library 43, ed. P. David, 1937, p.79. Kelly has observed that 'the Irish commentary on Luke ... depends heavily upon Bede's Lukan commentary' (1986, p.69).

201 *CCL* 108C, p.30, lines 68–78.

202 *CCL* 108C, p.34, lines 222–3.

203 *CCL* 108C, p.31, lines 83–93, translation in Farr, 1989, pp.102–3; Tyconius, *Liber Regularum*, III, p.28, lines 16–21; *see also* Farr, 1989, pp.102–5.

204 *See* the work of Ó Carragáin, 1994a, pp.9–36; Ó Carragáin, 1994b, 399–403.

205 Selmer, ed., 1959, pp.11–16, 37–45, 76–82; and in *The Age of Bede*, ed. D. H. Farmer, tr. J. F. Webb, 1983, pp.214–18, 227–30, 243–5. On the liturgical information provided in *The Voyage of St Brendan*, *see* Curran, 1984, 169–73.

206 Bede, *Life of Cuthbert*, Chapter 42, ed. and tr. Colgrave, pp.290–5.

207 Bede, *Life of Cuthbert*, ed. and tr. Colgrave, pp.296–7.

208 Callewaert, 1940b, p.538.

209 Maximus of Turin, Sermo 26, *PL* 67, 586, cited by Callewaert, 1940b, p.538; the Spanish Priscillianist, in the *Tractatus Paschae*, cited by Callewaert, 1940b, p.538.

210 *History of the Franks*, II.21, III.43, Thorpe, tr., 1974, pp.133–4, 474–75. Cited by Callewaert, 1940b, p.538.

211 *See also* Ó Carragáin, 1994a, pp.27–31, on the centrality of liturgical forms to expression of theological and political programmes and their artistic expression.

CHAPTER THREE

◄○►

Folio 114r, Arrest or Passion of Christ

Images, Texts, and Exegesis
The Prayer Pose, the Passion, and the Apocalypse

IN THE SYNOPTIC sense of the Gospels and in the sequence of the liturgical year, the illustration on fol. 114r (PLATE III) comes after the depiction of the Temptation of Christ, fol. 202v (PLATE I). Like the picture of the Temptation, this illustration presents a scene difficult to relate to the immediate Gospel text into which it is inserted, but, also like fol. 202v, fol. 114r clearly remains in its originally intended position in the manuscript.[1]

The illustration, placed in the text of Matthew 26.30, depicts the frontal figure of Christ standing with arms outstretched creating an 'X' shape. Two smaller, flanking figures stand in profile, each grasping an outstretched forearm of Christ. Out of bulbous forms immediately above the heads of the two attendant figures emerge two plants whose fruit-bearing tendrils both climb into the space above and descend symmetrically to frame Christ's head. The group of three figures stands beneath an arch decorated at its apex with opposed beast heads and supported on a pair of columns abstracted into flat geometric forms presenting vinescroll and geometric ornament. The capitals of the columns are depicted as flat cross-shapes decorated with animal interlace. The words of Matthew 26.30 are inscribed in the 'tympanum' of the arch: *Et ymno dicto exierunt in montem oliveti* ('And after reciting a hymn, they went out to Mount Olivet').

On the folio's verso, the incipit of Matthew 26.31, *Tunc dicit illis iesus: Omnes vos scan* (*dalum*) ('Then Jesus said to them: You will all be scandalized … ') enlarges to cover the page (PLATE IV). The words are ornamented with vinescroll and framed by a border ornamented with geometric and animal interlace and terminated with a large, snarling animal head at the top of the page. The beginning of the verse is repeated in smaller letters of red lead at the bottom of the page. In the text following, on fol. 115r, Christ quotes Zechariah 13.7:

Scriptum est enim percutiam pastorem & dispergentur oves gregis.
[For it has been written: I will strike through the shepherd, and the sheep of the flock will be scattered.]

The subject of the scene depicted seems even more difficult to determine than that of the Temptation of Christ. Clearly it does not represent the Last Supper nor the singing of the hymn afterwards. The compositionally static figures within an unmoving configuration cannot literally depict Christ walking with his disciples to Mount Olivet conversing about his death and their future acts of betrayal.[2] Traditional identifications of the subject as Christ in Gethsemene or the Arrest of Christ are awkward because arrival at Gethsemane (verse 36) is presented on fol. 115v and the arrest (verse 47) on fols 116v–117r. The illustration faces the text of Christ's Last Supper with the apostles, telling of the institution of the Eucharist, one of the most important events in Christian theology.

Until very recently, modern scholars have usually attempted to identify the scene as one of the events narrated in the surrounding text and to support their opinions by citing other Insular or Early Christian depictions of figures symmetrically arranged in poses resembling those in the illustration.[3] In addition to interpretations based on Matthew 26, one suggestion identifies it as a depiction of an Old Testament scene.[4] Recently Jennifer O'Reilly has connected it with a vast range of patristic and Insular exegesis as an image for contemplation in monastic *ruminatio*.[5] A few scholars, notably Éamonn Ó Carragáin, have considered its possible liturgical connections.[6] In the last twenty years, scholars have begun to question identification of the illustration's subject as the Arrest of Christ, especially as an illustration of the event in a strictly narrative sense. Several scholars now consider the image to refer to the Passion, specifically to the Crucifixion, and because of this reference it serves as a 'preface to the Passion', rather than presenting a narrative illustration in the strictest sense.

In spite of this recent progress, some questions concerning the reasons for representing the three figures in this seemingly peculiar manner still need investigation. First of all, the two figures on either side of Christ are often identified as disciples, but no one has asked why they are depicted as identical twins. Possibly the artist wished to enforce the rigid symmetry of Christ's pose in order to heighten its dramatic impact. However, if these are meant to represent disciples, one may still ask why they lack any apostolic attributes. Moreover, the plants above the two figures seem deliberately placed so as to appear to be sprouting from the figures' heads, and their lower leaves are made to frame the head of Christ in an unnecessarily ungraceful manner. This apparent clumsiness may be attributed to a lack of space within the arch of the frame, but one may also ask why an artist working within a tradition which had developed design skills refined enough to allow creation of highly detailed yet striking images, such as the Chi-Rho page, the Virgin and Child, and the Enthroned Christ, would resort to such awkwardness if he were obeying only the requirements imposed by the size of the picture.

Like the depiction of the Temptation, however, the scene presented on fol. 114r may represent the liturgical meaning of a feast day, not simply a gospel scene. Its imagery could overlap with or represent a response to the verbal figures used in interpretation of texts connected with the day. It could also and perhaps simultaneously refer to the visual conception of the day's significance presented in liturgical ritual. It could be connected in various ways with liturgical presentation of text.

Nearly every scholar who has written about the illustration has recognised that the central figure is depicted in a pose of prayer. The simple shape formed by the figure could be compared with the shape of the Temple topped with the bust of Christ in the picture of his Temptation. What could be the pose's significance as a multivalent *figura*?

The pose with hands uplifted was a sign of the Crucifixion, and Moses depicted at the battle against the Amalechites with his upraised hands supported by Aaron and Hur presented a well-known typological figure of the cross as a triumphal sign.[7] The Christian significance of the image of Moses praying during the battle against the Amalechites (Exod. 17.8–16) probably had origins in Jewish Messianic interpretation of the event.[8] According to Philo of Alexandria, Moses' upraised hands symbolise the superiority of the spiritual realm:[9]

> Thus, by symbols God showed that earth and the lowest regions of the universe were the portion assigned as their own to the one part and the ethereal, the highest region to the other; and that, just as heaven holds kingship in the universe and is superior to earth so this nation should be victorious over its opponents in war.[10]

The Israelites won because of the pose indicating alliance with heavenly powers.

The pose, because of its association with prayer and victory and its Messianic symbolism, was quickly taken up by Christians, among whom it became a popular symbol of the victory of the cross as well as the pose of prayer. Actual use of the pose during prayer is strongly suggested by the dozens of examples of orans figures known from the catacombs and sarcophagi, as well as works such as the fourth-century wall painting from Lullingstone in Kent and the Rotunda mosaic at Thessaloniki.[11] An ivory casket from Pola presents the figures of four priests with arms raised in the pose as they stand on either side of the altar of St Peter's, beneath the ciborium with its spiral columns.[12] The earliest Christian writers, beginning with Justin, attributed Moses' victory to his pose because it presented a sign of the cross pointed to the heavens.[13] Some early Christian writers, such as Tertullian, describe the pose as the appropriate one for the Christian to assume for prayer because a person in this position imitates the cross and thus recalls Christ's Passion.[14] The implications of this imitation of the Passion of Christ by praying with arms outstreched are graphically expressed in Eusebius' first-hand account of martyrdoms under Diocletian:

> You would see a youngster not yet twenty standing without fetters, spreading out his arms in the form of a cross, with a mind unafraid and unshakable occupying himself in the most unhurried prayers to the Almighty not budging in the least and not retreating an inch from the spot where he stood, though bears and panthers breathing fury and death almost touched his very flesh. Yet by some supernatural, mysterious power their mouths were stopped, and they ran back again to the rear.[15]

The passage not only describes prayer recited by a Christian standing in the cross pose but also expresses the martyr's assimilation to Christ by his suffering. The martyr has assumed the sign of Christ's victory over death while simultaneously re-enacting its significance.

By the fifth century, the pose had gained a rich field of associative meanings. Because of its by now inextricable connection with the passions of Christ and the martyrs, it found a place also in the iconography of the Transfiguration, an association presented notably in the apse mosaic of S. Apollinare in Classe.[16] Exegetical writings of the fifth and sixth centuries continued to connect the pose of prayer assumed by Moses with the Passion and with the salvation promised by Christ's resurrection.[17] Maximus of Turin, in his sermon *De Cruce et Resurrectione Domini* speaks of the meaning of the pose succinctly:

Ipsius etiam incessus hominis, cum manus levaverit, crucem pingit; atque ideo elevatis manibus orare praecipimur, ut ipso quoque membrorum gestu passionem domini fateamur. Tunc enim citius nostra exauditur oratio, cum Christum, quem mens loquitur, etiam corpus imitatur. Hoc etiam exemplo Moyses sanctus, cum contra Amalech bellum gereret, non armis non ferro sed elevatis eum ad deum manibus superavit.[18]

[Indeed the appearance of man himself, when he raises his hands, depicts a cross. Moreover, for this reason we are instructed to pray with raised hands, so that we may indicate the passion of the Lord with this gesture of our limbs. Then our prayer will be heard more quickly, when the body represents Christ, to whom the mind speaks. By this example, the holy man Moses, when he waged war against Amalech, was victorious not with weapons, not with the sword, but after they had lifted him up to God with his hands.]

Maximus describes the cross pose as a powerful spiritual weapon which increases the efficacy of prayer. Gregory the Great also interpreted the pose in terms of weaponry, but as a defence against temptations of the flesh, symbolising the raising of the mind above temptation by means of celestial contemplation and good acts.[19] Patristic writings of the fifth and sixth centuries provide evidence that Christians still prayed in the cross pose and that the pose signified Christ's victorious struggle, prefigured by Moses' battle against the Amalechites and continued in the present by the daily prayer and struggle of the faithful against the devil's temptation.

The Irish knew the pose as the *crossfigell,* the 'vigil of the cross' from the latin *crucis vigilia.*[20] Although many of the instances of its use often cited in scholarship from Irish hagiography date from a somewhat later period than the Book of Kells, the term and descriptions of the pose are known from the penitential *De Arreis,* probably written during the seventh century, and from the *Martyrology of Oengus, c.*800.[21] The Irish considered the pose to imitate Christ's passion, especially in the context of penance. The *De Arreis* explicitly instructs the penitent to contemplate the Passion of Christ while assuming the cross pose.[22]

Apparently members of Insular monastic communities performed the cross vigil regularly, as a component of ascetic practice, although the term is most frequently encountered in penitential literature.[23] Its penitential practice, however, was forbidden, along with penitential genuflexion, during the Easter octave and between Christmas and Epiphany.[24] Some evidence exists that it was associated especially with Lent. Insular hagiography often associates the *crossfigell* with Moses, who, besides being the Old Testament hero of the battle against the Amalechites, also performed a forty-day fast representing a type of Christ's fast and of Lent.[25] The Book of Leinster presents, at the end of a list of the members of an anchoritic unity, a note that the people of the unity would

... be together in Daire Ednech, no false order, practising devotion without extravagance, at cross vigil in Lent.[26]

Alcuin, according to the *Vita,* spent hours in prayer with outstretched arms, uttering sighs and shedding tears, a description recalling the vigil of Eadberht, Bishop of Lindisfarne, who passed Lent at one of Cuthbert's retreats, 'shedding tears of devotion'.[27] Possibly the *crossfigell* was widely practised among the monks of Ireland and Northumbria as part of their Lenten exercises.

Moreover, as a pose for prayer, it is often depicted in hagiography in the context of battle or defence from enemies.[28] Adomnán tells of Saint Columba who assumed the character of a fiery warlord when he prayed with hands upraised for divine vengeance upon the plundering band led by the magnate Ioan of the Cenél Gabhrain.[29] A less likely candidate for the role of fiery warrior, Wilfrid of York, nonetheless became endowed with the same sort of power when, defending his shipwrecked band of monks from the fierce East Saxons, he assumed the prayer pose of Moses and overcame the multitude of attacking pagans.[30] In addition to the militant character accorded to the cross pose in hagiography, the *Martyrology of Oengus* refers to it by a name that characterises it as spiritual armour, the *lúirech léire* or 'breastplate of devotion'.[31]

The figure of Christ depicted in this pose would indeed have presented an image appropriate for viewing by a monastic community on Holy Thursday. Holy Thursday marks the end of Lent proper and the beginning of the Holy Triduum, the three holy days before Easter. If Insular ascetic practices resembled those in Gaul, the spiritual leaders of the monastic community who had gone into retreats for solitary prayer and fasting during Lent would return on that day.[32] The entire community would have reached an important point in a long season of spiritual battle, the widely recognised sign of which was the cross pose, the heroic prayer pose of Moses and all holymen.

Furthermore, the pose not only symbolised Christ's suffering but also identified its practitioner with Christ as he suffered during his passion and crucifixion, the events to be re-enacted by the liturgy of the three holy days. As a sign of the cross, the pose also symbolised Christ's triumph obtained through his death on the cross. In this respect, Lewis' suggestion that the illustration presents a conflation of eucharistic iconography with that of the Passion deserves further consideration.[33] The cross pose may serve to unify the two texts in several ways.

The cross pose may serve as a linking *figura*, on one level, through associations with the iconography of the Transfiguration. In early exegeses, including at least one attributed to an Irish writer, the term *transfiguratio* is used to describe the transfiguration of the eucharistic bread and wine into the body of Christ, linking Transfiguration with Crucifixion.[34] Christ, flanked by Moses and Elias, assumes the cross pose in Early Christian representations of the Transfiguration, often creating an image resembling that presented by the Kells illustration.[35] The later Transfiguration scene, created about 1000, in the Evangeliary of Otto III (Munich, Bayerische Staatsbibliothek CLM 4453, fol. 113r), resembles the Kells illustration in several ways, especially in the similarity of the poses of Moses and Elias with those of the attendant figures in Kells. The illustration in the Book of Kells could depict Christ transfigured into the sacrifice, an idea which bridges the Last Supper and the Passion.[36]

Associations with the Ascension could be important, too, as Mount Olivet was also the site of Christ's Ascension. An image resembling that on fol. 114r appears on the Cross of Muiredach at Monasterboice, on one of the house cap panels. The carving shows a central figure in the orans pose flanked by two profile figures who hold his arms. The flanking figures may be depicted with wings or wearing stylised drapery. Harbison and Stalley have convincingly argued that the scene depicts the Ascension, with Christ borne aloft by angels.[37]

As the illustration of the Temptation of Christ presents in its depiction of the Temple a multivalent *figura*, so the cross pose on fol. 114r represents a figure possessing many levels of meaning. It refers to the Old Testament figure of Moses, to Christ, to the martyrs, to the image's viewers, and to the promise of future salvation. The picture further refers to Christ's spiritual battle, suffering, death, and ascension and to the sacrifice of the Eucharist, as will be discussed in more detail later. The significance of the cross pose alone, however, cannot fully explain the unusual iconography of the illustration and its placement in the Gospel text at verse 30. Like its companion illustration of the Temptation of Christ, the illustration's iconography probably results from its intended role in a specific context, which probably was a liturgical context.

The Text of Matthew 26 and the Prophecy of Zechariah

The illustration refers to elements of the text of Matthew 26.26–42. The illustration appears to be placed at a point of transition between the account of the Last Supper and the departure for Gethsemene via Mount Olivet. The text of verse 30, referring to a hymn recited after the meal, appears at the top of the illustration, but the picture does not appear to refer to any of the texts which patristic and early medieval exegetes set forth as the hymn.[38]

Beginning at verse 31, the text moves on to the theme of temptation and the need for vigilant prayer to triumph over it. Christ's words at verse 31 refer directly to this theme, since he tells his apostles that they are going to suffer temptation on his account and that all will fail. In Gethsemane (verses 37–8), he asks Peter and the two sons of Zebedee to watch with him, but they fail to stay awake. Christ, verse 41, warns Peter again, 'Watch and pray so that you will not fall into temptation'.

According to patristic interpretation, the temptation about which Christ warns the apostles is not simply the hardship and struggle that they are about to endure nor his own impending suffering. He is referring to the temptation that only begins with his Passion and death and continues through the deaths of the martyrs, to culminate in the final battle that precedes the Second Coming.[39] By this point in the Gospel, the devil has returned and entered Judas for the final Temptation of Christ, and this satanic temptation is to continue after the resurrection of Christ but is to be directed at the Church.[40] Justin, Ireneus, Tertullian, Origen, Augustine, Gregory and the Irish author of the eighth-century Lucan commentary all refer to the return of the devil at the Passion and his constant temptation of the Church until his defeat at the end of the world.[41]

The idea of the continuity of temptation after Christ's night at Gethsemane occurs in Insular hagiography. For example, Bede, in his *Life of Cuthbert*, tells of the saint delivering prophetic warnings to monks and lay people to 'watch and pray', quoting Christ's words to them on such festive occasions as the dedication of a church and the Feast of the Nativity.[42] Warnings for constant vigilance against the devil's temptations appear also in connection with celebration of Holy Thursday in the *Voyage of St Brendan*.[43] For the Irish or Northumbrian monk, Christ's struggle in Gethsemane extended through the present life.

While Christ's quotation of Zechariah 13.7, on the shepherd who will be 'struck through and his sheep scattered from the flock', may be of some significance in respect to the illustration, no exegesis of it is known to make clear any relationship between prophecy and illustration. However, a multivalent image which probably influenced the illustration appears in Zechariah 4.1–14.

Zechariah describes his vision of a stone with seven eyes and a golden candelabrum with seven lamps flanked by two olive-trees which feed it with oil. When the prophet asks the angel what the olive-trees are, the angel eventually replies that they are, to translate literally, 'the two sons of oil, who stand near the Lord of the entire earth' (verse 14). The reader is to understand that they are not merely plants which drip oil into the lamp, but they are olive-trees that are somehow anthropomorphised into attendants or guards.

Because Zechariah's prophecy concerns the rebuilding of the Temple and restoration of Jerusalem, Christianity interprets his book as prophecy of the founding of the New Covenant, accomplished by the Passion of Christ, and the Second Coming. Thus, as much of the text of Zechariah is eschatological in nature, the image of the two olive-trees reappears in the Apocalypse 11.3–13. The author of the book, having been instructed to measure the Temple and its altar and to count its worshippers, is then shown two witnesses clothed in sackcloth who will prophesy for one thousand two hundred and sixty days. They are the two olive trees and two lamps standing before the lord of the earth. If anyone will try to harm them, fire will come forth from their mouths and devour their enemies. They have the power to change the seas into blood and to inflict every plague upon the earth. When their period of witnessing and prophecy comes to an end, the beast, who will ascend from the abyss, will wage war against them and will defeat and kill them. After the beast kills them, the bodies of the two witnesses will lie in the streets of the city 'where their Lord was crucified'. When three and a half days have passed, they will resurrect and ascend to heaven on a cloud while a terrible earthquake wipes out one-tenth of the population of the city which refused them burial.

The Apocalypse represents the two olive-trees as types of Christ because of their death near the site of the Crucifixion and their resurrection after three and a half days.

The visual images of the two olive-trees presented in both texts and multivalent exegetical figures connected with them probably inspired, perhaps in connection with other scriptural images of triads of figures, the illustration in the Book of Kells depicting Christ with two attendant figures. Neither the stone nor the lamp of Zechariah are depicted literally in the illustration, but both stone and lamp are figures of Christ, as will be seen. The stone is the Messianic stone to be laid by Zorobabel, the cornerstone of Psalm 117.22 and Isaiah 28.16. Also, it has seven eyes, described more clearly in Zechariah 3.9: *Quia ecce lapis quem dedi coram Iesu, super lapidem unum septem oculi sunt.* The candelabrum, too, supports seven lamps. The seven lamps and the seven eyes of the stone appear again in the Apocalypse, as, for example, in the figure of the Lamb having seven eyes. All of these objects, which are figures of Christ, appear in the middle of the scenes of triads of figures and objects described in the Scriptures, just as Christ appears in the illustration in the Book of Kells.

In the illustration, the two attendant figures flanking Christ are depicted as anthropomorphised olive-trees. The bulbous forms on top of their heads, usually described as 'flower pots' holding vine-like plants, probably are meant to depict trunks of olive-trees with branches growing from them. Each tree and human figure form one attendant, with the tree branches growing from the attendants' heads, not from separate plants behind or above them. The text of Zechariah provides an explanation for the leaves which frame Christ's head in the illustration: they are the spouts pouring oil into the lamp, described in verse 12.

The plants depicted within the arch on fol. 114r are distinct from the flowing vine plants that appear below on the 'columns' and within the decoration of a number of other folios in the manuscript. They are gnarled and spikey, with thick branches and large round fruit growing in bunches of three, like the small clusters of fruit grown on olive-trees. Most of the fruits are yellow, which would not be naturalistic but could refer to their oil, probably the plant's most important product for humans in general and for ecclesiastics in particular. The olive tree, as Nordenfalk pointed out, was one of the distinct topological features of the Mount of Olives as presented in the *loci sancti* tradition.[44]

In the illustration, the arrangement of the two olive-trees with Christ posed in a group presenting a type of Moses with Aaron and Hur praying during battle underscores the trees' role as attendants in war. The illustration may in a sense depict a spiritual battle fought on two levels: Christ's battle waged against the devil during his passion and crucifixion and also the other battle to be fought against Satan by the Church, as described in the Apocalypse.

The illustration's iconography suggests that for some reason the Irish or Northumbrians brought together images presented by the texts of Exodus 17, Zechariah 4 and the Apocalypse into an association with Matthew 26.30–1. The logical place to look for an explanation is patristic and Insular exegesis of Exodus, Zechariah, Matthew 26 and the Apocalypse.

Exegesis of Exodus, Zechariah, the Apocalypse and Matthew 26

Is there any evidence of an exegetical tradition connecting Zechariah's vision, Exodus 17 and the Passion which could have inspired the figures depicted in the illustration? A hint of such a tradition surfaces in the interpretation given by Isidore of Seville on Moses, Aaron and Hur:

> Post haec Moyses ascendit in montem, Josue contra Amalech militat, tenet virgam Moyses, brachiaque sua in modum crucis extendit. Sicque hostis, id est, diabolus, vitam coelestis patriae intercludere molitus, signo crucis dominicae superatur. Dum levaret manus Moyses, vincebat Israel; rursus si inclinasset, superabat Amalech. Elevantibus enim nobis actus nostros ad coelum, rectores tenebrarum subjiciuntur. At contra remissis orantes manibus, hoc est, terrenam conversationem sectantes, hostis victor insequitur, sedet Moyses super lapidem qui in Zacharia septem habebat oculos et in Samuelis volumine appellatur Lapis adjutorii et utramque manum ejus, Aaron and Hur, quasi duo populi aut duo Testamenta sustenant.[45]
> [After this Moses went up onto the mountain and fought with Josua against Amalech. Moses held

his rod and extended his arms in the manner of a cross; and so the enemy, that is the devil, who endeavoured to blockade the way to the heavenly homeland, was overcome by the Lord's sign of the cross. As long as Moses raised his hands, Israel was victorious; on the contrary, when he inclined (them), Amalech would win. By addressing our prayers up to heaven, the leaders of darkness are brought down, and in contrast, those praying with lowered hands, that is, those who pursue earthly conversation, the enemy succeeds as victor. Moses sat upon the stone which in Zechariah had seven eyes and in the Book of Samuel is called the Stone of Help, and Aaron and Hur, just as the two people or the two testaments, held each hand of his.]

What Isidore says about the stone proves important. He says that it is the same stone the prophet Zechariah saw in his vision (3.9; 4.10) and the stone erected by Samuel to mark the point to which the Israelites, with God's help, had driven back the Philistines (1 Samuel 7.12). Because the Stone of Help represented a victory of God's people in battle against 'the enemy', it presents a type of Moses' stone. However, insofar as Christological interpretation is concerned, the stone of Zechariah appears in the richer context of an eschatological prophetic vision and presents features which equate it immediately with other symbols of Christ and the Church: the lamb with seven eyes and the candelabrum with seven lamps. Interpretation of Aaron and Hur as figures of the 'two testaments', however, parallels a widespread typological interpretation of the two olive-trees as the Law and the Prophets or as the two testaments, which will be discussed further on. Isidore implies, in his interpretation quoted above, that the two images are equivalent.

Isidore's *Quaestiones in Vetus Testamentum*, from which the above passage is quoted, was almost certainly known in Ireland, and possibly in Northumbria.[46] Isidore, however, draws only thin lines of connection between the prophecy of Zechariah and the battle pose of Moses. Nonetheless, neither this text nor any other known single work of exegesis provides a complete explanation of the picture. The recurring themes presented by surviving literature suggest that the basis of the association of the texts lies not in a single exegesis but rather in the image of the heroic saviour flanked by attendants.[47]

The earliest western commentary on Zechariah known to survive is that written by Jerome, who mentions as sources the commentaries of Hippolytus, Origen and Didymus.[48] Jerome explains the stone with seven eyes as the cornerstone of the Temple, which is also Christ, and lists several interpretations for the olive-trees, two of which are known to reappear in Insular exegesis.[49] Some writers, Jerome says, explain the two olive-trees as the two testaments, the law on the left and the Gospels on the right, but others believe the two trees to be Enoch and Elias, each of whom pleased God and so was carried up to heaven.[50] Didymus also brings up their possible identity as Enoch and Elias, citing as his source 'an apocryphal book'.[51]

The unusual aspect of the two witnesses as anthropomorphic olive-trees gave rise to many different interpretations, some explaining the figures according to an elaborate typology, others identifying them as two prophets.[52] However, it is in interpretations of the Apocalypse that the typological tradition seems to become merged with the exegetes' compulsion to identify the olive-trees, the most frequently occurring identification being as Enoch and Elias.

Besides Bede's *Explanatio Apocalypsis*, three early Irish Latin commentaries on the Apocalypse are known, two of which are known to survive but only one of which, the Pseudo-Isidoran or Pseudo-Hieronymian, has been published.[53]

The two commentaries reflect different approaches to texts and learning. Bede's commentary is organised and comprehensive, a compendium of the interpretations. That of the unknown Irish author presents the 'conference' approach of the monastic schools of Ireland, in which the text probably would have been accompanied by discussions between teachers and pupils.[54] Nonetheless, their dependence upon common sources is evident, and both may present interpretations unique to Insular exegesis.[55]

Bede begins by interpreting the Temple and its forecourt as the two nations of the Church.[56] He equates the 1,260 days of the olive-trees' prophecy with the three and a half years of Christ's preaching on earth.[57] An explanation of the two olive-trees follows:

> Ecclesia duorum Testamentorum lumine radiata, Domini semper jussis assistit. Nam et propheta Zacharias unum candelabrum vidit septiforme, et has duas olivas, id est, testamenta, inlundere oleum candelabro. Haec est Ecclesia cum oleo suo indeficiente, quod eam facit in lumine orbis ardere.[58]
> [The Church, irradiated with the light of the two Testaments, ever waits upon the commands of the Lord. So also the prophet Zechariah saw one candle-stick with seven branches, and these two olive-trees, that is, Testaments, pouring oil into the candle-stick. This is the Church with its unfailing oil, which makes it shine for the light of the world.]

The ensuing battle with the beast, Bede continues, signifies the final persecution, re-enacting the passion of Christ, but the three and a half days during which the olive-tree witnesses lay dead represent the time of the Antichrist's reign.[59] Bede then identifies the two witnesses:

> Quidam duos prophetas Enoch et Eliam interpretantur, qui, tribus semis annis praedicantes, contra mox secuturam Antichristi perfidiam fidelium corda confirment.[60]
> [Some understand the two prophets to be Enoch and Elias, who, preaching for three years and a half, will confirm the hearts of the faithful against the perfidy of the Antichrist, which is presently to follow.]

Compared with Bede's *Explanatio Apocalypsis*, the Irish commentary differs in content as well as form:

> *Metire templum dei* unicuique secundum mensuram in ecclesia praedicare; *et altare* fidem. *Atrium quod foris templum* haeretici et philosophi gentiles qui sunt foris ecclesiam; *civitatem sanctam ecclesiam; mensibus quadraginta* hoc tempus Antichristi; *duos testes* Heliam et Enoch. Per *olivas* unctio spiritualis; per *candelabrum* praedicatio intellegitur; *conspectu domini terrae* in conspectu Antichristi; *ignis* praedicatio.[61]
> [*To measure the temple of God* is for each one to preach in the Church according to measure; *and the altar* means faith. *The courtyard which is outside the temple* signify the heretics and pagan philosophers who are outside the Church; *the holy city*, the Church; *for forty months* this is the time of the Antichrist; *the two witnesses* Elias and Enoch. By *olive-trees* spiritual anointing; by *candelabrum*, prophecy; *in the presence of the Lord of the earth*, in the presence of the Antichrist; *fire* preaching.]

The Irish author seems to unify the two interpretations by placing the preaching of the witnesses in the context of the Church, existing in present and apocalyptic time.

As Jerome indicates in his commentary on Zechariah, the apocryphal interpretation of the two witnesses as Enoch and Elias was well-known to patristic exegesis, and it was called upon frequently in medieval interpretation.[62] The earliest known Irish reference occurs in *De mirabilibus sacrae scripturae*, dated 655:

> ... jamjamque Elias igneo curru receptus velut ad coelum, considerante Elisaeo, rapitur. Et hactenus ipse, sicut et Enoch in testimonium novissimi temporis, adhuc sine morte servatur, ut scilicet horum in ore duorum testium, novissimi testimonii sermo consistat, in extremo tempore, paulo antequam damnetur satanas, qui humanum genus aperto bello deprimat.[63]
>
> [... at that moment Elias was carried away in a fiery chariot into heaven, while Elisha watched attentively. And he himself [Elias] up till now is preserved without death just as Enoch in testimonial of the end of time, for, the word of final testimony will take place in the mouth of these two witnesses in that last time, shortly before Satan, who oppresses the human race with open warfare, will be condemned.]

The idea of paradise as an earthly waiting room for souls can be found in very early exegesis and apocrypha. Origen's belief that the souls of the faithful remain in the earthly paradise until the resurrection was current in the West until the time of Gregory, and the theme of Enoch and Elias waiting in paradise appears in the *Contra haereses* (V.5.1) of Irenaeus.[64] Insular exegetes sometimes refer to their ascension not into the same heaven into which Christ ascended but to some ethereal realm higher than the earth. References to Enoch and Elias in the heavens above earth occur in the eighth-century Pseudo-Bedan *Collectanea* as well as Bede's sermon on the Ascension.[65] The theme of their martyrdom by the hand of the Antichrist also occurs in early Irish literature, and probably derives, directly or indirectly from any of a number of early apocryphal and exegetical writings.[66] Enoch and Elias appear in the writings of Aldhelm and Blathmac, and in the 'Reference Bible.' They continue in middle Irish apocrypha and the homilies of Aelfric.[67] The idea that they remain in some zone between the ordinary world and heaven, preaching in the present time is an important one, for it endows them with the potential for reference to past, present, and future.

In this respect of reference to a typological layering of history, Mount Olivet also presents important connections. Association of the image of the candelabrum flanked by the two olive-trees with the text of Matthew 26.30–1 could result from Mount Olivet's history as a place of theophany. According to the account of the ascension in Acts 1.9–11, Christ not only ascended on a cloud from Mount Olivet but, by the word of two men who appeared to those watching, Christ would return in the same way, which is usually understood to mean that he will appear coming from a cloud over Mount Olivet.[68] In Insular literature, the mention of Mount Olivet often brings on a reference to Christ's ascension and the vigil of the faithful awaiting his return.[69] Adomnán and Bede both wrote of the footprints of Christ which were supposed to be visible at the site of the Ascension, a tradition originating in the prophecy of Zechariah 14.4.[70] The resemblance of the picture of Christ in the cross pose in the Book of Kells to the scene on the house cap panel of the Cross of Muiredach at Monasterboice has been pointed out above. The sculpted image is now being interpreted in scholarship as a multivalent depiction of the Ascension, referring addition-ally to the Passion and Apocalypse.[71]

Association of the Ascension with the Apocalypse is based, at least in part, on Zechariah 14.4, on the Lord's feet on Mount Olivet, which was also taken as a prophecy of Christ's second coming, when 'the Lord … will come and all his saints with him' (Zechariah 14.5) for the final battle. Because Mount Olivet is supposed to be the site of Christ's return as well as his Passion and Ascension, the olive-trees who are his witnesses and attendants become in exegesis inhabitants of this semiotic location, multivalent signs of past, present, and future theophany.[72]

The witnesses are often associated in literature with the structuring of the history of the world. Bede, in *De schematibus et tropis*, explains a reference in Ecclesiasticus (44.16), 'Enoch, the seventh descendant of Adam … carried out of the world', as an anagogical figure of the 'future bliss of the elect', reserved for them to enjoy at the end of the world, the seventh age.[73]

Some of the most interesting and imaginative uses of the imagery connected with the witnesses Enoch and Elias occur in Middle Irish literature. Fintan mac Bóchna, in the Mid-dle Irish story 'Settling of the manor of Tara', came to Ireland before the Flood and sur-vived into Christian times. Eventually he was taken away, 'people think … in his physical body … to some secret divine place as Elijah and Enoch were taken to paradise, so that they are awaiting the resurrection of that aged patriarch'.[74] Kim McCone has envisioned ways in which this antediluvian hero, whom the Irish ask to lay out 'the foundations of chronology of the hearth of Tara itself with the four quarters of Ireland around it', serves the assimi-lation of pre-Christian Irish past and Old Testament history with post-Patrician Irish and New Testament world order. According to McCone, such assimilation was needed in Chris-tianised society to enhance and maintain the authority of the Irish aristocratic *literati*, whose interests and identity were merged with those of the Church.[75] The equation of Fintan with the two Old Testament heroes reinforces this historical assimilation.[76] In McCone's inter-pretation, the story shapes with precision its identification of Fintan with particular Old Testament heroes. The five-ridged stone set by Fintan at the site of the meeting of the fifths in Uisnech suggests a reappearance of Old Testament stones. The stone of Uisnech, which signified Ireland and the place of the Uisnech and Tara within it, may have been meant to imitate the Old Testament stones set up by Samuel and Josua, associated in the Bible ac-counts with kingship and witness to divine truth.[77]

In an Old Irish context, such connection would be important because of Isidore's identification of the stone upon which Moses sat as the *Lapis Adiutorii* of Samuel and the stone of Zechariah's vision, with their Christological and eschatological significance. Moreo-ver, Fintan referred to himself as 'the truly learned witness who explains to all everything unknown'.[78] Perhaps he likened himself to the two olive-tree witnesses of Apocalypse 11.3 who now preach in Paradise. Like them, Fintan lectured to the Irish on the meaning of history and he served to link Old Testament, or pre-Patrician, antediluvian, past with the present existence of the Church and its future temptation in the Apocalypse.

Biblical visionary images linked by the exegesis of Isidore to Christian past and future may have presented considerable appeal to an aristocracy whose legitimacy and status were still based upon constructs surviving from a pre-Christian age. Historiographic allusions in Irish literature to the identification of indigenous past with historical 'markers' like the boundary stones and Old Testament heroes that are going to reappear at the end of the world make use of a framework of spiritual history.[79] The Irish aristocracy, who had an interest in merging themselves with the international order of Christianity, updated and enhanced their high status by placing their pre-Christian history within this framework of the story of universal salvation. Visual images intended to resonate with the significance of Old Testament, pre-Christian, and Christian history would have served the needs of a northern élite in an opulent, highly decorated copy of the Gospels.

Mount Olivet, like the Temple in Jerusalem, represented a kind of multivalent historical geography. As the site of Christ's cross pose in the picture on fol. 114r, it endows the image with an almost exponential multivalence. It evokes a layering of spiritual history, in which New Testament events – the Passion, the Ascension, and the end of the world – are sandwiched between layers of Old Testament references and addresses to the present condition of the Church. The Passion begins with the going out to Mount Olivet, Christ ascended into heaven from Mount Olivet, and he will return 'in the same way', which was assumed to mean in the same place, and he is to appear not only as he appeared ascending but also as he appeared during his passion, to both of which events the cross pose refers.[80] The image of the two witnesses is carried within this elaborate structure of salvation history.

The unifying factor in the textual interpretations and in the illustrations seems above all to be the image of the heroic saviour flanked by the two attendants. The use of the figure in the Book of Kells may have been connected as well with the visual images and multi-levelled verbal associations created by liturgical texts and ritual, the next area of investigation.

The Illustration and the Liturgy

The illustration depicting the praying Christ flanked by two attendants may represent, in visual form, the multivalent *figura* presented in Zechariah 4.1–14, and its variation in Apocalypse 11.3–12. Did this insertion of an image influenced by a prophetic vision into the text of Matthew result from the possible liturgical function of the Book of Kells, or was the influence more purely textual, arising from exegesis or apocryphal traditions? Another question concerns the reading of Matthew 26 as a gospel lection. Matthew 26.30 is known to have been included in gospel lections in a number of early liturgies but some question arises about how it was read. The illustration in Kells is not placed at the beginning of any usual pericope, but rather in the middle of text marked in other gospel books and the Bobbio Missal as the lection. What is the importance of the text at verses 30–1? Is the illustration connected with liturgical presentation of the text?

Matthew 26 in Early Lection Systems

In early lection systems presented by surviving gospel and liturgical manuscripts, Matthew

26 nearly always serves as a lection during Holy Week, either for Palm Sunday or Holy Thursday.

The known lection systems indicating readings from Matthew 26 for Palm Sunday fall into the category of early Roman liturgy. According to Chavasse, the Passion according to Matthew 26–7 was read in the papal liturgy on the Sunday before Easter as early as the third century.[81] The eighth–century Anglo-Saxon copy of a Roman lectionary of *c.*645 (Würzburg, Universitätsbibliothek, Mp. th. fol. 62) presents the same pericope for 'Ebdomada VI die dominico ad Lateranis', or the stational mass on the Sunday before Easter at the Lateran.[82] This Roman pericope is indicated again in a manuscript associated with eighth-century England. A marginal notation in the Northumbrian Burchard Gospels (Würzburg, Universitätsbibliothek, Mp. th. fol. 68) designates Matthew 26 as the text read on Palm Sunday, indicating the papal stational mass at St John Lateran.[83] Also, the quasi-capitularies of the Lindisfarne Gospels and Royal 1.B.vii may have indicated a lection beginning at Matthew 26.1, but these lists indicate a reading 'Die sabbati prima passionem domini nostri Ihesu xpi', probably meaning the text it originally indicated was to be read at prime on the Saturday before Palm Sunday.[84] While the notations in the Burchard Gospels and the quasi-capitularies in Lindisfarne and Royal 1.B.vii are known to present related systems of lections, these particular notations seem unrelated. The Burchard Gospels' notation for Matthew 26 clearly displays its Roman origins in its designation of the papal station, but the notation in the quasi-capitularies believed to correspond with Matthew 26 is of a different type and indicates a different day. For this reason, the notation in the quasi-capitularies may be considered to represent part of the Neapolitan system believed to have been combined with a Roman system to create the notations and lists preserved in these three Insular manuscripts.[85] The Roman lection of Matthew 26 on Palm Sunday also appears in capitularies and marginal notations of Carolingian manuscripts and later became the standard lection for Palm Sunday.[86]

In eight non-Roman liturgies, pericopes from Matthew 26 are known to have been read on Holy (Maundy) Thursday (Appendix 1, numbers 1, 3, 4, 5, 7, 8, 9, 10). A ninth manuscript, Paris, B.N., lat. 256 (Appendix 1, number 6), presents a skeletal cross in the margin to the right of the text of Matthew 26.30–1 (FIG. 24).[87] These pericopes exhibit a considerable variety in length and purpose, some being designated for the office, others for mass, and others without any specific designation.

The liturgies represented by the nine manuscripts can be described as early and non-Roman, like those indicating readings of the Temptation story from Luke 4.1. The Rabula Gospels, the earliest manuscript of the ten listed, indicates both lections. Furthermore, North Italian lection systems are prominent in both, but the group indicating lections from Matthew 26 for Holy Thursday also includes two manuscripts preserving early Gallican liturgies, the Lectionary of Luxeuil and the Bobbio Missal.[88]

The Paris Gospels presents a set of eighth-century non-Roman lections in its marginal notations.[89] The skeletal cross by the text of Matthew 26.30–1 in the Paris Gospels represents instruction within a liturgical reading of the text. The cross's position is of much interest because, as will be discussed in more detail later, it was placed at the same point in the text as an interlinear cross inscribed in the Bobbio Missal and also at the point where the 'Arrest' illustration was placed in the Book of Kells.[90]

An additional manuscript which is possibly important because of its firm attribution to an Irish context and its probable liturgical use is not listed: the Book of Dimma (Dublin, Trinity College MS 59, page 26), a pocket Gospelbook dating from the second half of the eighth century.[91] The margins in the Gospel text in the Book of Dimma were inscribed with dozens of small crosses, some at sections of text which served as lections in any number of liturgies but others at points which cannot be associated with any known lection system.[92] No written marginal notes indicating feast days are known to be associated with these crosses, making it difficult to imagine how such a myriad of markings could have usefully served liturgical gospel readings. Nonetheless, a small, faint cross was carefully drawn in double lines at the edge of the folio at Mt. 26.31, the initial of which, in double lines very similar to those delineating the cross, is enlarged a bit more than other letters marking the beginnings of sections. Two things are important here. Firstly, that the articulation of the text is in the same tradition at that of the Book of Kells and other manuscripts with block format where the emphasis occurs at verse 31, not at 30, which seems to be associated with a separate tradition of gospel division, to be discussed below.[93] Secondly, this is the same point at which crosses were inscribed into the Paris Gospels (*above*) and the Bobbio Missal, as well as that in which the picture on fol. 114r is placed in the Book of Kells.

The Barberini Gospels (Appendix 1, number 9; also FIG. 27) also provide important evidence for the reading in late eighth- and early ninth-century Anglo-Saxon England of a Holy Thursday lection beginning with Matthew 26.17, the same incipit as lections for the feast given in the Rabula Gospels, North Italian liturgies (Appendix 1, numbers 1, 4), and the Gospels of St Kilian (number 10). Produced by a Northumbrian-Mercian scribal team, the Barberini Gospels could have been made either North or South of the Humber, although Mercia seems more likely because its decoration closely resembles that of Southumbrian manuscripts.[94] Its interlinear figural decoration, lacertine display script, and certain other stylistic features of its script decoration connect it with the slightly later Book of Armagh and the contemporary Book of Kells.[95] The Barberini Gospels, therefore, demonstrate the practice of a non-Roman lection for Holy Thursday in a late eighth- to early ninth-century Anglo-Saxon centre. Furthermore, this centre was possibly in contact with contemporary Irish book production.

Besides lection systems which indicate reading of Matthew 26 or excerpts from it during the Mass or offices of Holy Week, another type of system indicates reading the Passion of Christ from a synoptic text or diatessaron constructed of excerpts from all four Gospels. This type of Passion reading was characteristic of the Spanish Church, although Augustine had suggested a Passion diatesseron be read at Hippo during Holy Week.[96] The best preserved and most accessible early example is that presented by the Liber Comicus (Paris, B.N., nouv. acq. lat. 2171), an eleventh-century Spanish manuscript preserving a Visigothic cathedral liturgy of the seventh century.[97] Within its Passion cento, one of the long narrative sections taken from a single Gospel begins with the words of Matthew 26.30. Verse 30 may have been an important transitional point in the passion narrative when read aloud in its liturgical context, as will be seen from further evidence given by the graphic and decorative articulation of this text in some manuscripts.

Evidence gathered from early lection systems suggests a few conclusions as well as additional questions. The evidence of lection systems suggests that the the Book of Kells may have belonged to a community in which the text of Matthew 26, or part of it, was read on Holy Thursday rather than on Palm Sunday. The Passion according to Matthew represents the Holy Thursday lection characteristic of the non-Roman liturgies indicating Quadragesima Sunday lections from Luke 4.1–13, a text preceded by the other illustration in the Book of Kells. While the capitularies and notes of the Burchard Gospels and Würzburg Mp.th. fol. 62 attest to knowledge of the Roman lection system in Anglo-Saxon England, the decoration of the Book of Kells does not necessarily indicate the influence of a Roman lection system. Moreover, the notation in the Barberini Gospels demonstrates the co-existence of Roman and non-Roman lection systems in Anglo-Saxon England. Further questions surface about the possible reading of the Passion from the Book of Kells and the function of the illustration in relation to liturgical reading of the text. Does any evidence exist to indicate the way in which the Passion may have been read in Insular liturgies? Is it possible to tell if Matthew 26.30 represented an important point in liturgical readings? Might other factors have been involved, such as traditions of chapter divisions? One possible source of information on such questions may lie in the decorative structuring of the text of Matthew 26 in early gospel manuscripts.

The Decorative Structuring of Matthew 26

A discussion of possible liturgical influences on the textual decoration of Matthew 26 will differ somewhat from a study of the decorative structuring of the Temptation texts. The most evident difference results from the absence of any verse or list within the text, in contrast to the position of the Lucan Temptation story after the genealogy of Christ. For this reason, the illustration on fol. 114r can be more readily seen as expressing a division or transition in the narrative text between verses 30 and 31. Furthermore, differences are created by Eusebius' division of the Passion text into small sections. In contrast to the two Eusebian sections comprising the text of the Temptation story in the Gospels of Matthew (4.1–11) and Luke (4.1–13), Matthew's account of the Last Supper and walk to Gethsemane (verses 21–35) is divided into twelve sections (279–90).[98] Decorative articulation of Matthew 26 often conforms to the structure of the sections, making it difficult for the modern eye to distinguish between possible liturgical influences and the pure expression of Eusebian sections. Another difference is the greater variety in pericope length. Known Passion lections from Matthew 26 display five different incipits, while Temptation lections begin consistently at Matthew 4.1 or Luke 4.1.[99] Finally, the lower survival rate for Insular manuscript texts of Matthew than for texts of Luke limits the available comparative material. Study of textual articulation of the Passion according to Matthew will focus on treatment of verses

30 and 31, the section into which the illustration is placed in the Book of Kells.

Manuscripts of Matthew 26 studied so far can be categorised into four groups: 1) manuscripts articulated *per cola et commata* (Appendix 2.II.a.), 2) those with block text format (Appendix 2.II.b.), 3) those with text articulated into short sections or paragraphs (Appendix 2.II.c.), and 4) those combining block text format with section articulation (Appendix 2.II.d.).

The first group includes the Lindisfarne Gospels, British Library Royal 1.B.vii, British Library Additional MS 5463, and British Library Harley 1775. Three of the manuscripts format the text in double columns, while the oldest – Harley 1775 – presents a single text column. Punctuation is minimal, being rendered superfluous by the *per cola et commata* articulation. All four manuscripts place greater emphasis on the incipit of verse 30 than 31, almost undoubtedly to articulate a chapter incipit, which Lindisfarne and the Beneventan manuscript (Additional MS 5463) number in marginal notations.

In the Lindisfarne Gospels (FIG. 17), neither incipit receives an extraordinary degree of emphasis.[100] Verse 30, *& hymno dicto exierunt*, presents a slightly greater emphasis, the first character expanding to touch the following letter of the word *hymno*, with colour and a triad of small circles, resembling a *distinctio* (point) punctuation mark, in the interval. The interior of the slightly enlarged first character of verse 31, *Tunc dicit illis ihs ...*, is filled with colour, but receives no further embellishment.

Royal 1.B.vii presents some features clearly indicating liturgical use.[101] For example, a neatly printed cross appears beside the incipit of verse 1, *& factum : cum* (FIG. 18), most probably marking the beginning of a lection, which further indicates the manuscript's place in a romanising milieu, since the verse represents the incipit of the Roman lection for Palm Sunday. In this part of the Gospel, the single, slightly enlarged letters seem to correspond to the Eusebian sections. The division incipit status of verse 30 (FIG. 19) is expressed graphically by rubrication and expansion of the first letter to a size approximating that of verse 1. At verse 31, however, only the initial is written with red lead.

Harley 1775 (FIG. 20), dated to the sixth century, provides an example of an early uncial manuscript from Italy, articulated *per cola et commata*.[102] Eusebian sections, noted in the left margin, begin with enlarged letters of uniform size at the left edge of the text, with no graphic or decorative variations indicating chapter incipits. The restraint of the uncial manuscript style, seen in this example, underlies the relatively minimal decoration and balanced graphic emphases of Royal 1.B.vii and, to an extent, the Lindisfarne Gospels.

A Beneventan uncial manuscript of the mid-eighth century British Library Additional MS 5463 (FIG. 21), presents the double column format and emphasis, by rubrication, on a chapter division at verse 30.[103] The entire verse is written in red, slightly enlarged letters, with the chapter number noted in the left margin below the notation of the Eusebian section. Additional MS 5463 adds *versus* marks, or commas, (without accompanying *punctus*) at line ends, an unusual use of punctuation in a *per cola et commata* system.[104] The emphasis of this verse with colour and slightly enlarged letters in the Lindisfarne Gospels and Royal 1.B.vii represents an emulation of Italian uncial manuscripts' articulation of this division and the degree to which the two Insular manuscripts follow the texts and systems of divi-

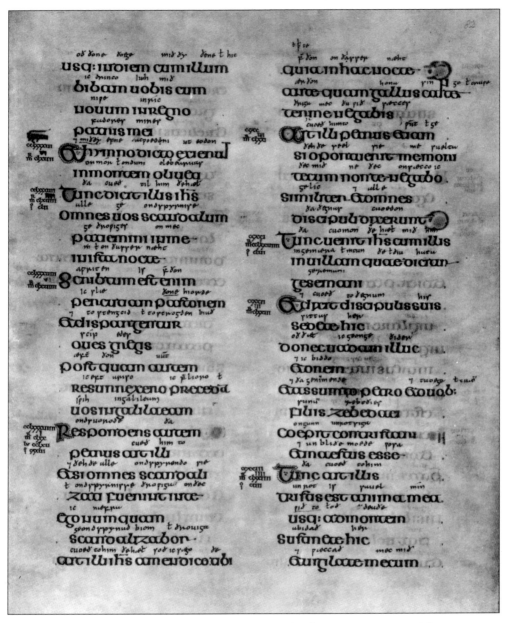

FIG. 17 Lindisfarne Gospels (London, British Library, Cotton Nero D.iv),
fol. 82r, Matthew 26.29–38

sion of their exemplars. Furthermore, it may indicate the manuscripts' contexts in a setting where Roman forms were used, with a Passion lection beginning with Matthew 26.1 read there on Palm Sunday. The Book of Kells, as Appendix 2.II.a. shows, does not emulate this articulation at all, putting by far the greatest graphic emphasis on verse 31 and punctuating the division with the full-page image of Christ and the olive-tree witnesses as well as a red *distinctio* at the end of verse 30.

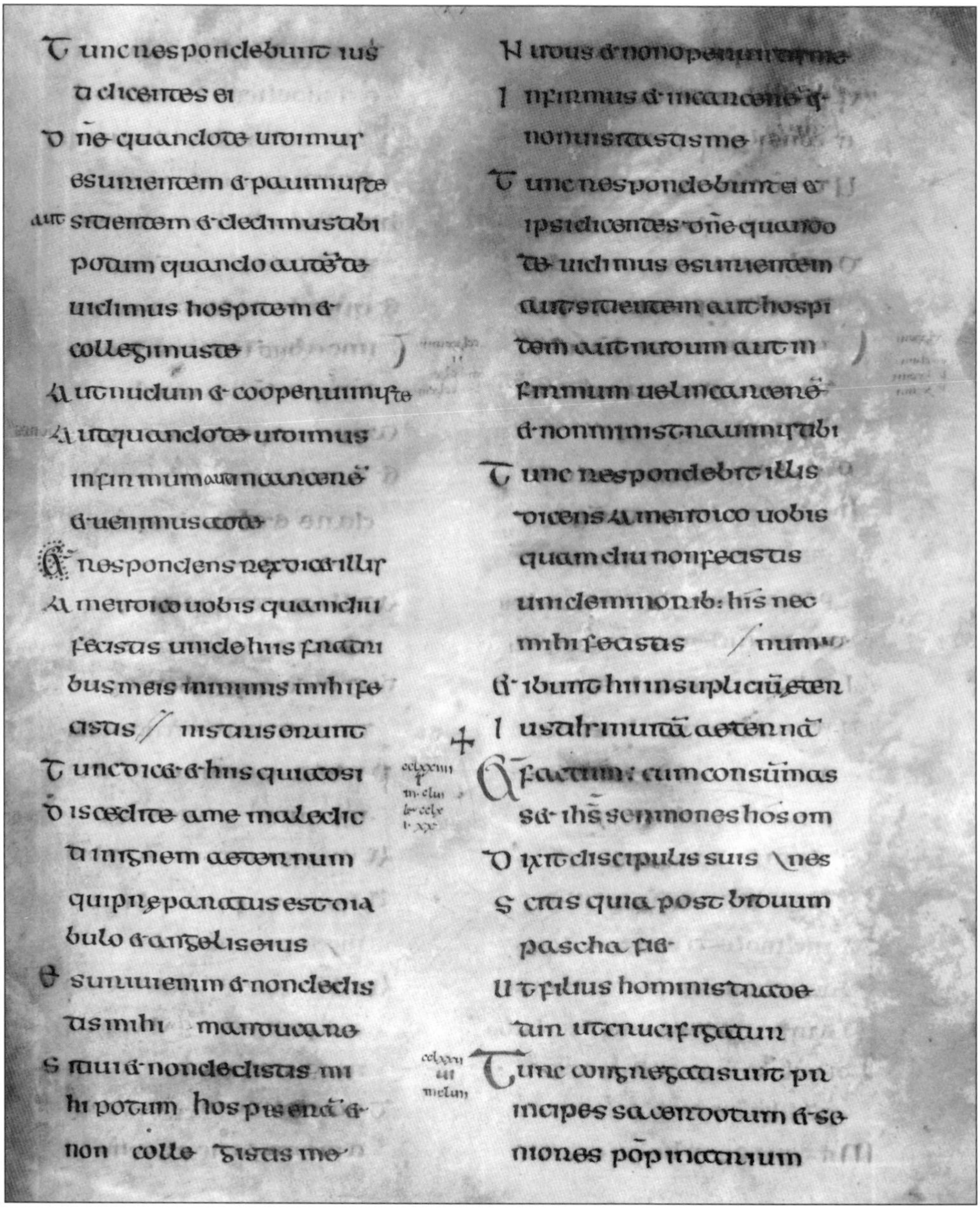

FIG. 18 London, British Library, Royal I.B.vii, fol. 46r,
Matthew 25.45–26.43

The tradition of textual articulation which the Book of Kells follows at this point in the text of Matthew is quite clearly a very old Irish tradition associated with gospel manuscripts presenting the text in block format. In these manuscripts a chapter division at the end of verse 30 is emphasised by extended punctuation and graphic emphasis on the beginning of verse 31. Appendix 2.II.b. presents analysis of several examples, all of which are Insular with the exception of the Gospels of St Gatien of Tours, probably from eighth-century

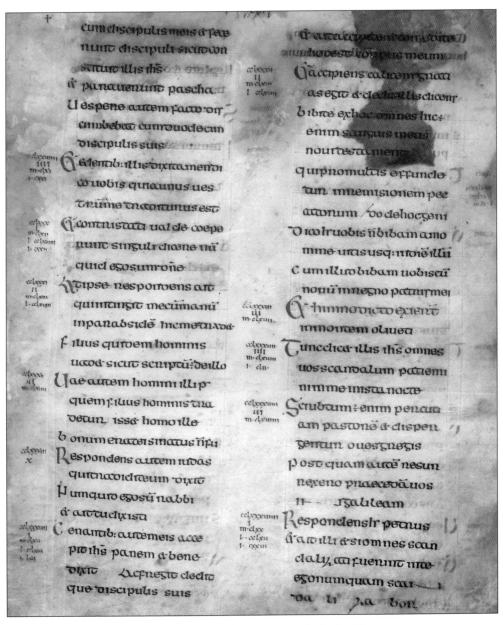

FIG. 19 London, British Library, Royal I.B.vii, fol. 47r,
Matthew 26.18–33

Brittany.[105] The tradition's antiquity is attested by the articulation of Matthew 26.30–1 in the Usher Gospels, or Codex Usserianus Primus, one of the oldest surviving manuscripts from Ireland.[106] An early to mid-seventh-century copy of a pre-Jeromian translation of the Gospels, Usserianus Primus articulates the text presented in block format with a series of red commas from the end of verse 30 at mid-line, continuing rubrication for verse 31.

This archaic tradition of structuring a chapter incipit from an Old Latin series of divi-

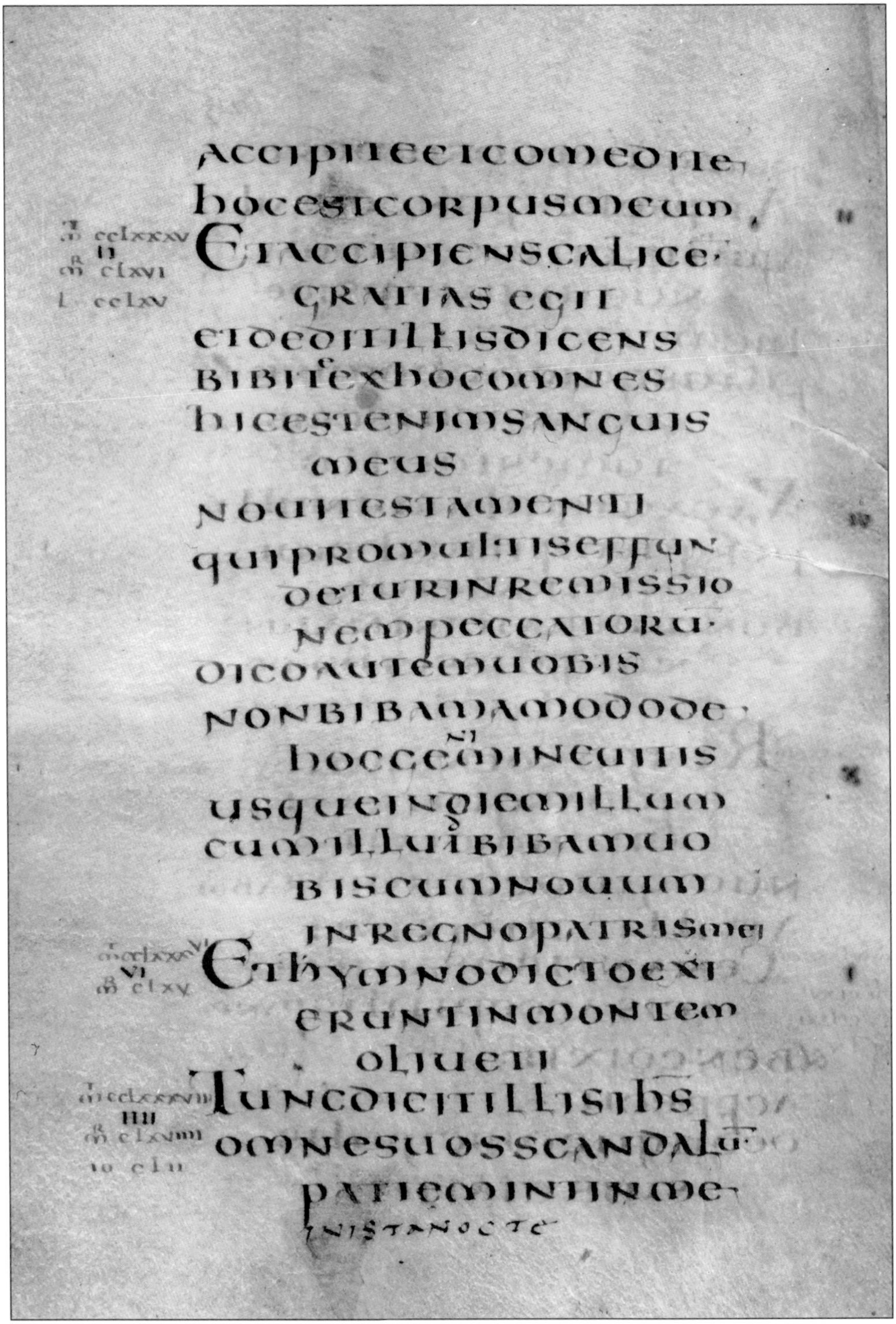

FIG. 20 London, British Library, Harley 1775, fol. 124v, Matthew 26.26–31

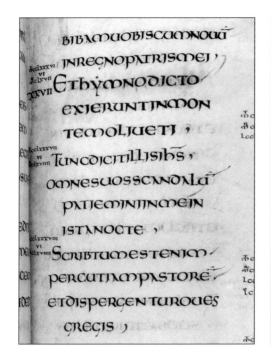

FIG. 21 London, British Library,
Additional 5463, fol. 67r,
Matthew 26.29–38

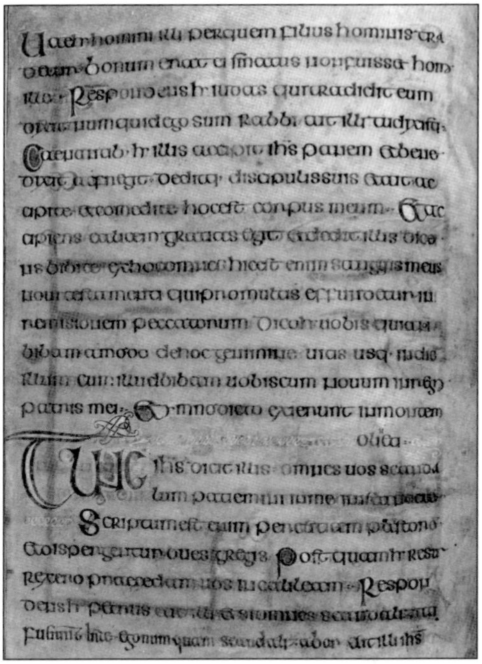

FIG. 22 Durham, Cathedral Library,
MS A.II.17, fol. 38(2)v,
Matthew 26.24–34

sions survives in Durham A.II.17 (FIG. 22). The incipit of verse 31 is elevated to the highest ranks of the manuscript's decorative hierarchy, while the incipit of verse 30 receives the ordinary articulation of an Eusebian section incipit. Placed at the left margin, the first word of verse 31, *Tunc*, begins with its first letter coloured, decorated with interlace and enlarged to extend above the height of three normal lines of script. The following letters gradually diminish in size, in the Insular manner of *diminuendo*, until its final letter is about twice the height of a normal line. A double contour of yellow dots borders the entire word, becoming at the end of the word a panel of dots containing the last letter. The letters are embellished further with spiral ornament and a coloured infill. The incipit of verse 30 seems a mere satellite of ornament which has somehow escaped from the flourishes below it. The interlace of the large letter **T** reaches up to it from the line below to capture it and the following word *ymno* with its contour of yellow dots. The yellow dots invade the interior space between the first two characters and fill it with meticulous rows, duplicating on a smaller scale the panel effect seen on the line below. This panel effect is emphasised by the squared corners of the dotted contour at the end of the word *ymno*. Like the illustration on fol. 114r of the Book of Kells, the decoration between the two verses functions graphically like punctuation, and also, as does the picture in the Book of Kells with its design and iconography, it unites the two sections of text visually.

Some Irish pocket Gospel books, for example, the Books of Mulling and Dimma (Appendix 2.II.b.), present articulation of the text of Matthew 26.30–1 closely resembling that

FIG. 23 Macregol Gospels
(Oxford, Bodleian Library, Auct. D.2.19),
fol. 44, Matthew 26.25–36

of Usserianus Primus.[107] Patrick McGurk has described other archaic features of pocket gospel books as well as Breton manuscripts such as the Gospels of St Gatien of Tours.[108] Perhaps these archaic features bear some relation to the placing of the small, double-lined cross in the margin at the beginning of verse 31, on page 26, in the Book of Dimma, discussed above.[109]

The latest Insular book in the table of block format gospel manuscripts is the early ninth-century Macregol, or Rushworth, Gospels (FIG. 23), produced at Birr, in County Offaly.[110] An impressive manuscript because of its size, full-page gospel incipits, evangelist portraits, and massive text blocks, it presents this part of Matthew 26 with modest decoration. Originally just the first letter of verse 31 (*Tunc ait*) was emphasised with a red dotted contour. Only later, probably at the time the tenth-century Old English gloss was added in Northumbria, was the interior of the first letter of verse 30 (*& imno*) filled in with red lead, now oxidised to dark grey, and a *punctus versus* mark added to the end of the verse. When the Macregol Gospels was made, therefore, it maintained in an abbreviated way the archaic division tradition. Its text block impresses by its sheer size, but it shows little regard for the functional articulation seen in earlier manuscripts. This priority of blatant visual impressiveness indicates the participation of the scribe Macregol in the new concern for virtuoso calligraphic textual presentation seen in Southumbrian and other late eighth- and early ninth-century Insular manuscripts.[111] The Macregol manuscript, however, seems to have been used at some point for liturgical reading because, from verse 10 to 64, Christ's speeches are marked with a cross, suggesting public presentation of the Passion text in two or more voices.

The third group of manuscripts (Appendix 2.II.c.) is important in relation to the Book of Kells in three ways. First, the oldest of the manuscripts with section articulation, the fifth-century Italian uncial gospel book called the Codex Corbeiensis, presents a pre-Jeromian Latin gospel text with chapter division at Matthew 26.31, the first line of the verse articulated with red letters following the chapter number.[112] Codex Corbeiensis's structuring of this division – seen also in Usserianus Primus, another Old Latin text – strongly suggests that the text break presented in Kells and other Insular, especially Irish, gospel books in block format represents an archaic tradition. Two other manuscripts in this group, the Paris

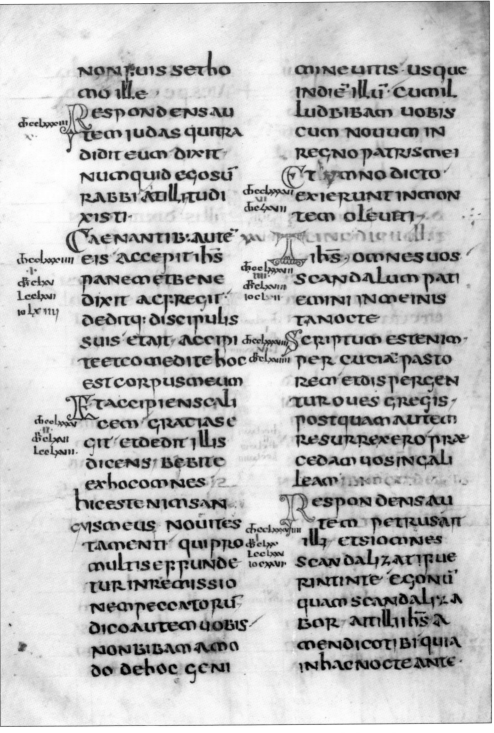

NON fuis setho
mo ille
RESPONDENS AU
tem iudas quitra
didit eum dixit
numquid egosu
RABBI ATILL'TUDI
XISTI
CAENANTIB: AUTE
eis accepit ihs
PANEMETBENE
dixit acfregit
deditq discipulis
suis etait accipi
TEETCOMEDITE hoc
ESTCORPUSMEUM
ETACCIPIENSCALI
cem gracias e
git etdedit illis
dicens BEBITE
exhocomnes
hicestenimsan
cvismeus Nouites
TAMENTI quipro
multiseffunde
TUR INREMISSIO
NEMPECCATORU
dicoautem uobis
NONBIBAM AMO
do dehoc geni

COMNEUITIS usque
INDIE illu cumil
ludbibam uobis
cum Nouum in
REGNO PATRISMEI
ET ymno dicto
exierunt inmon
tem oleuum
Ihs omnes uos
scandalum pati
emini inmeinis
TANOCTE
Scriptum estenim
per curia pasto
rem etdispergen
turoues gregis
postquam autem
resurrexero prae
cedam uosingali
leam
Respondens au
tem petrusan
illi etsiomnes
scandalizatifue
rintinte egonu
quam scandaliza
bor amlihs a
mendicoti bi quia
inhacnocteante

FIG. 24 Paris Gospels (Paris, Bibliothèque nationale, lat. 256),
fol. 60v, Matthew 26.24–34

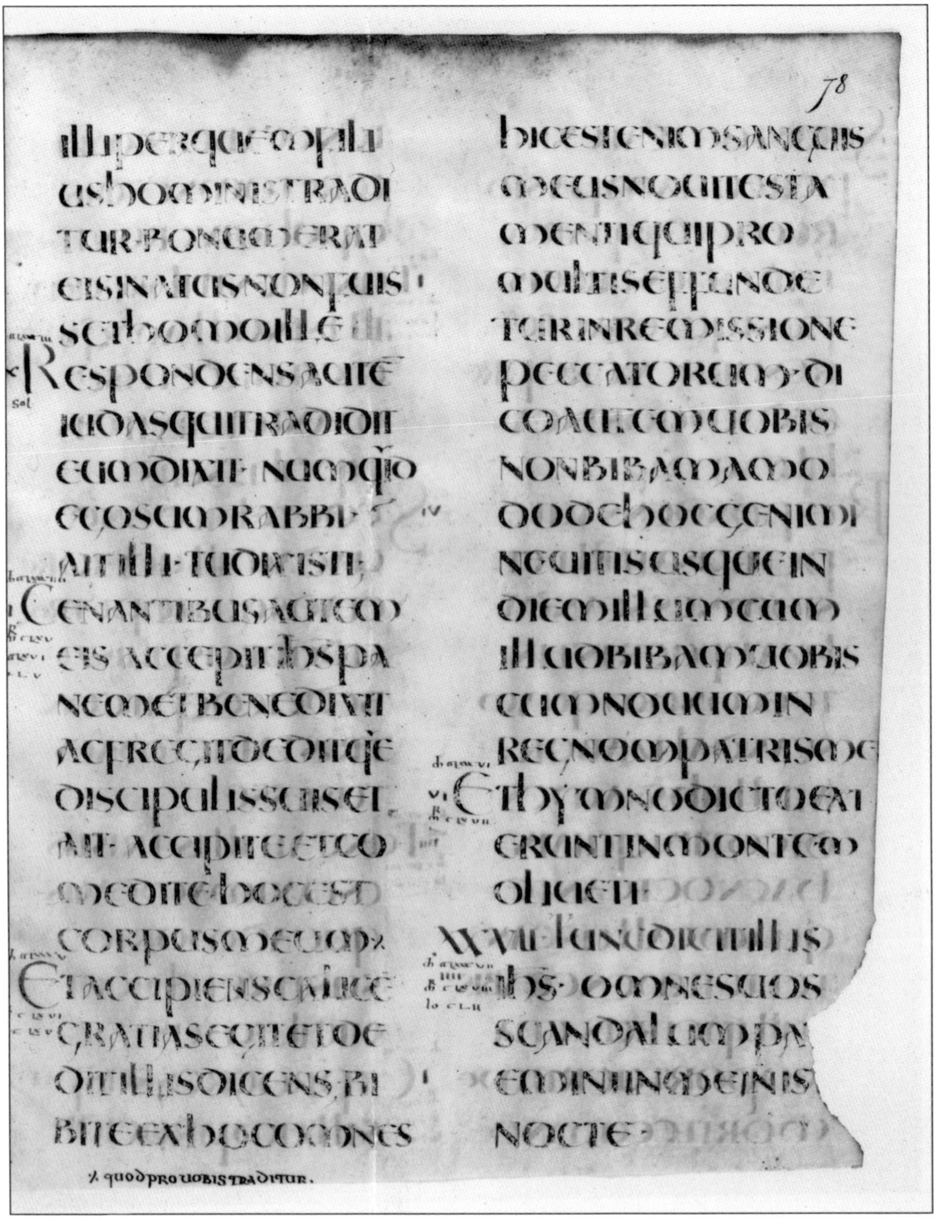

FIG. 25 Paris, Bibliothèque nationale, lat. 17226, fol. 78r,
Matthew 26.24–31

Gospels (Paris, B.N., lat. 256, FIG. 24) and a seventh- to eighth-century uncial manuscript from Italy (Paris, B.N., lat. 17226; FIG. 25) place graphic emphasis on a chapter division at verse 31, showing the persistence of this tradition of division in manuscripts not articulated *per cola et commata*.[113] A third manuscript, from Tours and written in Caroline minuscule at the end of the eighth century (Paris, B.N., lat. 260; FIG. 26), indicates the chapter division at verse 31 with an interlinear notation.[114] These three also place punctuation between the

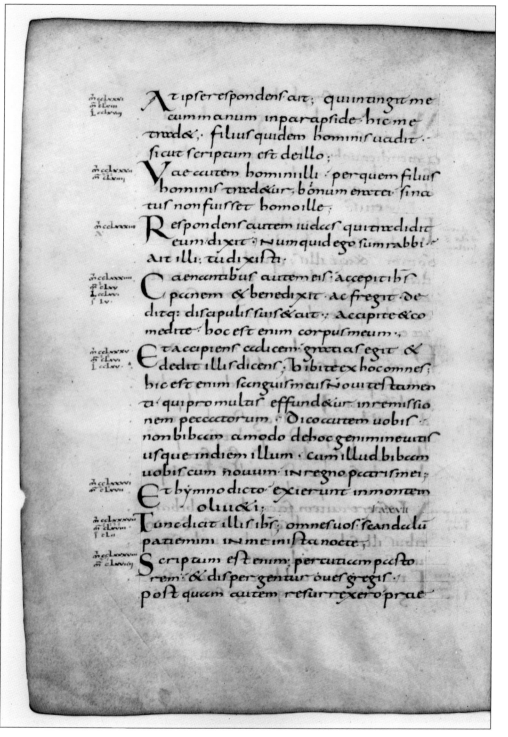

FIG. 26 Paris, Bibliothèque nationale, lat. 260, fol. 68v,
Matthew 26.23–32

two sections. Second on the list of important points, evidence for liturgical reading of the text appears in the Paris Gospels (FIG. 24), a seventh-century manuscript from the environs of Paris.[115] A skeletal cross hovers in the right margin between verses 30 and 31. The shape and decoration of the initial T perhaps refer to the eucharistic and liturgical significance of the text, as will be discussed in more detail later.[116] Third notable point: sectional structuring of text, usually based on Eusebian sections, with each 'paragraph' articulated with an enlarged, often coloured or even decorated initial, seems to have become increasingly popular with scribes producing both luxury and utilitarian manuscripts of the last half of the eighth and early ninth century. It combines the virtues of clarity of organisation and economy – the visually disciplined *per cola et commata* articulation being materially extravagant – with the prestigious authority of continental associations and possibilities for many kinds of decorative embellishment, all the more to express prestige, structure and meaning. It is a flexible kind of articulation, and Insular scribes of the late eighth and early ninth centuries exploited its fluidity.

The fourth group of manuscripts (Appendix 2.II.d.) includes three Insular ones of the late eighth and early ninth century which seem to combine section articulation, usually Eusebian sections, with block format. The Book of Kells itself fits well into this category because its block text is often divided corresponding to Eusebian sections, with conspicuously large and decorated initial letters placed at the left margin. The text of Matthew 26 is presented in this way. Within the blocks of the sections, smaller enlarged letters, infilled with colour and sometimes embellished with decoration, structure the text, following roughly the *per cola et commata* articulation of the Lindisfarne Gospels, seen also in its text of Luke 4.1–13.

The three manuscripts analysed here share selectively and to different degrees the variety of types of articulation presented in the Book of Kells. None of the three maintain the archaic division at verse 31, either giving nearly equal emphasis to both verse beginnings (Barberini Gospels) or emphasising the division at verse 30 found in the *per cola et commata* group (Hereford Gospels and Book of Armagh). The Hereford and Barberini Gospels (FIGS 15, 27) format the text in short sections resembling paragraphs, but sometimes articulate sense structures within the section block with colour infills or slightly enlarged letters.[117] This is particularly true of Hereford. In the Book of Armagh (Dublin, Trinity College Library, MS 52), text is presented in double-column blocks which are divided into sections by enlarged initials or abbreviated words offset in the left margin.[118] If a line preceding the division initial falls short of the right text block edge, the gap is filled in with a flourish of small, repeated punctuation marks. Occasionally in the Book of Armagh, lines within the block are broken up into short sense units, as in the section of text narrating the breaking of bread at the Last Supper, on fol. 49v. Otherwise, emphasis within the column block is just perceptible, accomplished by slight enlargement of initial letters and judicious use of spacing. Punctuation may or may not be used in the Book of Armagh. It is absent from the interval between verses 30 and 31 (fol. 49v), while the other two manuscripts include it, the Barberini Gospels presenting a graceful, elongated red *distinctio*. Two of the manuscripts in

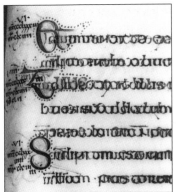

FIG. 27 Barberini Gospels (Vatican, Biblioteca Apostolica, Barb. Lat. 570), fols 42v–43r, Matthew 26.15–42

this group, the Barberini Gospels and the Hereford Gospels, almost undoubtedly served as lection books, despite the wealth of decoration of the former, the poverty of the latter.[119]

To sum up this analysis of textual articulation of Matthew 26.30–1, one may say that at least two important points have been made about the Book of Kells. First, it preserves an archaic text block type articulation of a gospel division known from Old Latin gospel manuscripts. The only other manuscripts to articulate the division in the same way, i.e., within block formatted text, are Insular manuscripts, most if not all of them Irish or presenting Irish connections. Those dating from the last half of the eighth and early ninth century, with one exception (Macregol), have been described as preserving other archaic features. Why did the scribes and artists who created the Book of Kells preserve this archaic feature when they were clearly in touch with advanced Italianate manuscript art as well as the most recent developments in textual presentation, where such archaic features seem to have been increasingly ignored? Second, the manuscript evidence suggests that this textual break had taken on significance beyond that of textual division. The elaborate emphasis given to it in the Durham A.II.17 gospel fragment, as well as its preservation in later archaicising books, probably were not simply intended to reproduce existing divisions. The Paris Gospels provide further evidence of liturgical importance, as well as a simple example of liturgical influence upon initial forms, where, as will be discussed further, a T comes to resemble a cross on an altar or table. The possibility remains, also, that the small cross inscribed in the margin of the Book of Dimma at Matthew 26.31, with its archaicising articulation, could refer to a liturgical importance of this point in the text in an Irish context.

Function and Audience: Salvation in the Past, Present, and Future

The harmony of textual articulation by decoration with the visual images in the Book of Kells seems as apparent as the complexity of its graphic forms. Part of this harmony, as seen in the analysis of the articulation of the text preceding and following the Temptation illustration, is created by the way that decoration and images function within the block format. This seems to be a peculiar feature of Insular manuscripts presenting text in block format. The emphases imparted by *per cola et commata* articulation and the intervals or breaks expressing divisions in block formatted text differ in their structural and interpretative effects. Where the former emphasises the beginning of text and eliminates the need for punctuating divisions, the latter can emphasise the gap between sections as well as unify them graphically by use of punctuation or other kinds of decoration. The multivalent iconography of the illustration discussed above in this chapter and by others, such as O'Reilly and Ó Carragáin, in referring to and expanding the meaning of adjacent texts may be seen as a complementary part of the full-page punctuation marks and *figurae* inserted into the text of the Book of Kells.[120]

Still more evidence of the liturgical importance of this point in the text of the Matthew Passion may be provided by a liturgical manuscript, the Bobbio Missal. As seen earlier (Appendix 1), the Bobbio Missal presents the pericope Matthew 26.20–35 as the gospel lection for Holy Thursday. In the text presented in the manuscript, a cross is inserted between verses 30 and 31, between *in monte olivite* and *tunc dicit illis*.[121] On the preceding folio a cross has been inscribed in the right margin next to the end of verse 25, with indication in the text at the beginning of the institution of the Eucharist.[122] This section of text, verses 26–30, may also have been deliberately isolated in the Book of Kells: verses 26–9 represent the sole text written on fol. 113v, facing the illustration and verse 30 on fol. 114r, an arrangement determined by careful spacing on the preceding folio.[123] Exactly how the cross between verses 30 and 31 in the Bobbio Missal functioned in the context of the Holy Thursday liturgy cannot be known, but it indicates the importance of the point between the two verses in a liturgical reading. It is not simply a division to organise the text graphically.

The liturgical significance of the point between verses 30 and 31 is further suggested by the skeletal cross inscribed in the margin of the Paris Gospels (FIG. 24). Moreover, the first letter of verse 31, T, is drawn in black and set upon a 'platform', giving it the appearance of a cross on an altar or stand. The *figura* or shape of the uncial T, like the cross shape of the Greek *Tau*, easily transforms into a sign with liturgical and textual significance: Eucharist, Passion, Crucifixion, and salvation.[124] The *figura* of the Insular half-uncial T, for all its potential formal expressionism, cannot so easily take on the semiosis of a cross-shape, unless historiated in some way.[125]

The illustration of Christ praying in the cross pose flanked by the olive trees on fol. 114r could be compared with a multivalently historiated letter or even a multi-levelled elaboration of punctuation. This inflated punctuation becomes a *figura* articulating and linking the Eucharistic text facing it, into a whole with the story of the sacrifice and martyrdom of Christ that follows.[126] But also it expands the meaning of the events to include past, present, and future significance, as seen earlier in discussion of the cross pose and olive trees.

In addition to its references to the Passion and Crucifixion, the illustration presents a Eucharistic image in specific relation to the text facing it. Suzanne Lewis has already suggested that the chiastic *figura* of Christ's body grasped on either side may depict the *cofractio panis* of Iona's Eucharistic rite.[127] The unique text of the institution of the Eucharist presented in Kells supports her suggestion. To the end of verse 26 (*hoc est enim corpus meum*), the text of Kells adds *quod confringitur pro seculi vita*, 'which is broken in pieces for the life of the world', using the verb, *confringo*, the root of the term for shared breaking of the host.[128] The variant text, together with the picture, places the liturgical re-enactment of passion and martyrdom within the spiritual history of the world where it serves as the manifestation of the promise of salvation during the time of the present Church until the end of the world. This connection is expressed verbally in the Eucharistic formula of the Stowe Missal and in the hymn 'Quando commonicarent sacerdotes' (or 'Sancti venite') in the Antiphonary of Bangor, with their apocalyptic reference to the Last Judgement and Second Coming, as pointed out by Fritz Saxl.[129]

If, as evidence from non-Roman lection systems and graphic articulation in early gospel books suggests, the illustration and decoration of Matthew 26 in the Book of Kells participated in some way in liturgical reading of the Gospel's Passion on Holy Thursday, how might the iconography of the picture on fol. 114r have been specifically connected with the feast's liturgy?

The rituals of Holy Week commemorate Christ's Passion, Crucifixion and Resurrection, but in early liturgies this week also saw the culmination of the Lenten preparation of catechumens and the restoration of penitents. In a sense, the week also begins the new year: the old communion hosts are buried, the old paschal candle dismantled, and new oil and chrism for the coming year are concocted and blessed. The liturgy of Holy Week symbolises the renewal of the Church by Christ's resurrection and the tangible fulfilment of the new covenant by baptism, penance and the Eucharist.[130] Several themes expressed in the liturgy of Holy Week which seem related to the themes seen in the illustration, for example, the promise of salvation in the Eucharist, rituals of anointing with oil, vigilance against evil, and looking forward to the ultimate vision of resurrection and salvation. These themes are most prominent in the early liturgy of Holy Thursday.

Holy Thursday is one of the most liturgically complex days of the year. In some early liturgies, at least two masses were celebrated in order to accomplish the various rituals proper to the day. During one mass, the reconciliation of the penitents may take place, another may accomplish the blessing of the oils.[131] The Gregorian, Gallican, North Italian and Spanish liturgies appear to have celebrated only one mass on Holy Thursday, but lection systems associated with these liturgies often designate gospel or Old Testament lections for one or two of the day's offices.[132] In relation to the illustration in the Book of Kells, perhaps one of the most significant rituals performed on Holy Thursday is that of the consecration of the oils.

Two oils were necessary for baptism: one, 'oil of exorcism', for anointing before baptism, the other, chrism, for unction after baptism.[133] The 'oil of exorcism' was pure olive oil, chrism a mixture of oil and balsam.[134] Chrism was used for baptism and confirmation, in the consecration of bishops, churches, and liturgical furnishings, and in the ordination of priests.[135] Because of the need in the early Church for a fresh supply of oil for the baptisms to be performed at the end of Holy Week, Holy Thursday quickly became the day of consecration of the oils.[136]

Early papal consecration of oils is recorded in documents of the Gelasian and Gregorian liturgies, while the liturgy of other Roman churches of the second half of the eighth century is documented in four manuscripts, published by Andrieu as *Ordo 24*.[137] In the Gelasian Mass, the consecration of the oils takes place on the altar during the Mass between the fraction of the Eucharist and Communion.[138] Two acolytes bring two ampullae containing the oils to two deacons who present, first the chrism, then the oil of exorcism, to the pope.[139] Having completed the consecration, the pope then continues with distribution of Communion. The Roman cathedral ceremony of Ordo 24 nearly duplicates the papal ceremony except that a bishop takes the place of the pope and no mention is made of a stational basilica.[140] Both documents give a sense of the integration of the ceremony of consecration of the oils into the Eucharist. They describe the setting aside of the chalice and paten while the pope or bishop turns his attention to the ampullae which the two acolytes have brought to the altar and passed to the subdeacons and archdeacons.[141] Consecration of the oils becomes part of the Eucharist in the Holy Thursday liturgy. The oils would have constituted part of the basic equipment for the Irish and Northumbrian Churches with their emphasis on conversion and church foundation, so that a need would have existed for a similar ritual for consecration of the two oils in Insular Churches having the equivalent function of cathedrals, most probably on Holy Thursday.

If the iconography of the illustration on fol. 114r is connected in some way with a lection from Matthew 26 for Holy Thursday, then it seems possible that the liturgical image of the bishop flanked by two deacons holding two ampullae of oil, enacted between the fraction of the host and Communion, would be very effectively echoed by the illustration, especially if viewed on Holy Thursday.

Holy Thursday, moreover, represents the liturgical turning point from Lent to the promised victory over death in its commemoration and re-enactment of turning points in salvation history: the institution of the Eucharist and the beginning of the Passion. The illustration of the Temptation of Christ overlays the gospel narrative with liturgical texts and interpretative images that, on one level, represent Lent in terms of salvation history – past, present, and future. The illustration on fol. 114r articulates a turning point in the gospel narrative and unites two sections of text – altered to emphasise the apocalyptic significance of the Eucharist – with a multivalent *figura* that places text, liturgy, and Insular audience within universal, salvation history. That the Book of Kells places this image at a point in the text which had a long history as a point of emphasis in native Christian tradition is surely significant in its commemoration of indigenous forms connected with early holymen and their aristocratic networks. The audience of monastic and clerical élite of a Columban community who would have seen the illustration in this setting would have understood all the more fully the significance of the texts and liturgy of Holy Thursday and would thus have been able to pass on the one, orthodox truth of the gospel to the Christian community.

Notes to Chapter Three

1 Powell in Henry, 1974, p.223. Also, the inscription of the text of Matthew 26.30 in the arch above Christ's head serves as the actual text and is not simply a caption.

2 *See* Alexander, in Fox, 1990, p.282, and Ó Carragáin, 1994b, p.418–19, on this 'contradiction' of movement and immobility.

3 Henry, 1974, pp.188–9; Nordenfalk, 1977a, pp.275–6; Nordenfalk, 1977b, p.124; Schapiro, 1973b, pp.53–4; Harbison, 1985, pp.185–6; Henderson, 1987, p.162–3. *See* Harbison, 1985, pp.184–6, on the early attempts to identify the picture, beginning in the sixteenth century. Scholarship to 1989 summarised in Farr, 1989, pp.218–26.

4 Porter, 1931, pp.51–3; Henderson, 1987, 162–3.

5 1988–1989; 1993.

6 Ó Carragáin, 1994; Lewis, 1980, p.155; *see also* Farr, 1989, Chapter 3.

7 Porter, 1931, pp.52–3.

8 Schapiro, 1973, p.18.

9 *Allegory of the Laws* III.186, cited by Schapiro (1973, fn. 19, p.51) and Danielou (1950, fn. 1, p.190); *Every Good Man is Free* (vol. 9, p.27); *Moses* I.39 (vol. 10, pp.389–91).

10 *Moses* I.39, tr. F. H. Colson, vol. 6, p.389, lines 217–19.

11 Klauser, 1960, pp.112–33; Thérel, 1973, pp.125–33; Kleinbauer, 1982, pp.25–45.

12 Kleinbauer, 1982, pp.36, 38.

13 Lindblom, 1925, pp.109–11.

14 Tertullian, *De oratione* 11, 13, cited in Lindblom, 1925, pp.110–11.

15 Eusebius, *Ecclesiastical History* VIII.7., ed. Lawlor, 1932, vol. 2, p.272; tr. G. A. Williamson, 1965, p.336.

16 von Simson, 1987, pp.40–8.

17 Gougaud, 1927, pp.6–10.

18 Sermo XXXVIII.3, *CCL* 23, pp.149–50, lines 32–41

19 Gregory, *In Primum Regum Expositiones* 6.3–4, *PL* 79,409B–410A.

20 Godel, 1963, p.314; Gougaud, 1927, p.10.

21 Gougaud, 1927, pp.10–11; McNeill and Gamber, 1938, pp.31–2; Godel, 1963, pp.314–15; Lapidge and Sharpe, 1985, No. 603; O'Dwyer, 1981, pp.108–10.

22 Godel, 1963, p.314.

23 Godel, 1963, pp.314–15; Gougaud, 1927, pp.10–12.

24 Godel, 1963, p.314.

25 Kelly, 1979, p.260; Schapiro, 1973, p.21; Hennig, 1949–51, pp.251–60.

26 Hughes, 1958, pp.263–4; the original text of the Lebor Laignech (Dublin, Trinity College, MS 1337) is available in *Corpus Genealogiarum Hiberniae* 1, ed. O'Brien, and in the facsimile by the Royal Irish Academy, 1880.

27 On Alcuin, Godel, 1963, p.315; on Cuthbert, Bede, *Vita Sancti Cuthberti*, Colgrave, ed. and tr., 1940, pp.292–3.

28 *See also* Farr, 1996.

29 Smyth, 1984, p.95; *also* Godel (1963, pp.314–15) and Gougaud (1927, pp.11–12) for other examples.

30 (Eddius) Stephanus, *Life of Wilfrid*, Colgrave, ed. and tr., 1927, pp.26–9.

31 Epilogue 7, in Stokes, 1905, p.267; O'Dwyer, 1981, p.108.

32 *See* Chapter 2, pp.93–4.

33 Lewis, 1980, p.155; O'Reilly (1994) and Ó Carragáin (1994b) have now discussed the exegetical and liturgical connections in detail.

34 Ó Laoghaire, 1987, p.155; von Simson, 1987, p.47; Wilmart, 1911, pp.282–92. Wilmart cited Pseudo-Jerome, *Commentarius in Marcam* (*PL* 30, 632A=655A), which Morin (1910, pp.357–62) attributed to Italy and dated fifth century, but Bischoff (1976, no. 27, pp.129–31) gave it to Cummianus. Some accept Bischoff's attribution (Lapidge and Sharpe, 1985, no. 345, p.99; Kelly, 1974, p.xii, and 1986, p.69; Ó Cróinín, 1986, p.449), although it has been questioned recently (Cahill, 1994).

35 Mütherich (1977–78, p.102) finds its closest iconographic parallel in the Transfiguration depicted in the triumphal arch mosaic, SS. Nereo e Achilleo, Rome. The Evangeliary of Otto III is one of two Reichenau manuscripts presenting illustrations of the Temptation of Christ which parallel the Kells depiction of the head and shoulders of Christ above the Temple (*see* Chapter 2). *See also* Schiller, 1972, vol. 1, p.146.

36 von Simson, 1987, pp.41–58; Ó Carragáin, 1986, pp.385–8.

37 Harbison, 1980, pp.319–20; Stalley, 1990, pp.138–41. *See also* Farr, 1996, pp.241–2; Ó Carragáin, 1988, pp.20–31, 42–3; Ó Carragáin, 1994b, pp.429–36; Roe, 1981, pp.33–4.

38 *See* Farr, 1989, pp.239–41.

39 Jeremias, 1957, pp.57–8.

40 Raponi, 1983, pp.210–11, 225–7; Baltzer, 1965, pp.263–74.

41 Raponi, 1983, pp.226–7; Irish Lucan commentary, edition in *CCL* 108C, p.34, lines 219–23. *See also* Chapter 2, pp.58, 73, 91–2.

42 Bede, *Vita Cuthberti,* 28, Colgrave, ed. and tr., 1940, pp.292–3.

43 6–7, 15, in Selmer, 1959 (1989), pp.6–7, 12–16, 40–5.

44 Nordenfalk, 1977a, pp.275–6.

45 *Quaestiones in Vetus Testamentum, PL* 83, 299C–D.

46 On Irish knowledge of Isidore, Hillgarth, 1984, pp.7–8; Bischoff, 1966, p.181; according to Bischoff (1966, p.183) and Laistner (1935, p.265), Bede may have known *Quaestiones in Vetus Testamentum* by the eighth century.

47 *See also* the work of Ó Carragáin, on the liturgical, ritual images of the *sustenatio* and *in medio duorum animalium,* in Ó Carragáin, 1994b, pp.417–35.

48 Jerome, *In Zachariam, CCL* 76A, p.748, lines 28–34. Didymus' commentary, Doutreleau, ed. and tr., 1962. The commentaries of Hippolytus (AD 160–230) and Origen (AD 185–254) do not survive (Adriaen, in *CCL* 76A, p.748, notes 29 and 30). Other early commentators on Zechariah include Theodore of Mopsuestia, who wrote his commentary between 380 and 383, and Ephrem, whose work Jerome probably did not know because it apparently was never translated from Syriac (Doutreleau, ed., pp.33–5).

49 *CCL* 76A, pp.781–3, lines 160–220.

50 *CCL* 76A, p.785, lines 276–81, 284–6. For further discussion of exegesis of Mount Olivet, *see* Farr, 1989, pp.264–9; O'Reilly, 1993, pp.110–12.

51 McGinn, 1988, pp.5–6; in Didymus, Doutreleau, ed., 1962, pp.375–7.

52 On typologies of the figures, *see* LoBue, 1963, p.145; as prophets: Didymus (Doutreleau, ed., vol. 1, pp.371–7) and Jerome (*CCL* 76A, pp.784–5, lines 265–94) list examples.

53 Kelly, 1982, pp.394–5); Bischoff, 1976, No. 1, pp.97–102.

54 Bischoff, 1976, No. 37, p.143.

55 Kelly, 1982, pp.404–6; Bischoff, 1976, p.143; Bonner, 1966, pp.7–8.

56 *PL* 93, 162B–C.

57 *PL* 93, 162C.

58 *Explanatio Apocalypsis* 2.11, *PL* 93, 162D; *also* Marshall, tr., 1878, p.73.

59 *PL* 93, 162D–64A.

60 *Explanatio Apocalypsis* 2.1, *PL* 93, col. 164C; *also* Marshall, tr., 1878, p.77.

61 Pseudo-Isidore, *Commentarius in Apocalypsin*, *PLS* 4, 1859.

62 Rauh, 1973, pp.75–6; for Jerome's commentary, *see above*, p.112.

63 Augustinus Hibernicus, *De Mirabilibus Sacrae Scripturae*, 22, *PL* 35, col. 2184

64 Dottin, 1909, p.350, footnote 1.

65 Pseudo-Bede, *Collectanea*, *PL* 94, 543B. Note that although Migne attributed this work to Bede, it is no longer accepted as his but rather that of an anonymous Irish or Anglo-Saxon writer. Bede's Ascension sermon, Homilia II.15, *CCL* 122, p.286–7, lines 277–80.

66 McNamara, 1975, pp.26–7; Dottin, 1909, 349–52.

67 Aldhelm, 'De virginitate, Carmen,' in *Aldhelmi Opera*, Ehwald, 1961 (1919), pp.363–5, lines 248–82; 'The Carmen de virginitate, Lapidge and Rosier, tr., 1985, pp.108–9; Blathmac, Poem to Our Lady, quatrains 256–9, Carney, ed. and tr., 1964, pp.87–8; 'Reference Bible' cited by McNamara, 1987, p.99; middle Irish apocrypha, McNamara, 1975, pp.1–3, 6, 26, 139; *The Two Sorrows of the Kingdom of Heaven, Descensus ad inferos, Vision of Adomnán, and Antichrist*, in Herbert and McNamara, 1989, pp.19–21, 86, 147, 150; Aelfric, *Dominica* 1 *in Quadragesima*, Thorpe, ed., 1844–6, rep. 1971, II, pp.100–1; *see also* Green, 1989, pp.13–19.

68 Thérel, 1973, pp.178–9, quotes in translation Eusebius' account in *A Preparation for the Gospel* 6.18 (*PG* 22, col. 452); further discussion of exegesis on Mount Olivet and Gethsemane in Farr, 1989, pp.264–7.

69 For example, the Irish Pseudo-Jeromian commentary on Mark, *PL* 30, 655D: '*Exierunt in montem Olivarum … In monte Oliveti Jesus tenetur, et inde ad coelos ascendit: ut nos sciamus quia inde ascendimus ad coelos, unde vigilamus, et oramus, et ligmur, nec repugnamus in terra*'.

70 Zechariah 14.4: 'That day his feet shall rest upon the Mount of Olives, which is opposite Jerusalem to the east'. *See* Schapiro, 1943, rep. 1979, p.273.

71 *See above*, pp.108–9 and Harbison, 1980, pp.319–20; Stalley, 1990, pp.138–41. *See also* Farr, 1996, pp.241–2; Ó Carragáin, 1988, pp.20–31, 42–3; Ó Carragáin, 1994b, pp.429–36.

72 In *Das Bibelwerk*, cited by McNamara, 1987, p.99; *also* Adso, *De ortu et tempore Antichristo*, *PL* 40, 1134, cited in Green, 1989, pp.20–21. Green also discusses later Enoch imagery, in the *Old English Genesis*, and iconography in Anglo-Saxon manuscripts, pp.19–20. *See also* the examples in the *Gospel of Nicodemus* in which Enoch and Elias are associated with the appearance of Christ on Mount Olivet after his Resurrection and prior to his Ascension, in Herbert and McNamara, 1989, pp.73–7.

73 Bede, *Concerning figures and tropes*, in Miller, Prosser, and Benson, 1973, p.120.

74 *Do Suidigud Tellaich Temra*, ed. R. I. Best, 1910, 121–72, at §36, page 160: 'Is indemin immorro cía baile in rohadhnocht, acht is dóig leo is ina chorp chollaigi rucad i nnach ndíamair ndíada amail rucad Ele 7 Enóch i pardus condafil ic ernaidi eiseiséirgi in sruthseanóir sáeghlach sin. I. Fintan mac Bóchra meic Eithieir meic Rúail meic Annida meic Caim meic Náe meic Laimiach'. Cited in McCone, 1990, p.76; Ó Corráin, 1987, p.294.

75 McCone, 1990, pp.75–6; text and translation in Best, 1910, §20, pp.144, 145.

76 O Corráin, 1987, pp.293–4.

77 McCone, 1990, p.76; text and translation in Best, 1910, §32, pp.152, 153.

78 Best, 1910, §20, pp.144, 145: '… ar is mesea in fíada firéolach foillsiges cech n-ainfis do chách'. Apocalypse 3.3: '*Et dabo duobus testibus meis, et prophetabunt diebus mille ducentis sexaginta, amicti saccis*'.

79 *See also* Carey, 1989; Farr, 1996, pp.242–8.

80 Vaesen, 1988, p.55; Ó Carragáin, 1994b, pp.432–4; Farr, 1994, pp.445–9.

81 Chavasse, 1952, pp.81–2, 94, 96–7.

82 Klauser, 1972, pp.3–4; Bischoff and Hofmann, p.96; Klauser, 1972, no. 85, p.23; Morin, 1911, p.304.

83 Bischoff and Hofman, 1952, pp.93–4; *see also* T. J. Brown's references to the lections marked in the Burchard Gospels in relation to the quasi-capitularies of Lindisfarne and Royal 1.B.vii, in Kendrick *et al.*, 1956–60, vol. 2, pp.34–8; Morin, 1893b, pp.113–26, *esp.* p.120; Beissel, 1907, p.122.

84 Morin, 1891, no. 63, p.488; Brown in Kendrick *et al.*, vol. 2, List IV, no. 4, p.40.

85   *See* Brown, in Kendrick, *et al.*, 1956–60, vol. 2, pp.34–41; Bischoff and Hofmann, 1952, p.93; Chapman, 1908, pp.23–9, 45–72; Morin, 1891, pp.481–93, 529–37.

86   Klauser, 1972, pp.69 (no. 99), 110 (no. 95), 149 (108), 176 (101); Beissel, 1907, pp.127–31, 135. On the reading of the Passion according to Matthew on Palm Sunday in the Roman rite, *see* Tyrer, 1932, pp.66–8.

87   A small cross, carefully drawn in double lines, appears in the margin of the Book of Dimma (Dublin, Trinity College MS 59, page 26) at Mat. 26.30–1, discussed *below*, p.118.

88   On North Italian lection systems, the Codex Forojuliensis (Cividale, R. Museo Archeologico s.n.; Prague, Bibl. Metr. CIM.1; Venice, S. Marco s.n.), which presents a marginal notation marking Mt. 26.1 as the incipit of a lection 'De autentica III filia', or the third ferial (Tuesday) after Palm Sunday (De Bruyne, 1913, p.214).

89   Morin, 1893c.

90   Lowe, 1917, fols 96v–97r; Lowe, 1920, vol. 1, p.61; Farr, 1994, pp.442–3.

91   While unanimous agreement on the function of pocket Gospel books does not seem to exist (*see* McGurk, 1987, p.169, on their possible personal function; Gameson, 1994, on their 'working' liturgical use), the Book of Dimma, along with the Books of Mulling, Armagh, and Deer and St Gall MS 1394–5, presents later liturgical material relating to the Office of the Visitation of the Sick. Most liturgicologists who have written on these texts have commented, however, on their limited nature and associated them with private or personal use. *See* Kenney, 1993 (1968), pp.701–3; Warren, 1987 (1881), pp.167–71, 173–4. *See also* Brown, 1996, pp.78, 97, 177, relating it to contemporary manuscripts; *also* Alexander, 1978, p.69, on its connection with the monastery of Roscrea, County Tipperary.

92   Often, however, these are texts of prayers and hymns, such as the *Pater noster* (Mt. 6.9, page 7) and *Magnificat* (Lk. 1.46, page 57).

93   *See* the discussion *below* on decorative articulation, pp.119–32, and Appendix 2.

94   Brown, 1996, pp.62, 95, 120–1, 167–8; Brown, in Keynes and Brown, 1991, pp.195, 205; Alexander, 1978, p.61.

95   Brown, 1996, pp.66, 95, 120–1, 124, 167; Brown, 1994, pp.338–9.

96   Thurston, 1904, p.230.

97   Morin, ed., 1893a; Morin, 1892, 442–7. The more recent edition of Perez de Urbel and Gonzalez y Ruiz-Zorrilla (1950–55) is based upon several lectionaries of this type.

98   de Bruyne, 1914, p.506.

99   *See* Beissel's index of pericopes (1907, p.201).

100 *See* Kendrick, *et al.*, eds., vol. 1, 1956, fol. 82r.

101 *See also* Gameson, 1994, pp.32–52.

102 Lowe, *CLA* 2, no. 197, p.23. The correction in sloping uncial at the bottom of fol. 124v is, according to Lowe (p.23), in a contemporary hand.

103 Lowe, *CLA* 2, p.13.

104 According to Lowe (*CLA* 2, p.13) the comma-shaped marks ('virgula') and citation marks are contemporary with the script of the text.

105 Alexander, 1978, pp.78–9; Bischoff, 1990, p.90; McGurk, 1987, p.176; McGurk, 1961, no. 63; Lowe, *CLA* 5, no. 684.

106 McGurk, 1961, p.79; McGurk, 1987, p.172; Lowe, *CLA* 2, p.271; *see* Farr, 1994, Pl 67.

107 For the Book of Mulling, fol. 47v, *see* Farr, 1994, Pl 113.

108 McGurk, 1956, pp.64, 249–70; McGurk, 1987, pp.165–70, 176; *also* T. J. Brown, 1982, p.113; Farr, 1994, p.441–2.

109 *See* p.118.

110 Lowe, *CLA* 2, no. 231, p.32.; McGurk, 1987, pp.172–3; McGurk, 1990b, pp.59, 61; Brown, 1982, pp.109–10; Brown, 1984, p.326.

111 On Southumbrian manuscripts, *see* Brown, 1996, pp.15–18, 60–2, 162–84; Brown, 1985.

112 Paris, B.N., lat. 17225; Lowe, *CLA* 5, no. 666, p.42; McGurk, 1961, no. 61; McGurk, 1990, pp.42–3; Vezin, 1987, pp.55–6; *see* Farr, 1994, Pl 76.

113 Lowe, *CLA* 5, p.42, No. 667; Vezin, 1987, p.58.

114 McGurk, 1961, no. 57; Lowe, *CLA* 5, no. 525.

115 *See* Appendix 1 for bibliography.

116 *See also* Farr, 1994, p.443.

117 On Hereford: Alexander, 1978, no. 38; McGurk, 1987, pp.174–5; Brown, 1984, p.326. On Barberini: Alexander, 1978, pp.61, 84; Brown in Keynes and Brown, 1991, pp.195, 205; Brown, 1994, pp.336–8; Brown, 1996, pp.62, 116, 120–1, 124, 125, FIGS 39, 40.

118 Alexander, 1978, no. 53; McGurk, 1987, pp.165–7, 171–2, 173; Brown, 1982, p.113; Brown, 1996, pp.116, 117, 118, Fig. 45.

119 Gameson, 1994, pp.39–43, 47–8; McGurk, 1994, pp.19–22; *see also* the discussion of lections in this chapter, p.118.

120 In addition to the discussion *above*, see especially O'Reilly, 1994; O'Reilly, 1993; Ó Carragáin, 1994b.

121 Lowe, ed., vol. 58, 1920, p.61 (fol. 97r).

122 Lowe, ed., vol. 58, 1920, fol. 96v.

123 *See* Fox, vol. 1, fol. 113r.

124 On *figurae*, *see* Parkes, 1987, pp.16–19, 28; Irvine, 1986, 16–17, 21–2; Stevenson, 1990, pp.21–2. On the multivalency of the Tau, *see* O'Reilly, 1987, p.154; *also*, Raw, 1990, pp.80–1, 116.

125 *See* Nordenfalk, 1970, p.122; Harmon, 1984, pp.107–8.

126 *See* Lewis, 1980, p.155.

127 Lewis, 1980, p.155; *see also*, Ó Carragáin, 1988, pp.9–16, 40–4; and Ó Carragáin, 1994b, pp.419–21 on further Eucharistic connections.

128 McGurk, 1990, pp.65, 97; I am grateful to Paul Meyvaert, in personal communication, July 1989, for pointing out this variant text and its importance.

129 Stowe Missal in Warner, 1906, 1915 (1989 reprint), vol. 1, fols 36r–36v, vol. 2, p.18; Antiphonary of Bangor in Warren, 1893, 1895, vol. 2, pp.10–11, 5–7; Warren, 1881, pp.187–9; Curran, 1984, pp.47–9. See Saxl, 1943, p.4.

130 Tyrer, 1932, pp.19–44.

131 Tyrer, 1932, pp.92–3; Morin, 1891, pp.531, 536.

132 Tyrer, 1932, p.93; Morin, 1903, p.382; Morin, 1902, p.7.

133 Tyrer, 1932, p.96.

134 Tyrer, 1932, p.100.

135 Thurston, 1904, p.318.

136 Tyrer, 1932, pp.96–7; Thurston, 1904, pp.315–16.

137 Albi 42, Brussels 10127–44, Saint Gall 614 and Wolfenbüttel 4175, in Andrieu, ed., vol. 3, 1951, pp.281–98.

138 Tyrer, 1932, pp.97–9; Thurston, 1902, p.319.

139 Tyrer, 1932, pp.100–1.

140 Andrieu, vol. 3, 1951, pp.280, 281.

141 Andrieu, ed., vol. 3, 1951, p.290: 14. 'Postquam communicaverit, ponit calicem super altare; deinde, accepta a subdiacono patena, ponit iuxta calicem de latere sinistro et statim coopereritur a duobus diaconibus de sindone munda ... 15. Et continuo duo acoliti involutas ampullas cum sindone alba syrica, ... '.

CHAPTER FOUR

Conclusion

A T THE END of this study, questions remain to be asked about the illustrations' function and about their place within the manuscript as a whole. How do the two illustrations fit together within the larger group of the manuscript's decorated pages? How might the manuscript have been used in the liturgy? What can this liturgical function reveal about the other full-page illuminations in the Book of Kells? Can something be said of the church in which it was used? Could it have been made for the use of a particular individual or for the commemoration of a founder or patron? Answers to these questions and some of the conclusions drawn from the study are probably more accurately termed suggestions for further study. Nonetheless, the effort will prove fruitful. The significance of the full-page images can be clarified, but also more may be learned about the Book of Kells as a liturgical manuscript.

Reading, Learning, Preaching: Pastoral Functions of Insular Monasteries

Who could have formed the audience of the full-page illustrations in the Book of Kells? While ordinary people associated with a church or monastery may have viewed the images and understood them in their liturgical context, the emphasis on interpretation and preaching seen in the Temptation image, as well as its luxurious presentation, suggests a primary audience of élite ecclesiastics, possibly in the context of a monastic school or somehow connected with one.[1] Such an audience and its Gospel book would not, however, have been isolated from a community of monks and laity who may have been literate in a rudimentary way or illiterate. Recent historical and archaeological studies are making apparent the pastoral function and lay involvement of monasteries in early medieval Ireland and Britain.[2] In this context, studies of grammar, language, and interpretation, produced in monastic schools, played their part in making text understandable to the ordinary faithful who heard the Gospel read by the clergy and listened to their sermons.

If specific liturgical contexts are vital to the meaning of the illustrations in the Book of Kells, the next questions are how the pictures might have been used or displayed in the liturgy and who would have been able to see them.

As a gospel lection book, the Book of Kells could have been read from either during the mass or during the divine office. Some modern liturgical and manuscript scholars conclude that gospel books were used only during the mass and not during the office, which would have required an entire Bible.[3] Some early lectionaries are known to include readings for mass and office, and some early gospel lection systems indicate readings for both.[4] Careful designation of mass lections 'ad missa' seems to have been especially necessary for the final three days of Holy Week, with their liturgical complexity and blurred distinctions between mass and office.[5] Therefore, it seems at least equally possible that the Book of Kells was used at both mass and office or only mass. A double use seems especially possible for the liturgy of Quadragesima Sunday and Holy Thursday, for which early lection systems sometimes indicate multiple gospel lections, with or without designations for mass or office.[6]

If the Book of Kells was displayed for viewing at mass, it probably would have been set on the altar, perhaps on important feast days, open to the illustration or decorated incipit. Such an arrangement might have worked satisfactorily for the Quadragesima illustration depicting the Temptation of Christ. Those close enough to the altar would have seen the picture while verses from Psalm 90 were read and sung and probably also during the reading of the Epistle from 2 Corinthians 6.2–10. After the Epistle, a deacon would have picked up the book and carried it to an ambo to read the lection, so that the illustration would not have been visible during the gospel reading.

On the other hand, the illustration for Holy Thursday seems to fit less satisfactorily into this arrangement because it is placed in what would probably have been the middle of the lection and the full-page incipit at verse 31 is presented on the overleaf. At least two possible ways of displaying the picture can be suggested. First, the gospel book could have been returned to the altar open to the picture so that it could have been seen during the Eucharist and consecration of the oils, although these rituals probably would have obscured the view, or the picture might have been superfluous in the presence of the ritual. A second possibility is that the Passion was not read straight through from Matthew 26. The picture at verse 30 could have indicated a pause or interruption in the lection, perhaps because of the intrusion of another Passion text in a cento reading from separate gospel books or perhaps for some other kind of liturgical intrusion. However, even if such an interruption or intrusion could be proved, it is difficult to understand how the picture could have been viewed by anyone other than the deacon, unless the gospel book were positioned upright for display during reading or temporarily replaced on the altar. Ironically, one of the clearest bits of evidence suggesting that the manuscript was used for public reading appears on fol. 114v, below the full-page, elaborately decorated text of verse 31, the words are rewritten in red at the bottom of the folio presenting the important passage in script more legible than that above.

Fewer difficulties would interfere with collective viewing of the illustrations during the office than during mass. If the manuscript saw duty during a night office, such as matins or a similar nocturnal office, the pictures could have been viewed during a complex round of lections, accompanied by verses, antiphons and responses as well as the cursus of Psalms for the day. Even though the usual biblical lections for night offices are read from the Old Testament, such offices often include, as do the Benedictine matins, readings of sermons and homilies on Sundays and important feast days. The second reading on such days is usually a sermon taken from a patristic commentary, often on the significance of the feast or liturgical season. The third reading, a homily, is taken from a patristic commentary on a short gospel pericope, which would probably have been cited if not read in full.[7]

Little is known of biblical and patristic office lections in Insular liturgies. While some Celtic writings mention the office of matins, the only known reference to office lections in a document associated with a Celtic context occurs in the *Regula cuiusdam patris*, which calls for Old and New Testament readings at the night office.[8] Curran, in his reconstruction of the office of matins at Bangor from the collects of the 'antiphonary', places a gospel reading with collect in the second half of matins. However, because all the gospel collects of the Antiphonary of Bangor express a uniform theme, Curran believes that the lection was invariably the Gospel of the Resurrection, known also in several early cathedral liturgies.[9] For Northumbria, Bede's homilies provide the night office readings at Jarrow.[10] Other collections of sermons and homilies compiled from patristic writings, such as that of Paul the Deacon, contributed to the eighth-century move toward standardisation, but in fact, the readings for matins were still the choice of the abbot, as were other aspects of the divine office.[11] Despite calls for 'correct' recitation of the office, such as Chapter XV of the Acts of the Council of Clofesho of 747, one cannot assume uniform office lections in Insular liturgies.[12] One can only consider the possibilities by placing the illustrations alongside lections known from early liturgical documents and homiliaries.

The illustration of the Temptation of Christ may be better suited to display during the office than mass, especially if part of Augustine's commentary on Psalm 90 were read as a patristic lection. However, no known liturgical document or homiliary dated before 800 indicates a reading from his commentary for Quadragesima Sunday. Some Continental *ordines* and homiliaries list readings from the *Enarrationes in Psalmos* during Lent and Holy Week, but never for Quadragesima Sunday.[13] The homiliary of Paul the Deacon lists the Quadragesimal homilies of Gregory and Leo, neither of which seem especially relevant to the picture.[14] Nonetheless, the illustration clearly refers to the liturgical texts of Quadragesima Sunday. It would still be generally relevant when viewed during a reading of nearly any known patristic Quadragesimal homily because the Church fathers often emphasise the devil's temptation of the Church or the individual, and they usually speak of Christ's lesson for the faithful in defeating Satan's efforts. Also, the apparent influence of Augustine's exegesis upon Insular titles for Psalm 90 and the presence of the 'Head and Body' figure in some Irish and Anglo-Saxon interpretations of the Temptation should not be forgotten when considering these possibilities. The Psalm titles indicate a liturgical context for interpretations, and in particular Augustine's interpretation, of Psalm 90 using the Tyconian figure.

The other illustration, depicting Christ in prayer with his two attendants, may also fit into the context of a night office with multiple biblical and patristic readings. Although no known single text satisfactorily explains the picture's iconography, the point is precisely its resonances with multiple texts and liturgical forms. One possible lection from Matthew 26 at matins on Holy Thursday is known, that presented in the Lectionary of Luxeuil, although the designation *ad matutinum* could mean a morning mass.[15] An interpretation of one of the Psalms associated with the Passion presents another possibility for reading. The most well known of these, Psalm 21, is quoted by Jerome and Bede in their interpretations of the departure to Mount Olivet and the suffering at Gethsemane.[16] Other possibilities include commentaries on Psalm 63. Some eighth- and ninth-century Continental *ordines* indicate lections from Augustine's *Enarratio in Psalmo LXIII*, but the *enarratio* neither refers to this verse of Matthew nor to anything particularly related to the picture.[17] Even though no single interpretation unifying the image of the *filii olei* with the text of Matthew is known, it is precisely the lack of a clear connection between the picture's iconography and the gospel text that suggests the influence of texts and images brought together by exegesis and liturgy. Because such a variety of texts were read during the night office of special days and because the office readings had a didactic as well as a devotional aspect, the office liturgy might have provided a suitable context for interpretive images depicting the meaning of special feast days.[18]

Moreover, the illustrations could perhaps have been more effectively displayed during the office than during the mass because the mass ritual may have blocked them from view. The illustrations would not have been visible during the gospel reading, unless the Gospel were read from another book. As images for viewing during the office, the illustrations could have been displayed during the reading and chanting of other texts. Under nearly any conditions, however, the number of viewers would have been limited. If viewed in the actual context of liturgy, only one person, the deacon who read from the book, undoubtedly saw the illustrations. Nevertheless, even though the illustrations may present special significance for the deacon, as will be seen, there must have been some reason for creating such a large and boldly decorated gospel book which exceeds the scale necessary for private viewing.

Another possible viewing context might have been that of the monastic schools or conferences, where exegesis was produced and consumed on a conspicuous scale. The schools operated on several levels to shape the Christianization of Irish society. The sons of kings often were placed in fosterage with the monasteries. These students were among those trained to become abbots, bishops, scholars, and holy men.[19] The whole Book of Kells, and especially its illustrations, might have been viewed as a prestigious and effective tool for teaching the way to unveiling the divine truth of the Scriptures and revealing that truth to the faithful.

The Other Full-Page Illuminations

The illustrations depicting the Temptation of Christ and the Passion of Christ should also be considered in relation to the other full-page images presented in the Book of Kells. These include the two surviving evangelist portraits, the four-symbols pages, the Virgin and Child, the Enthroned Christ, the carpet page, the depiction of the Crucifixion which may have been planned, and the full-page incipits.

The evangelist portraits belong to a well-established and extensively studied type of book image, the author portrait. Although the two evangelist portraits in the Book of Kells present some unusual features, modern scholars understand their function as introductory portraits relatively well within the corpus of images surviving in early gospel manuscripts.[20] The four-symbols pages also present a type of introductory image, but one unique to Insular gospel books. As a type of evangelist image, the four-symbols page is less well understood than evangelist portraits, but still its function as an introductory image is clear.[21] The four pages presenting images of this type in the Book of Kells serve to introduce each Gospel, and the layout of the pages may be reflect a four-part division of early gospel book covers.[22] The evangelist portraits and four-symbols pages serve to introduce books of the Gospel by reference to their authors and to their place within the four-part division of the entire gospel book.

On the other hand, questions remain about the role of the other full-page illuminations. The two portraits of Christ (PLATES V, VI: the Virgin and Child, and the Enthroned Christ) appear independent of the gospel text because of their blank overleaves and lack of narrative content. Moreover, their formats separate them from the two illustrations. Their borders frame them with bands of interlace ornament emphasised with heavy, squared corners, as opposed to the 'arched' format of the two illustrations. Were these two originally inserted somewhere in the gospel text or were they independent of it?

The Virgin and Child portrait (PLATE V) can be compared with known prefatory images. Some aspects of its layout and ornament resemble those of surviving book shrines and covers. The three half-circles which mark the horizontal and vertical visual axes of the picture create a cross-shaped configuration, completed visually by the throne and body of the Virgin. Some surviving book covers and shrines present a central cross creating a four-part division resembling the layout of the picture of the Virgin and Child.[23] Also, the square panel filled with six male busts which intrudes into the right-hand side of the border of animal ornament resembles the catch which would have fastened the cover of the book. Moreover, some aspects of the ornament– the flat yellow bands around the half circles and border and also the golden throne with coloured 'inlay' – seem to mimic metalwork. The picture may take on the aspect of a metalwork shrine or cover in order to refer to the additional function of the gospel book as a sacred object. If the image was meant to express this iconic aspect of the Gospels, then its visual reference by its design and layout to an exterior shrine or cover would help make it understood as an introductory image, different from images that refer to a specific part of the text.

Furthermore, the picture presents some similarities with a particular type of introductory image, the dedication portrait. Dedication portraits may depict a manuscript's living patron, or the patron saint or sacred personage to whom the manuscript is dedicated. The earliest surviving dedication portrait, of Anicia Juliana in the early sixth-century Vienna Dioscurides (Vienna, Nationalbibliothek, cod. med. gr. I, fol. 6v), presents the enthroned Byzantine princess attended by a 'court' of allegorical figures.[24]

Perhaps the angels attending the enthroned Virgin and Child in the illustration in the Book of Kells serve a function similar to that of the allegorical figures in the Vienna

Dioscurides. The pair of angels at the top of the illustration point toward the Virgin and hold sceptre-like objects, usually said to represent the liturgical fans called flabella.[25] At the bottom of the illustration, another pair of angels flanks the Virgin's throne. One of these holds an object also identified in modern scholarship as a flabellum, and the other holds, in a downward position, a short, dull yellow wand terminating in a pair of tri-lobed foliate forms.[26] Although the identification of the sceptres held by the top pair of angels as flabella may be questioned because of their short handles and small disc terminals, the wands held by the other pair of angels may represent identifiable liturgical objects. The angel in the lower left corner may hold a flabellum since the object is of an appropriate size and he grasps it with both hands as if he sweeps it through the air. The angel in the lower right corner may hold a branch of hyssop, the plant prescribed in the Old Testament and in Christian liturgy for ritual sprinkling in the purification of sanctuaries.[27] The angel holds the foliate wand upside down, perhaps to lustrate the 'floor' of the sanctuary in which the Virgin and Child sit enthroned. These liturgical objects symbolising purification, the flabellum and hyssop, may represent attributes indicating the presence of the Virgin and Child in the sanctuary or dwelling place of God on earth, the Church. If this is so, the picture could refer to the Church on earth in a symbolic sense, perhaps representing the Virgin as the 'earthly Tabernacle', or it could refer to an actual church.

If the picture does represent the Virgin and Child enthroned in a church and if it was created as a dedication image, it is possible that it depicts the Virgin and Child in this way because the church for which the Book of Kells was made might have been dedicated to the Virgin. The picture may present a prefatory image identifying the gospel book as part of the furnishings of a church given to the Virgin. This suggestion assumes that the overleaf is blank because this image of the Virgin and Child was not created to accompany a particular gospel text. On the other hand, the picture could have been made to accompany a gospel pericope, its iconography influenced by exegetical texts on the Virgin or by the liturgy of the feast day. Determining where the picture would have been inserted into the gospel text and what interpretations might have influenced its iconography would comprise a full-length study in itself.[28] Furthermore, images of the Virgin and Child Enthroned are known to have been made for churches not dedicated to the Virgin. However, because the picture's resemblance to prefatory images such as book covers and dedication pages and its lack of any clear references to narrative or text, it seems more plausible as a portrait which, like a dedication page, explains something about the book's identity and overall purpose.

The portrait of the Enthroned Christ (PLATE VI) may also present a prefatory image. It is painted on a folio presenting no text *recto* or *verso* and does not allude to any specific narrative. Although Christ is depicted holding a codex in the manner of an evangelist, this portrait may present an Apocalyptic image of Christ, or Christ enthroned in the heavenly Tabernacle. It is comparable with other full-page frontispieces known from Insular and Carolingian manuscripts presenting portraits of Christ combining evangelist author portrait and Apocalyptic imagery.

One of these, the frontispiece for the New Testament in the Codex Amiatinus conflates the Apocalyptic vision of Christ enthroned in the heavenly Jerusalem with author portrait iconography of the evangelists. In the Amiatinus frontispiece, Christ sits enthroned and surrounded by the rainbow and the four animals, based on the Apocalypse 4.3 and 4.6. Christ holds a codex, not the scroll with seven seals, and he is flanked by two angels holding sceptres. Furthermore, the animals are 'naturalistic' creatures having pairs of wings, a type believed to have been developed in the author portrait tradition, and they accompany four full-length portraits of the evangelists, placed in the corners of the page.[29] The Codex Amiatinus frontispiece combines an image of the fulfilment of the Gospels – the events of the Apocalypse – with the conventional introductory imagery of the author portrait.[30]

Evangelist symbols and portraits do not influence the portrait of Christ Enthroned presented in the Book of Kells, but he is depicted flanked by angels and within an apse-like setting which may refer to Advent or Second Coming imagery. Other Insular full-page depictions of events related to the Second Coming depict Christ enthroned and flanked by angels in settings that resemble that of the Kells portrait. In the depiction of the Last Judgement in St Gall Codex 51, angels blowing trumpets flank a half-length portrait of Christ, while the twelve apostles look up at him from the bottom of the page.[31] The page is divided up into an arrangement of four 'panels' into which the figures are inserted. Another example, the Ascension depicted on a double folio surviving from an Irish gospel book in the Turin library, resembles the St Gall Last Judgement, with a half-length portrait of Christ in a central panel flanked by angels.[32] The picture's inscription from Acts 1.11 explains the resemblance: Christ will return in the same way he ascended.[33] The portrait of Christ in the Book of Kells also separates the figure of Christ from the angels by placing the angels within rectangular panels, but Christ's panel is arched, taking on the appearance of an apse. While the St Gall and Turin illuminations may be based upon the Apocalyptic descriptions of the 'abstract' shape of the heavenly Jerusalem, the setting of the Kells portrait seems based on artistic traditions of Second Coming imagery descending from Imperial iconography and associated with architectural decoration.[34]

The architectural setting of the portrait of Christ Enthroned can be compared with the setting of the enthroned Christ of the Godescalc Evangelistary (Paris, Bibliothèque nationale, nouv. acq. lat. 1203, fol. 3r). The Godescalc portrait follows a series of four evangelist portraits at the beginning of the manuscript.[35] While the Godescalc portrait of Christ belongs to a cycle of evangelist portraits, it may combine Apocalyptic imagery with an author portrait type.[36] Its architectural setting may have been intended to depict the heavenly Jerusalem in tangible visual language, ·like the depictions known from Early Christian apse mosaics of the Apocalyptic vision.[37] The Kells portrait may present a similar type, having the same significance.

The Kells portrait presents further indications of its setting. At the top of the panel on the right, a wingless figure shoulders a green stalk with leaves sprouting from its upper end, which could represent a stalk of hyssop. Like the angels holding liturgical objects in the portrait of the Virgin and Child, this figure holding hyssop could indicate the portrait's setting in the church to which the Book of Kells belonged. However, since the portrait presents Apocalyptic imagery, it may instead depict Christ enthroned in the heavenly Temple with the symbols of his New Covenant: the Eucharist and the vine, presented by peacocks, symbols of resurrection.

A possibility remains that the portrait of the Enthroned Christ was created to accompany a gospel lection. Because of its connections with the iconography of the Second Coming and other events of the Apocalypse, it may have been designed as an illustration for one of the Sundays in Advent, the lections for which sometimes refer to the Second Advent. Alternatively it may have accompanied a reading for the Ascension as a 'double-sided' image like the full-page illumination of the Ascension surviving from the Turin gospel book, even though the latter probably served as a frontispiece. However, because the illumination presents no connection with any particular gospel text, searching for a probable liturgical context would be a difficult and perhaps fruitless task. Furthermore, the picture's iconography fits in much more easily with that of known frontispieces than with any known early narrative iconography, and it does not present unconventional iconography like that seen in the two illustrations remaining in the gospel text of the Book of Kells. It seems to express the book's liturgical function by referring to the heavenly liturgy described in the Apocalypse.

The carpet page now bound at fol. 33r opposite the Christ Enthroned also lacks clear textual connections and probably served as an introductory image. The carpet pages in the Book of Durrow and the Lindisfarne Gospels appear to have been bound at the beginning of each gospel, with a fifth in the Lindisfarne Gospels serving as frontispiece for the manuscript.[38]

The Book of Kells probably originally presented multiple introductory images based on established types of portraits of Christ, author portraits and ornamental pages. The sequence of these images and their possible distribution between the different types of prefatory material remain unknown. All the full-page figural illuminations, however, appear to possess thematic connections. The two portraits of Christ seem to refer to the presence of Christ in his Church on earth and in heaven, echoing the theme of the two illustrations within the text. The introductory images proclaim the manuscript's function as a liturgical book, while the illustrations interpret the meaning of the liturgy in which the book was used.

Probably the creators of the Book of Kells planned, but never executed, one more full-page illustration on the blank fol. 123v, opposite the text of the Crucifixion as told by Matthew 27.38 (PLATE VII). The absence of a Crucifixion illustration may seem puzzling because surviving eighth-century Insular examples present a well-established iconography for the subject.[39] On the other hand, the unconventional iconography of the two surviving illustrations discourages 'reconstruction' of the intended Crucifixion image. The inventiveness seen in the other illustrations surfaces again in the full-page, richly decorated incipit of verse 38, *Tunc crucifixerant Xri cum eo duos latrones*, facing the blank folio. Fierce animals ornament the text, one fantastic beast becoming a border of interlace panels into which are set three small panels of profile human busts, all facing the blank page opposite. The text is arranged in a figure to express its content: after the word *crucifixerant* the words are written along opposing diagonal lines, forming an 'X'. This expressively decorated text possibly was meant to face an equally complex illustration, influenced by its liturgical context.[40] Matthew's account of the Crucifixion was read in non-Roman liturgies – in Northern Italy, Gaul and Spain – on Good Friday, during offices and mass.[41] However, the way in which the pericope was read varies considerably. In some liturgies, the reading of the Passion from Matthew was distributed over all the offices and masses of Good Friday in lections varying in length. The complexity of the Good Friday liturgy would have presented a rich context for the decorated page, especially if it faced an image of the Crucifixion.

The other full-page incipits also appear to reflect the influence of a non-Roman lection system. The most unusual pericope presented with a full-page incipit and figural imagery begins the Crucifixion according to Mark 15.24–5, *Erat autem hora tercia & crucifigentes eum divise ....* (FIG. 28), on fol. 183r. The ornament bordering the sides of the text becomes a human figure, with head emerging from the top right, feet at bottom left. Within the text an angel hovers, presenting a book. Aside from the scrambled Vulgate text combining and inverting Verses 24 and 25, the elaborate presentation of the text is remarkable because, as McGurk has pointed out, no other Insular gospel book emphasises this text to such a degree.[42] Even in the broad context of western liturgies, the pericope finds no place among known lection systems. The only published lection system known to indicate readings from Mark 15 is the system presented in the Rabula Gospels. The sixth-century Syriac notations indicate a reading beginning at Mark 15.1 'for the Friday of the Crucifixion', and another beginning at 15.33 'for Friday of the Passion, for *none*'.[43] Although there can be no direct connection between the Syriac liturgy represented by the Rabula Gospels and Insular liturgies, this is not the only coincidence of emphasised Insular incipit and the lections marked in the Rabula Gospels.

This coincidence occurs again for the text of the visit of the two Maries to Christ's tomb, beginning at Luke 24.1, *Una autem sabbati valde dilu ....* (FIG. 29), fol. 285r. The body of a fantastic beast borders the text, becoming a band of animal interlace. The text, embellished with bird interlace, is inhabited by four angels, two of whom hold closed books or tablets, two others holding what may be a flabellum and another liturgical object, perhaps hyssop. A notation in the Rabula Gospels marks a lection beginning at Luke 24.1 as the 'Lection for the Sunday of Our Lord's Resurrection'.[44] However, several other Insular gospel books also emphasise this passage, and two known western liturgies indicate a pericope beginning with Luke 24.1 as a lection for Easter Sunday.[45] The seventh-century 'Gallican' lection system compiled by Beissel from the Lectionary of Luxeuil and the lection list in the Paris Gospels (Bibliothèque nationale lat. 256) indicates a lection beginning with Luke 24.1 for 'Pascha'.[46] Notations in the 'Gospels of St Kilian' (Würzburg Mp. th. q. 1a) suggest that Luke 24.1–12 was read as part of a Resurrection cento taken from the four Gospels on Easter Sunday in the liturgy of an unknown Church in Gaul during the seventh to ninth century.[47] The text beginning with Luke 24.1 served as the lection for the most important day of the liturgical year in some western liturgies, as well as the Eastern liturgy represented by the lection system of the Rabula Gospels, a system of lections corresponding in some respects with the emphasised texts of Insular gospel books.[48]

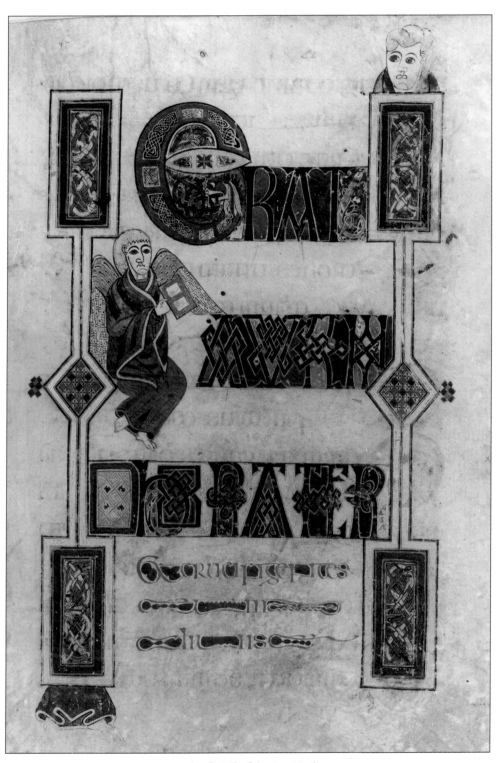

FIG. 28 Book of Kells, fol. 183r, Mark 15.24–25

The other full-page gospel incipits in the Book of Kells include the opening words of each gospel (fols 29r, 130r, 188r, and 292r) and the Chi Rho (fol. 34r). Also fols 127v (Matthew 28.1) and 188v (Luke 1.5) present enlarged incipits distinctively embellished with colour and ornament. Some of these texts probably were decorated because they served as liturgical readings, others probably were not, or at least not only on account of their importance in the liturgy.

The Chi Rho, at Matthew 1.18 (fol. 34r), may have been important both as the beginning of the lection for the Vigil of the Nativity and as the beginning of the narrative of Matthew following the genealogy. If the Chi Rho initial in the Book of Kells reflects a liturgical influence, the influence was probably not Roman. All known Roman lections of Matthew 1.18 begin with the second part of the verse, *Cum esset desponsata mater eius Maria*, not with the preceding phrase which actually closes the genealogy, *Xpi autem generatio sic erat*.[49] The homily of Bede also begins with the phrase *Cum esset...*, as does the homily in the collections of Alcuin and Paul the Deacon and the pericope for the Vigil of the Nativity in the Godescalc Evangelistary.[50] The only known lection systems designating a lection beginning *Xpi autem...* are North Italian systems and the Northumbrian notations in the Gospels of Burchard of Würzburg (Würzburg, Mp. th. fol. 68), believed to represent a Neapolitan system with Roman intrusions.[51] The Chi Rho incipit is elevated to the upper levels of the decorative hierarchy in many Insular manuscripts.[52] A few Continental gospel manuscripts – such as the Paris Gospels (FIG. 30), which also indicates liturgical reading of Matthew 26.30–1, discussed in Chapter 3 – give it emphasis as a chapter division.[53] Whether this emphasis results from an Insular tradition of textual structuring such a series of chapter divisions or whether the emphasis reflects influence of a non-Roman lection system has never been resolved. Nevertheless, the incipit of the Roman lection hardly ever receives more than very slight emphasis in Insular manuscripts.

The incipit of Matthew 28.1 (fol. 127v), *Vespere autem*, also emphasised with colour and decoration, probably reflects liturgical influence. All the letters of the phrase are coloured purple and set against a solid yellow panel which stretches across the top of the page. The enlarged incipit is formed of two intertwined beasts. Matthew 28.1 represents the incipit of a nearly universal lection for the Easter vigil.[54] It was read during the evening of Holy Saturday as early as the fourth century.[55] As McGurk has pointed out, Matthew 28.1 begins the Resurrection text having 'great liturgical significance', but its smaller size and more modest decoration in comparison with the incipit of the Resurrection text at Luke 24.1 seem to defy any explanation in terms of liturgical lections.[56] However, in a few liturgies in Gaul and in the Syrian liturgy represented by the notations in the Rabula Gospels, the Resurrection text from Luke was read on Easter Sunday. Perhaps this same arrangement of readings for the Vigil of Easter and Easter Sunday survived in Insular liturgies. The markedly greater emphasis given to the incipit of Luke 24.1 than to Matthew 28.1 may have resulted from differences in the liturgical symbolism of the Easter vigil and Easter Sunday as much as the importance of the feast days.

The full-page incipits of each gospel probably do not reflect liturgical influence but serve

FIG. 29 Book of Kells, fol. 285r, Luke 24.1

within the overall structure of the manuscript to open the gospel texts. The enlarged, coloured and ornamented words *Fuit in diebus hero...* beginning Luke 1.5, also emphasised in other Insular gospel books, open the narrative of Luke after the prologue.[57] But also this text on the annunciation to Zachariah of the birth of John the Baptist was read in many western liturgies for the vigil of the Feast of St John.[58] In addition to these, much of the minor ornament of the manuscript may have been influenced by the liturgy, but the questions posed by the minor ornament throughout the text await further study.

Observations on the full-page and large incipits in the Book of Kells suggest that the decoration of the manuscript's text may have been influenced by a non-Roman liturgy retaining a very early type of lection system. This lection system can be characterised by an emphasis on readings for Lent and Holy Week, perhaps including Passion centos or a distribution of Passion texts over the offices and masses of Holy Week. Tracing sources in known liturgies is still problematic because the emphasised incipits in the Book of Kells do not coincide exactly with the lections of any known system. Similarities exist between several non-Roman liturgies and the decorated texts of the Book of Kells, as well as many other Insular gospel books. Particular correspondences have been observed in the Passion lections of the Visigothic *Liber Comicus,* some of the lections of the 'Gospels of St Kilian', and the Quadragesimal lections of the liturgies connected with Aquileia. Unexpected parallels have been discovered in the sixth-century lection system of the Rabula Gospels, a Syriac gospel manuscript. While direct influence of a Syriac liturgy upon an Insular one would have been impossible, it is possible that the ornament of the Book of Kells was influenced by an early lection system related to a western liturgy, such as that of Aquileia, which had felt influences from eastern liturgies. Another possibility is that the Book of Kells was used in a liturgy retaining a very old lection system, perhaps a survivor of a fifth or sixth-century western system resembling that of the early systems cited here in its extensive readings for Lent and Holy Week, or that, for some reason, the decoration of the Book of Kells memorializes an old set of lections or a venerable liturgy.

The Book of Kells as a Liturgical Gospel Book

The remaining questions concern the manuscript as whole. What can the full-page illustrations and illuminations taken together reveal about the context of the Book of Kells? Was it made for a particular person or in commemoration of a saint? For what type of church – cathedral or monastery – was it made? How do the full-page images express the book's function and purpose?

Although nothing has been discovered in the full-page illustrations which would indicate a particular founder commemorated by the Book of Kells, such a commemoration remains a possibility. The recent publications of Meyvaert and O'Reilly, following suggestions originally made by Nordenfalk and Henry, have argued cogently the Columban significance of the decoration of the Lucan genealogy.[59] The illustrations appear to arise from the context of Celtic or Northumbrian asceticism, especially as known from the surviving literature on founder saints. They interpret gospel texts in terms of the Lenten

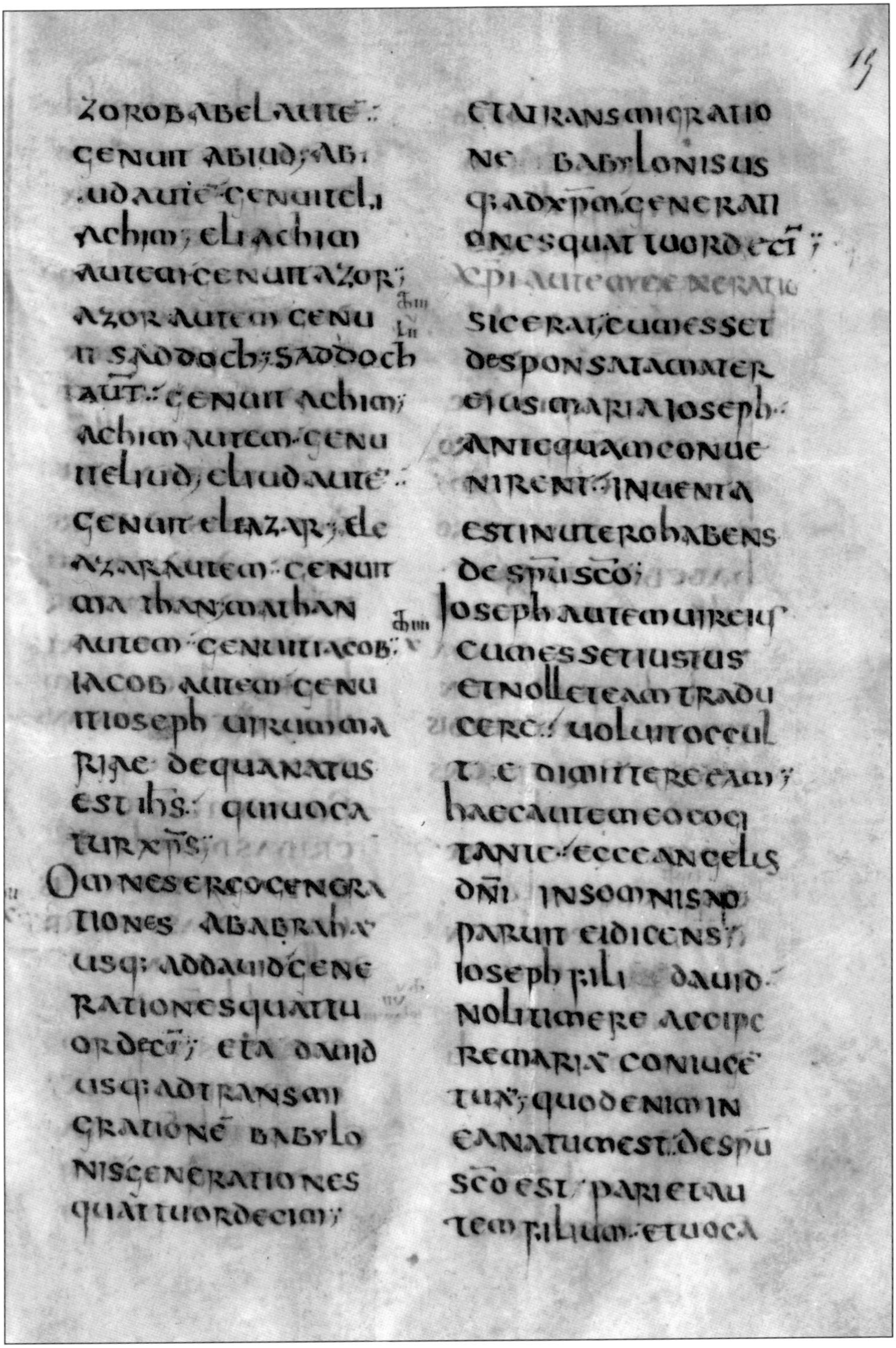

ZOROBABELAUTE
GENUIT ABIUD AB
IUD AUTE GENUIT EL
IACHIM ELIACHIM
AUTEM GENUIT AZOR
AZOR AUTEM GENU
IT SADDOCH SADDOCH
AUT GENUIT ACHIM
ACHIM AUTEM GENU
IT ELIUD ELIUD AUTE
GENUIT ELEAZAR ELE
AZAR AUTEM GENUIT
MATHAN MATHAN
AUTEM GENUIT IACOB
IACOB AUTEM GENU
IT IOSEPH UIRUM MA
RIAE DE QUA NATUS
EST IHS QUI UOCA
TUR XPS
OMNES ERGO GENERA
TIONES AB ABRAHA
USQ AD DAUID GENE
RATIONES QUATTU
OR DECI ET A DAUID
USQ AD TRANSMI
GRATIONE BABYLO
NIS GENERATIONES
QUATTUORDECIM

ET TRANSMIGRATIO
NE BABYLONIS US
Q AD XPM GENERATI
ONES QUATTUORDECI
XPI AUTEM GENERATIO
SIC ERAT CUM ESSET
DESPONSATA MATER
EIUS MARIA IOSEPH
ANTEQUAM CONUE
NIRENT INUENTA
EST IN UTERO HABENS
DE SPU SCO
IOSEPH AUTEM UIR EIUS
CUM ESSET IUSTUS
ET NOLLET EAM TRADU
CERE UOLUIT OCCUL
TE E DIMITTERE EAM
HAEC AUTEM EO COGI
TANTE ECCE ANGELUS
DNI INSOMNIS AD
PARUIT EI DICENS
IOSEPH FILI DAUID
NOLI TIMERE ACCIPE
RE MARIAM CONIUCE
TU QUOD ENIM IN
EA NATUM EST DE SPU
SCO EST PARIET AU
TEM FILIUM ET UOCA

FIG. 30 Paris Gospels (Paris, Bibliothèque nationale, lat. 256), fol. 15, Matthew 1.13–21

peregrinatio and the monk-hero's cross vigil and seem to integrate the Insular concepts of martyrdom into the events of Christ's life. Perhaps also the church in which the Book of Kells was used was dedicated to the Virgin, as suggested above.

Otherwise, the full-page illuminations presented in the Book of Kells may refer to the order of deacon, or the equivalent rank in the church to which the Book of Kells belonged. The deacons of the church would have been most familiar with the book because they read from it during the liturgy. The eighth-century pseudo-Bedan *Collectanea* describes the office of deacon, the sixth of the seven orders[60]:

> ... et ipsa vasa corporis et sanguinis Domini diaconis offerunt [subdiaconi]. Diaconus super altare ponit, et inde recipit. Levitae in veteri testamento excubabant custodientes universa, quae pertinebant ad cultum tabernaculi, servientes in ministerio; in novo testamento providebant universa quae necessaria erant multidini, cor unum et animam unam habenti. Igitur modo custodientes ministerium sibi commissum, quaecunque necessaria sunt ad coeleste convivium, disponunt super mensam Domini ...[61]
>
> [... and (the subdeacons) present the chalice of the body and blood of the Lord to the deacons. The deacon places it on the altar, and from there he takes it back. The Levite guardians in the Old Testament kept watch over all things that pertained to the cult of the Tabernacle, the keepers in the ministry; in the New Testament they provided all things that were necessary to the multitude, to the one having one heart and one soul. Accordingly now those keeping the ministry entrusted to them arrange upon the table of the Lord all things that are necessary for the heavenly banquet ...]

The passage is connected with Irish interpretations of the orders of the clergy in terms of the cult of the Tabernacle described in the Old Testament.[62] Following the section on the seven orders, an exegesis of liturgical vestments mentions further duties assigned the deacon in its explanation of the chasuble:

> Casula circumdatus aliquando Evangelium legit diaconus, ut expeditus ad evangelium possit accedere, vel mensam Domini praeparare. Casula aperta est in dextera parte unde emittitur brachium, quia auctor evanglii, quem debet diaconus imitari, in dextro latere lancea perfossus est.[63]
>
> [Whenever the deacon reads the Gospel he has been wrapped in the chasuble, so that he can be ready to approach the gospel book, or to prepare the table of the Lord. The chasuble is open on the right side from where the arm emerges, because the author of the Gospel, whom the deacon should imitate, was pierced through on the right side.]

The deacon prepared the altar, read the gospel and delivered sermons. Bede, who was deacon before his ordination as a priest in about 703, wrote about the role of the deacon in 'building the house of God' in his commentary on Ezra and Nehemiah.[64] Bede speaks of the importance of the deacons who delivered and explained the word of God to the people in order to 'drive them away from captivity of their sins to the vision of true peace', in the context of explaining the responsibilities of laity and all ranks of the faithful in maintaining proper pastoral care.[65] Like the author of the *Collectanea*, Bede speaks of the deacon in terms of the Levites or priestly cast of the Old Testament. In this way, Insular exegetes explained the deacon's role in the founding of the New Jerusalem on earth.[66]

While the appearance of liturgical vestments of the period can be known only from fragments of evidence, such as the references made in the *Collectanea*, it is possible that several of the illuminations of the Book of Kells refer to the deacon. First, there are the many figures holding books (PLATE VIII). The enthroned Christ, most of the angels and human figures, except for the evangelists, present books with the hand extended from the right side of an enveloping mantle which covers the left hand. The garment worn by the figures resembles the *casula*, the vestment worn by the deacon when he takes the gospel book from the altar for reading, according to the *Collectanea*. Moreover, different kinds of liturgical books are associated with different clerical orders. In Anglo-Saxon England, bishops presented special symbolic books to ordinates. Lectors, who read the office lections, received a *redeboc*, and exorcists, a *halsungboc*, neither of which would have been used to read from but which served as symbols of the powers and duties of clerics.[67] Presumably, the figures in the Book of Kells hold gospel books, the type of book appropriate to the deacon. Also, certain minor figures, such as the figure of Abraham holding a cup in the genealogy in the Gospel of Luke (fol. 201), may refer not only to biblical texts but also to the deacon's ministry and role as preparer of the altar.

The two illustrations may have special significance for the order of deacon. The depiction of the Temptation of Christ was probably influenced by typological interpretations of the Temple and Tabernacle, in which the deacon's Old Testament type, the Levites, served important functions, as the *Collectanea* mentions and Bede explains in detail. If the illustration of the Passion of Christ (fol. 114r) was influenced by the consecration of the oils, the reason for such influence might have involved deacons, who bear the oils and set them on the altar during the Eucharist. The attendants depicted supporting Christ also represent the two olive-tree witnesses of Christ who become the final martyrs. The Apocalypse describes their death at the hands of the Antichrist in terms which parallel the Passion and Resurrection of Christ. Deacons resemble the two witnesses because they deliver the testament of God and, according to the *Collectanea*, were supposed to imitate the martyred Christ when they donned the *casula* to approach altar and gospel book. Moreover, since the illustrations present interpretations of the Gospels, they may have been addressed especially to the deacon, who would have been charged with reading correctly the gospel lection and often would have been learning how to explain the meaning of the Gospel and the feast day. The possibility remains that the figures refer to additional clerical orders, especially that of priest or bishop, since all are said to resemble Christ, but the grade of deacon seems especially prominent in the iconography of the Book of Kells.

Whether or not the pictures and decoration were intended to refer to the deacon, the Book of Kells certainly presents numerous references to the liturgy and seems to depict the place of the gospel book in both a heavenly and an earthly liturgy. The kind of liturgy for which it was made seems to have been that of an important monastic church which used a non-Roman lection system. The structuring of the manuscript does not coincide with known Roman lection systems. The emphasis given to Quadragesima Sunday and Holy Week by the full-page illustrations and illuminated incipits might be explained by the Roman stational system because masses for Quadragesima Sunday, Palm Sunday and Holy Thursday were held at St John Lateran in the papal liturgy. This suggestion cannot hold true because no

Roman lection system is known to indicate a reading of Luke 4.1–13, besides the fact that without an urban context the Roman stational system loses its purpose.[68] The manuscript's concentration of full-page images at the Quadragesimal, Holy Thursday and Resurrection lections probably results from a lection system with a well-developed cycle of readings for Lent and Holy Week but fewer lections for Advent and the weeks following the Nativity. The lection systems found to present readings coincident with the manuscript's illuminated incipits and illustrations tend to fit this description.[69] Such systems may reflect the importance of Lent and Holy Week for early liturgies when conversions and baptisms were a major activity. Moreover, Lent and Holy Week must have been especially important to Insular monastic communities, with their emphasis on evangelism and developed concepts of asceticism and martyrdom.

The Book of Kells appears to reflect the influence of a liturgy suited to a Columban monastic context. Even though the iconography of the illustration of the Passion of Christ may have been influenced by an episcopal ceremony, the blessing of the oils, usually considered to have been performed in a cathedral and the manuscript's possible association with the office of deacon may indicate a pastoral context, rigid distinctions of monastic and pastoral do not apply to the eighth- and early ninth-century churches of Ireland and Anglo-Saxon England. Their functions overlapped in Insular monastic foundations. Irish monasteries blended the contemplative life with pastoral functions, creating a situation in which a deacon could be attached to a monastic church.[70] In any context, however, chrism could only be consecrated by a bishop. In Gaul, churches obtained chrism from the bishop by paying a tax, an arrangement contributing significantly to the income and power of the bishop.[71] The full-page decoration presented in the Book of Kells suggests that its most likely context may be found in a large Insular monastic foundation involved in training clergy as well as pastoral concerns, a context which would not be at all unusual in eighth- or ninth-century Ireland.

Function and Audience: the Figure of Interpretation

The two illustrations (PLATES I, III) seem especially related to a monastic context of high status in which the process of interpretation and archaic traditions of textual presentation occupied important positions. Both illustrate events from the gospel narrative, but the 'narrative' they illustrate is multi-levelled, based upon interpretative figures which layer images taken from the texts and rituals of the illustrations' liturgical context. Furthermore, the illustrations work within an archaic tradition of textual division, and their positions in the text appear to have determined the interpretative figures they present.

Their multivalence could function on levels beyond that of the single viewer posited in the context of Lent or Holy Thursday. Not only does it connect with liturgical themes of Lent and Holy Thursday, but also they seem to represent paradigms of how orthodox truth is revealed and passed on.

The Temptation illustration can even be seen as being about public, authoritative interpretation. It depicts an exegetical contest, between the two 'Heads', and this contest has an audience who witness the triumph of divine truth. Depiction of the contest by means of an interpretative figure, the Church as Head and Body of Christ, elevates it beyond any simple equivalence with a text. The image of the Head and Body, involved in exegetical struggle, becomes a figure applied to text to articulate and interpret it. The figure of Head and Body as set out by Tyconius in the *Liber Regularum* is neither words nor image but an idea, a figure, which has a shape that can reveal divine mystery in Scripture. The purpose of Tyconius's seven rules is to provide guidelines for correct, authoritative Christian interpretation that function on several interpretative levels, to include not only static symbolic relationships but also changing relationships of dialogue (the Body sings to the Head) or time (the temporal senses of existence of Tabernacle and Temple in past, present, and future). The Rules' flexibility and their potential to provide a framework for a unified Christian view of Old Testament Scripture and Christian salvation history must have been crucial factors in their adoption by influential patristic writers, Augustine in particular. The unified doctrine they made possible responded to the needs of the early medieval Church, especially in its period of evangelisation of non-Mediterranean people, because this doctrine, with its historical construct that emphasised the present-day Church, provided access for northern *gens* to enter and join themselves, their history, and culture into the universal Body.

In the Insular context of learning and interpreting, the image of the Body and Head in the Book of Kells is a *figura*, a shape like a letter or an elaborate punctuation mark articulating text. Such merging of interpretative forms and figures can be seen in the work of the early medieval (probably Irish) grammarian, Vergilius Maro Grammaticus, who saw the physical *littera*, or letter, as similar to the human body: '… its shape, its function, and its pronunciation, … are its joints and limbs …'. The letter has a soul in its meaning, and a spirit 'in its higher form of contemplation'.[72] Eccentric as Vergilius's metaphor may seem, it is not an isolated oddity but belongs within a continuum of textual study and exegesis that formed the interface between the divine Word and the body of the Church, the audience of the Word. This interface would be especially important at the beginning of Lent, the time of spiritual renewal when pastoral contact was particularly intense, with emphasis on preaching and its complex liturgy drawing in nearly daily lay participation.[73]

The Passion image on fol. 114r also presents a *figura*, a shape, that simultaneously articulates gospel text, relates the meaning of the text to the liturgical context of Holy Thursday, and expands this meaning to refer specifically to the context of the Church of the past, present, and future. With its allusion to the two olive-tree witnesses, probably seen by the picture's audience as the Old Testament heroes Enoch and Elias, it may also include within that context the history of the Insular world, which assimilated heroes such as Fintan to them. These layers of meaning are carried in a sign which consists of a triad of figures: the two flanking olive-tree figures on either side of a cross-shaped one. Placed at the point of division and transition at Matthew 26.30–31, the semiosis of the *figura* becomes fully exploited, causing the picture to operate as merged image, letter, and punctuation mark. It almost seems a lesson in how a shape can evoke multiple meanings and shift functions, unifying and harmonizing the visual and verbal in expression of complex thoughts.

The picture on folio 114r seems especially important because of its preservation and even glorification of an archaic textual division. That such an image with its historical semiosis would be placed at such a point and conceived to function in the way that it does suggests that it may have been seen to connect founder, monastic community, or other holder of the manuscript with the structure of Christian history. Furthermore, it would do this in connection with imagery, such as the figure of the Head and Body in the Temptation illustration, which expresses not only the divine authority of the Gospels themselves but also the methods of learning and communicating their truth.

The Book of Kells is an object of authority and prestige, but these qualities do not seem to have resided statically within it. Its absolute, material value certainly would have been obvious to its audience, but its expression of high status goes beyond its visual and material opulence. Much of its decoration functions to control, as well as to facilitate, understanding of text. In its two full-page illustrations, its audiences saw the process of understanding and statement of the divine truth. The pictures of the Temptation and Passion of Christ, seen within the context of the liturgy of Quadragesima Sunday and Holy Thursday, referred to and included the audiences, placing them within the history of the Earthly and Heavenly Church.

Notes to Chapter Four

1   On Irish monastic schools, *see* Ó Cróinín, 1995, pp.169–93; 203–22.

2   Thacker, 1992; Foot, 1992; Sharpe, 1992; Doherty, 1985; Ó Corráin, Breatnach, and Breen, 1984; Bitel, 1990.

3   Gneuss, 1985, pp.105–9, 110–11, 120–2; Cabrol, 'Bangor (Antiphonaire de)', *DACL* 2.1, col. 187.

4   For example, the notes in the 'Gospels of St Kilian' (Salmon, 1951, 1952); in the Codex Rehdigeranus (Morin, 1902, 3–11); and Codex Forojuliensis (de Bruyne, 1913, 208–18).

5   Hughes, 1982, p.271. For early examples, *see* any of the systems cited *above*, but especially the notation in the 'Gospels of St Kilian': 'Cena Dni in missa ad nona' (Salmon, 1951, p.43).

6   *See* Appendix 1 and Chapter 3, pp.116–19.

7   Clayton, 1985, pp.208–10; Salmon, 1959a, pp.135–54; Battifol, 1912, pp.78–86; Hughes, 1982, pp.60–1.

8   Curran, 1984, p.168, citing *PL* 66, col. 994: 'Orationes vero et duae lectiones, una de Veteri Testamento et alia de Novo, in singulis noctis conventibus dicendae sunt'. On matins, Curran (1984, pp.160–2) cites Columbanus, *Reg. mon.* 7 (ed. Walker, 1957, pp.130, 132), and Adomnán, *Life of Columcille* (ed. Anderson and Anderson, references in Introduction, pp.121–2), as well as the office in the Antiphonary of Bangor (pp.183–91).

9   Curran, 1984, pp.184, 186–7.

10 Clayton, 1984, p.210.

11 Salmon, 1959a, pp.144–9; Battifol, 1912, pp.81–2; Cabrol, cols. 188–9.

12 Haddan and Stubbs, vol. 3, 1871, p.367; Fisher, 1973, pp.166, 170–2; Wormald, 1982, p.100; Cubbitt, 1995.

13 Ordines in Andrieu, 1948–51, Ordo XIIIA, vol. 2, pp.482–3, Ordo XIIIC, vol. 2, p.513; Ordo XXVIII, vol. 3, pp.393, 397; Ordines XXXA–B, vol. 3, pp.455–6, 466–7. Homiliaries in Étaix, 1986, pp.3–4; Étaix, 1976, p.102.

14 Homilia LXXI and LXII, *PL* 95, 1210; *see also* Étaix, 1986, p.6. Gregory, Homilia 16, *PL* 76, 1135–8. Leo, Tractatus XL, *CCL* 138A, 223–31.

15 Salmon, vol. 7, 1944, pp.87–8, with footnote 1, p.88.

16 *See* Farr, 1989, p.317, for other patristic exegesis of Psalm 21.

17 Ordines XIIIA, XIIIC (Andrieu, vol. 2, 1948, pp.482, 513); Ordines XXXA, XXXB (vol. 3, 1951, pp.455, 467). Others leave the choice open: '… leguntur homeliae sanctorum patrum ad ipsum diem pertinentes' (Ordo XIIIB, Andrieu, vol. 2, 1948, p.499).

18 Salmon, 1959, p.142.

19 Ó Cróinín, 1995, pp.178–89.

20 Henry, 1974, pp.183–4.

21 Henry, 1974, pp.198–9; Nordenfalk, 1968, 1973; Schapiro, 1973a; Brown, 1996, pp.73–115.

22 Nees, 1978, pp.4–6.

23 For example, the first Lindau bookcover and the Soiscél Molaise (Henderson, 1987, Ill. 49). *Also*, depictions of gospel book covers, such as that held by the Matthew symbol in the Codex Milinarius (Braunfels, vol. 3, 1965, Pl. XXX).

24 Weitzmann, 1977, p.61.

25 Henry, 1974, p.188; Werner, 1972.

26 Henry, 1974, p.188; cf. Nordenfalk, 1977b, p.116; Farr, 1989, pp.322–4.

27 Farr, 1989, pp.178–87.

28 Possibilities for placement within the gospel text include the texts of the Nativity and Adoration of the Magi, pericopes read for the anniversary of the dedication of Sta Maria Maggiore and lections for feasts from the Sanctorale.

29 Kitzinger, 1956, pp.229–36; Nilgen, pp.533–5, 559–60.

30 *See* Friend, 1926.

31 McGurk, 1961, p.98.

32 Turin, University Library, MS O.IV.20, fol. 1a verso; Henry, 1974, pp.173–4; Alexander, 1978, pp.80–1.

33 Alexander, 1978, p.81.

34 Grabar, 1961, p.44.

35 Mütherich in Braunfels, vol. 3, 1965, p.31; Mütherich and Gaehde, 1976, PLATE 1.

36 Mütherich in Braunfels, vol. 3, 1965, pp.31–4.

37 Perrer, 1983, pp.81–91, 200–1.

38 Alexander, 1978, pp.31–2, 36; McGurk, 1961, pp.33–5, 70–81.

39 Henderson, 1987, pp.80–8; Alexander, 1978, pp.40–2, 67.

40 Farr, 1989, p.331.

41 Northern Italy: Codex Rehdigeranus (Beissel, p.99; Godu, 'Evangiles', no. 48 in chart after col. 880); Codex Forojuliensis (Godu, 'Evangiles', no. 38 in chart after col. 880); *see* Martimort, 1992, p.23. Gaul: 'Gospels of St Kilian' (Würzburg Mp. th. q. 1a, from Gaul, liturgical notes seventh to ninth century) note at Mt. 27.37 '+ ad sex ...', end of lection marked at verse 44, 'T' (Salmon, 1951, pp.43–4). The many notes throughout Mt. 27 in the 'Gospels of St Kilian' suggest that much of the text was read as part of a Passion cento on Good Friday. Spain: The Liber Comicus, ed. Perez de Urbel and Gonzalez Y Ruiz–Zorrilla, vol. 1, 1950, pp.345–52, *esp.* p.350.

42 McGurk, 1955, pp.106–7.

43 Merk, 1912, pp.206, 213.

44 Merk, 1912, pp.208, 214.

45 McGurk (1961, p.119) lists Durham A.II.16; Hereford Gospels; Bodley Auct. D.2.19 (Macregol); Bodeleian Rawlinson G.167; Paris, B. N. Lat. 9389 (Echternach); St Gall 51; Vatican, Barberini lat. 570.

46 Beissel, 1907, p.72.

47 Salmon (1951, p.46) lists at Lk. 24.1 the notation 'L', indicating 'lectio;' another notation at verse 12 reads 'Transi ad Iohannes ...'.

48 Several other non–Roman liturgies indicate lections beginning with Lk. 24.1 as readings for ferials of the week following Easter. *See* Beissel, 1907, pp.44, 48, 80, 123; Klauser, 1972, p.51, no. 131. *Also,* Bede wrote a homily on Luke 24.1–9 for a day following Easter (Homilia II.10, 'Post Pascha', CCL 122, pp.246–52).

49 Klauser, 1972, pp.43 (no. 234), 90 (no. 270), 127 (no. 274), 140 (no. 1), 169 (no. 328), 183 (295). All are for the Vigil of the Nativity.

50 Bede, Homelia I.5, 'In Vigilia Nativitatis Domini', CCL 122, pp.32–6; Alcuin and Paul the Deacon, *see* Beissel, 1907, p.150; Godescalc Evangelistary, *see* Gaehde in Mütherich and Gaehde, 1976, pp.34–5.

51 North Italian: Godu ('Evangiles', DACL 5.1, chart following col. 830) lists Codex Rehdigeranus (no. 6); Milan, Ambr. C. 39 inf. (no. 1); Codex Forojuliensis (no. 4); and Codex Valerianus (no. 3). Beissel (1907, p.91) also lists Sermones 145 and 146 of Peter Chrysologus, from fifth-century Ravenna. All lections beginning Mt. 1.18 are for the Vigil of the Nativity. The beginning of Matthew is missing from the Rabula Gospels (Merk, 1912, p.204) and the 'Gospels of St Kilian' (Salmon, 1951, p.38). Burchard Gospels: Morin, 1893b, pp.114–15, 118; for the Vigil of the Nativity. On the date and origin of the manuscript's text, notations and canon tables, *see* Bischoff and Hofmann, 1952, p.93.

52 McGurk, 1961, p.118.

53 *See also* Appendix 2.II.c.

54 *See* the indices in Beissel, 1907, p.202; Klauser, 1972, p.188. *Also,* Godu, 'Evangiles', *DACL* 5.1, chart following col. 880; Merk, 1912, p.206; Morin, 1911, p.304.

55 Augustine's homily for the Easter vigil, cited in Beissel, 1907, pp.44, 46.

56 McGurk, 1955, p.106.

57 McGurk, 1955, p.107; McGurk, 1961, p.118.

58 *See* the indices in Beissel, 1907, p.204; Klauser, 1972, p.189; and Godu, 'Evangiles', chart following col. 880.

59 Meyvaert, 1989; O'Reilly, 1994; Nordenfalk, revised paper for the Medieval Academy of America, 1978, cited in Lewis, 1980, p.139; Henry, 1974, p.221.

60 The *Collectanea*, which Bede did not write, has been attributed to both Ireland and Anglo–Saxon England. *See* Kitson, 1983, pp.100–1; Kenney, 1966, no. 541; Dekkers and Gaar, 1961, no. 1129; Glorieux, 1952, p.52.

61 Pseudo–Bede, *PL* 94, col. 554A.

62 For discussion of Irish interpretations of the orders, *see* Stevenson in introduction to Warren, 1987, p.lvii; O Corráin, 1984, pp.396, 405.

63 *PL* 94, col. 555A

64 Mayr–Harting, 1991, p.215.

65 *In Ezram et Neemiam* I, *CCL* 119A, pp.277–8, lines 1446–70.

66 Mayr–Harting, 1991, pp.218–19. I am most grateful for Henry Mayr–Harting's generous and patient discussion of this passage.

67 Gneuss, 1985, pp.121, 135.

68 Chavasse (1982) has demonstrated how the stationals distribute the masses and rituals of Lent and Holy Week around the city of Rome to fulfill an urban pastoral function. Ó Carragáin now sees specific relationships between Roman stational liturgies and Insular liturgies of Holy Week; *see* Ó Carragáin, 1994a.

69 Rabula Gospels (Merk, 1912); 'Gospels of St Kilian' (Salmon, 1951, 1952); Codex Forojuliensis (de Bruyne, 1913); Valerianus Gospels (Morin, 1893d); Liber Comicus (Morin, 1893a; Perez de Urbel and Gonzalez y Ruiz–Zorrilla, 1950–55). Cf. Klauser's 'pure Roman' systems (1972).

70 Thacker, 1992; Foot, 1992; Sharpe, 1984a; Sharpe, 1992; Etchingham, 1991, 1993, 1994; Stevenson, in her introduction to Warren, 1987, pp.xxxvi–xl. Mayr–Harting, 1991, pp.62–3, 134–5, 244–6; Fisher, 1973, pp.94–6.

71 Mayr–Harting, 1991, p.135.

72 In Law, 1995, pp.67–9.

73 On later Anglo–Saxon England, *see* Gatch, 1992, pp.164–5; on Lent, Jungman, 1959, 254–65.

APPENDICES

APPENDIX I

CAPITULARIES AND MARGINAL NOTATIONS
OF LUKE 4.1–13 AND MATTHEW 26.30–31
AS LITURGICAL LECTIONS

TEXT	NOTATION	ORIGIN / DATE
1	Wroclaw (Breslau), Stadtbibliothek, MS R 169, Codex Rehdigeranus[1]	
Mt 26.17	In cena dni	Pre-Vulgate text 7–8th cent., 8–9th cent. capitulary; N. Italy[2]
2	Cividale, R. Museo Archeologico S.N.; Prague, bibl. Metr. CIM.1; Venice, S. Marco S.N.; Codex Forojuliensis[3]	
Lk 4.1	In caput quadragisime	attr. Aquileia, 6th cent.;
Mt 4.1	In caput quatragiseme dom. III	notes 7–8th cent.
3	Florence, Laurentian Library, cod. Plt. I.56, Rabula Gospels[4]	
Lk 4.1	Sunday of the beginning of Lent	St John of Zagba,
Mt 4.1	Sunday of the beginning of Lent	Mespotamia, AD 586
Mt. 26.17	Lection for Thursday of the Mystery	
4	Milan, Bibl. Ambros. C 39 inf.[5]	
Mt 26.17–75	In cena dni ad missa	Text 6th cent., notes 7–9th cent., Northern Italy (Verona)[6]
5	Munich, Bayerische Staatsbibliothek, Clm 6224, Codex Valerianus[7]	
Lk 4.1	+Domineca in caput quadrageseme	?N. Italian or Danubian,
Mt 7.13	In caput quadragesim	text 7th cent.;
Mt 26.13	Coena Dni	notes 7–8th or 9th cent.
6	Paris, B.N. lat. 256, Paris Gospels[8]	
Mt 26.30–31	['Skeletal' cross in right margin]	c.700, N. France (S. Denis)[9]

1   Morin, 1902, pp. 2, 7.

2   Martimort, 1992, pp. 29, 49; Lowe, *CLA* 8, No. 1073, p. 16.

3   de Bruyne, 1913, p. 212; Godu, *DACL* 5.1, table following col. 882; Martimort, 1992, p. 49; Lowe, *CLA* 3, No. 285; Klauser, 1972, p. XXX; Gamber, 1963, p. 38.

4   Merk, 1912, pp. 206, 207, 213.

5   Morin, 1903, p. 378.

6   Martimort, 1992, pp. 23, 50; Cau, 1968, p. 18; Morin, 1903, pp. 375–6.

7   White, 1888, pp. liii, 78; Godu, *DACL* 5.1, table following col. 882; Martimort, 1992, pp. 23, 49; Lowe, *CLA* 9, No. 1249; Klauser, 1972, p. XXXIII; McGurk, 1961, No. 74.

8   Morin, 1893e, on lection notations; *see also* Plate 22.

9   Martimort, 1992, pp. 24, 48; Mütherich, 1989, pp. 320–1; Lowe, *CLA* 5, No. 524, p. 3; Klauser, 1972, p. xxxiii; McGurk, 1961, pp. 57–8; Morin, 1893e, 439–431.

Text	Notation	Origin / Date
7 Paris, B.N. lat. 9427, Lectionary of Luxeuil[10]		
Mt 26.2	Coena Domini, Ad Matutinos	7–8th cent.; Gaul[11]
8 Paris, B.N. lat. 13246, Bobbio Missal[12]		
Mt 26.20–35	in cena domini	Southeast France, 8th cent.[13]
9 Vatican, Biblioteca Apostolica, Barberini lat. 470, Barberini Gospels[14]		
Mt 26.17	in cena dni	c.800, Mercia or Northumbria[15]
10 Würzburg, Universitätsbibliothek Ms. Mp.th.q. 1a, 'Gospels of St Kilian'[16]		
Lk 4.1	Secunda die rogationis ad sexta in dominico	France or Italy,
Mt 26.17	Cena Dni in missa ad nona	text 6–7th cent.;
Mt 26.31–35	In parasceve in nocte	notes 7–9th cent.

10 Salmon, vol. 7, 1944, pp. 87–8. However, eight folios are missing from the manuscript's Holy Thursday lections. They would have presented most of the reading from Matthew for matins, then the reading for the mass (Salmon, vol. 7, 1944, fn. 1, p. 88).

11 Salmon (vol. 9, 1953, pp. 64–75) attributes it to the cathedral of Langres.

12 Lowe, vol. 58, 1920, p. 61, vol. 61, 1924, p. 157.

13 Lowe, CLA vol. 5, No. 654.

14 See Fig. 27.

15 Brown, 1996, pp. 167–78; Brown, in Keynes and Brown, 1991, pp. 195, 205; Alexander, 1978, p. 61.

16 Salmon, 1951, pp. 38, 43, 45–51; Salmon, 1952, pp. 294–6; Morin, 1911, p. 329; Martimort, 1992, pp. 23, 48–9; Hofmann in Bischoff and Hofmann, 1952, p. 92; McGurk, 1961, No. 78; Lowe, CLA 9, No. 1429; Klauser, 1972, p. XXXV.

APPENDIX 2

TEXTUAL ARTICULATION OF LUKE 4.1–13 AND
MATTHEW 26.30–31 IN GOSPEL MANUSCRIPTS:
COMPARATIVE TABLES

SIGLA

Manuscripts

B	Vatican, Biblioteca Apostolica, Barb. lat. 570 (Barberini Gospels)
D	Dublin, Trinity College, MS. 57 (Book of Durrow)
Ef	Durham, Cathedral Library, A.II.17
Hf	Hereford, Cathedral Library, P. I. 2
Ho	Oxford, Bodleian Library, Rawlinson G.167
O	Oxford, Bodleian Library, Auct. D.2.14 (St. Augustine Gospels)
Q	Dublin, Trinity College, MS. 58 (Book of Kells)
R	Oxford, Bodleian Library, Auct. D.2.19 (Macregol Gospels)
Ro	London, British Library, Royal 1.B.vii (Royal Gospels)
Y	London, British Library, Cotton Nero D.iv (Lindisfarne Gospels)

Graphic Articulation

*Number indicates number of consecutive letters emphasised; all are at the left margin
unless indicated as within text block (i).*

3	(in bold) Enlarged
*	Decorated
+	Colored
.	Medial point or other punctuation precedes the letter(s)
b	An undecorated letter of ordinary or slightly enlarged size at the left margin beginning a cola or commata line or section
t	Top of page or column
i	Within text block or mid-line
o	Initial offset in left margin
x	Interlinear or marginal cross
,	Punctuation within interval (Mt. 26.30–1)
–	Text missing

Dates of later additions noted in parentheses (i.e.: 10c).

1. Luke 4.1–13

[Eusebian sections fall at verse 1 (*Iesus autem*) and in 2 (*et nihil manducavit*).]

1. a. Book of Kells and Gospel Manuscripts Articulated *per cola et commata*.[1]

	Modern Verse, Text	Q	Y	Ro	O	D
1	Ihs autem plenus	20*+	3*+	b+ t	1+	7*+
	regressus est					
	a iordane				b	
	& agebatur a spiritu	+ i	b	b	b	b
2	& tentabatur		b	b	b	b
	& nihil manducavit	2*+	2*+	b+	b	3*+
	& consummatis illis		b	b	b	b
3	dixit autem		b	**b**	b	3
	Si filius dei es		b t	b	b	
4	& respondit	+ i	b	b	b	b t
	scriptum est		b	b	b	
	quia non in solo				b	
5	& duxit illum	2*+	b	b	b	2*+.i
	et ostendit illi				b	
6	& ait illi	+ i	b+	b	b	
	quia mihi tradita		b	**b**	b	
	& cui volo do illa			b	b	
7	tu ergo		b	b	b	
8	& respondens Ihs	+	b	b	b	
	scriptum est		b	b	b	
	dominum deum tuum				b	
9	& duxit illum	2*+ i	b+	b	b	2*+
	& statuit eum supra		b	**b**	b	
	& dixit illi		b	.	b	
	si filius dei es		b	b	b	
10	scriptum est		b	b	b	
	quod angelis suis		b		b	
	ne forte offendas				b	
12	& respondens	2*+.i	b+	b	b	2*+.i
	dictum est non tent		b			
13	& consummata omni	1+.i	b	b	b	

1   *See* Plates I–II and Figs 5–10.

167

1. b. Book of Kells and Manuscripts With Block Text Format[2]

	Modern Verse, Text	Q	Ef	Ho	Hf	R	B
1	Ihs autem plenus regressus est a iordane	20*+	—	8*+	3	3*+	2+ 2*+t
	& agebatur a spiritu	+ i		I			
2	& tentabatur & nihil manducavit & consummatis illis	2*+		1*+.i 1*+i	I i		
3	dixit autem Si filius dei es		5*+.i	1*+.i	I i	1*+	I
4	& respondit scriptum est quia non in solo	+ i		1*+.i			
5	& duxit illum et ostendit illi	2*+	6*+.i	1*+...i	I i		I
6	& ait illi quia mihi tradita & cui volo do illa	+ i		1*+.i			
7	tu ergo			2*+.i			
8	& respondens Ihs scriptum est dominum deum tuum	+	1+.i	1*+. 1*+	I i		I
9	& duxit illum & statuit eum supra & dixit illi si filius dei es	2*+ i	6*+.i 1+.i	1*+.. 1*.i		1*+.i	I t
10	scriptum est quod angelis suis ne forte offendas			.i 1*+t			I+
12	& respondens dictum est non tent	1*+.i	4*+.i	1*+.	I i		I+
13	& consummata omni	I+.i		1*+.i	I i		I i

2   *See* Plates I–II and Figs 11–16.

11. Matthew 26.30–31

11 a. Book of Kells and Manuscripts Articulated Per cola et commata.[3]

Manuscript	Verse 30	Interval	Verse 31
Book of Kells (Q)	1 + *	, * +	29 * +
Lindisfarne Gospels (Y)	1b * +		b *
Royal 1.B.vii (Ro)	1 16 +		b +
B.L., Additional 5463	27 +	, +	b
B.L., Harley 1775	1		1

11. b. Book of Kells and Manuscripts with Block Text Format[4]

Manuscript	Verse 30	Interval	Verse 31
Book of Kells (Q)	1 + *	, * +	29 * +
Usserianus Primus[5]	i	, + i	34 +
Durham A.II.17 (Ef)	6 +* (1) i	, * +	4 + *
Book of Mulling[6]	i	, i	0 2
Book of Dimma[7]	i	,	0 2 *
Gospels of St Gatien[8]	4 + i	, i	9 (1) * +
Macregol Gospels (R)	1 + i (10c)	, (10c)	1 * i

11. c. Book of Kells and Manuscripts with Section Articulation[9]

Manuscript	Verse 30	Interval	Verse 31
Book of Kells (Q)	1 + *	, * +	29 * +
Codex Corbeiensis[10]	b	,	17 +
Paris, B.N., lat. 256	1 0 +	, x	14 (1) *+
Paris, B.N., lat. 17226	1 0	,	14 (1) +
Paris, B.N., lat. 260	1 0	,	1 0

3   See Plates III–IV and Figs 17–21.
4   See Plates III–IV and Figs 22–3.
5   Dublin, Trinity College, MS. 55, fol. 25v; see Farr, 1994, Pl. 67.
6   Dublin, Trinity College Library, MS. 60, fol. 47v; see Farr, 1994, Pl. 113.
7   Dublin, Trinity College, MS. 59, p. 26.
8   Paris, B.N. nouv. acq. lat. 1587, fol. 28r; see Farr, 1994, Pl. 130.
9   See Plates III–IV and Figs 24–6.
10 Paris, B.N. lat. 17225, fol. 33r; see Farr, 1994, Pl. 76.

II. d. Book of Kells and Manuscripts Combining Block Text with Section Articulation[11]

Manuscript	Verse 30	Interval	Verse 31
Book of Kells (Q)	I + *	, * +	**29** * +
Hereford Gospels (Hf)[12]	**2** o	,	**I**
Barberini Gospels (B)	5(**I**)o+*t	, +	4(**I**)o+*
Book of Armagh[13]	**I** o		**I** i

11 *See* Plates III–IV and Fig. 27
12 fol. 31v.
13 Dublin, Trinity College Library, MS. 52, fol. 49v.

BIBLIOGRAPHY

Abbreviations

ASE   *Anglo-Saxon England*

Blair   Blair, John, and Richard Sharpe, eds. *Pastoral Care Before the Parish.* Studies in the Early History of Britain. Leicester, 1992.

Bonner   Bonner, Gerald, David Rollason, and Clare Stancliffe, eds. *St. Cuthbert, His Cult and His Community to AD 1200.* Woodbridge, 1989.

CCL   *Corpus Christianorum, Series Latina.* Turnhout, 1953–.

CLA   *Codices Latini Antiquiores: a palaeographical guide to Latin manuscripts,* ed. E.A. Lowe, Oxford, 1934–72.

CSEL   *Corpus Scriptorum Ecclesiasticorum Latinorum.* Vienna, 1866–.

DACL   *Dictionnaire d'archéologie chrétienne et de liturgie,* ed. F. Cabrol and H. Leclerq, 15 vols. Paris, 1907–53.

Fox   Fox, Peter, ed. *The Book of Kells:* MS *58 Trinity College Library Dublin.* Facsimile and Commentary. Luzern, 1990.

Gameson   Gameson, Richard, ed. *The Medieval Bible: Its Production, Decoration and Use.* Cambridge Studies in Paleography Codicology. Cambridge, 1994.

HBS   *Henry Bradshaw Society*

Ní Chatháin 1984   Ní Chatháin, P., and M. Richter, eds. *Irland und Europa: Die Kirche im Frühmittelalter.* Stuttgart, 1984.

Ní Chatháin 1987   Ní Chatháin, P., and M. Richter, eds. *Irland und die Christenheit: Bibelstudien und Mission.* Stuttgart, 1987.

O'Mahony   O'Mahony, Felicity, ed. *The Book of Kells: Proceedings of a Conference at Trinity College Dublin, 6–9 September 1992.* Aldershot, Hampshire, 1994.

PG   *Patrologia Graeca,* ed. J.P. Migne, 168 vols. Paris, 1857–68.

PL   *Patrologia Latina,* ed. J.P. Migne, 222 vols. Paris, 1844–55.

RB   *Revue bénédictine*

Ryan   Ryan, Michael, ed. *Ireland and Insular Art A.D. 500–1200.* Dublin, 1987.

Spearman   Spearman, Michael, and John Higgitt, eds. *The Age of Migrating Ideas: Early Medieval Art in Northern Britain and Ireland.* Edinburgh, 1993.

Szarmach   Szarmach, Paul, and Virginia Darrow Oggins, eds. *Sources of Anglo-Saxon Culture,* ed. Paul E. Szarmach and Virginia D. Oggins. Studies in Medieval Culture 20, Medieval Institute Publications. Kalamazoo, MI, 1986.

ADOMNÁN. *Adamnan's Life of Columba*. ed. A. O. and M. O. Anderson. London, 1961.

AELFRIC. *The Homilies of the Anglo-Saxon Church*. B. Thorpe, ed. and tr. 2 vols. New York, 1971 (repr. London 1844–46).

ALDHELM. 'The *Carmen de Virginitate*'. James L. Rosier, tr. In *Aldhelm: The Poetic Works*, Michael Lapidge and James L. Rosier, ed. and tr., 97–259. Cambridge, 1985.
De Virginitate. Carmen. In *Aldhelmi Opera*, Rudolf Ehwald, tr., 350–471. Monumenta germaniae historica. Berlin, 1961 (reprint of 1919).

ALEXANDER, Jonathan J. G. 'The Illumination'. In Fox, *Commentary*, 265–303.
Insular Manuscripts 6th to the 9th Century. London, 1978.

ALTON, E. H. and P. MEYER, eds. *Evangeliorum Quattuor Codex Cennannensis*, 3 vols. Berne, 1950–51.

AMOS, Thomas L. 'Monks and Pastoral Care in the Early Middle Ages'. In *Religion, Culture, and Society in the Early Middle Ages: Studies in Honor of Richard E. Sullivan*, Thomas F. X. Noble and John J. Contreni, eds., 165–80. Studies in Medieval Culture 23. Kalamazoo, Michigan, 1987.

ANDERSON, D. L. 'The Book of Rules of Tyconius: an Introduction and Translation with Commentary'. Ph.D. diss. Southern Baptist Theological Seminary, 1974.

ANDRÉ, Jacques. *Etude sur les termes de couleur dans la langue latine*. Paris, 1949.

ANDRIEU, Michel, ed. *Les Ordines Romani du haut moyen âge*, 5 vols. Spicilegium Sacrum Lovaniense, études et documents, fasc. 11, 23–4, 28–9. Louvain, 1931, 1948–51, 1956–61.

ATKINSON, Robert, ed. *The Passions and the Homilies in the Leabhar Breac: Text, Translation and Glossary*. R. I. A. Todd Lecture Series, vol. II. Dublin, 1887.

AUGUSTINE. *De Doctrina Christiana*. CSEL 80.
Enarrationes in Psalmos. CCL 39.
On Christian Doctrine. D. W. Robertson, Jr., tr. New York, 1958.

AUGUSTINUS HIBERNICUS. *De Mirabilibus Sacrae Scripturae*. PL 35, 2149–200.

BACKHOUSE, Janet. *The Lindisfarne Gospels*. Oxford, 1981.

BAILEY, Richard N. 'Bede's Text of Cassiodorus' Commentary on the Psalms'. *The Journal of Theological Studies* 34 (1983) 189–93.
'The Cultural and Social Setting'. In *Prehistoric, Roman and Early Medieval. The Cambridge Guide to the Arts in Britain,* vol. 1, Boris Ford, ed., 100–20. Cambridge, 1988.
Viking Age Sculpture in Northern England. London, 1981.

BALTZER, Klaus. 'The Meaning of the Temple in the Lucan Writings'. *Harvard Theological Review* 58 (1965) 263–77.

BANNERMAN, John. '*Comarba Coluim Chille* and the Relics of Columba'. *Innes Review* 44 (1993) 14–47.

BASSETT, Steven. 'Church and Diocese in the West Midlands: The Transition from British to Anglo-Saxon Control'. In Blair, 13–40.

BATIFFOL, Pierre. *History of the Roman Breviary*. Atwell M. Y. Baylay, tr. London, 1912.

BECKER, Alfred. *Franks Casket*. Regensburg, 1973.

BECKWITH, John. *Ivory Carvings in Early Medieval England*. London, 1972.

BEDE. *Concerning Figures and Tropes*. Gussie Hecht Tannenhaus, tr. In *Readings in Medieval Rhetoric*, Joseph Miller, Michael Prosser, and Thomas Benson, eds., 96–122. Bloomington, Indiana, 1973.
De Tabernaculo et Vasis eius ac Vestibus Sacerdotum. CCL 119A, 1–139.
De Templo. CCL 119A, 141–234.
Explanatio Apocalypsis. PL 93, 129–206.
A History of the English Church and People. L. Sherley-Price, tr. New York, 1968.
Homiliarum Evangelii, Libri II. CCL 122, 1–403.
In Evangelium Lucae Libros VI. CCL 120, 5–425.
In Ezram et Neemiam. CCL 119A, 235–392.
In Marci Evangelium Expositio. CCL 120, 431–648.

Lives of the Abbots of Wearmouth and Jarrow. In *The Age of Bede*, D. H. Farmer, ed. and tr., 185–210. New York, 1983.
On the Tabernacle. Arthur G. Holder, tr. Translated Texts for Historians. Liverpool, 1994.
On the Temple. Seán Connolly, tr. Translated Texts for Historians. Liverpool, 1995.
Vita Sancti Cuthberti. In *Two Lives of Saint Cuthbert: A Life by an Anonymous Monk of Lindisfarne and Bede's Prose Life*, Bernard Colgrave, ed. and tr., 141–308. Cambridge, 1940.

BEISSEL, Stephan. 'Entstehung der Perikopen des römischen Messbuches: zur Geschichte der Evangelienbücher in der ersten Hälfte des Mittelalters'. *Ergänzungshefte zu den 'Stimmen aus Maria-Laach'*, bd. 24, Ergänzungsheft 96, Freiburg im Breisgau, 1907, pp. 401–620.

BERSCHIN, Walter. '*Opus Deliberatum Ac Perfectum*: Why Did the Venerable Bede Write a Second Prose Life of St. Cuthbert?' In Bonner, 95–102.

BEST, R. I. 'The Settling of the Manor of Tara', *Eriu* 4 (1910) 121–72.

BEST, R. I., and H. J. LAWLOR, eds. *The Martyrology of Tallaght*. HBS 68. London, 1931.

BINCHY, D. A., 'The Fair of Tailtiu and the Feast of Tara', *Eriu* 18 (1958) 113–38.

BISCHOFF, Bernhard. 'Die europäische Verbreitung der Werke Isidors von Sevilla'. *Mittelalterliche Studien* 1 (1966) 171–94.
'Kreuz und Buch im Frühmittelalter'. In *Mittelalterliche Studien: ausgewählte Aufsätze zur Schriftkunde und Literaturgeschichte*, Bernhard Bischoff, ed., vol. 2, 284–303. Stuttgart, 1967.
Latin Paleography: Antiquity and the Middle Ages. Dáibhí O Cróinín and David Ganz, trs. Cambridge, 1990.
'Turning Points in the History of Latin Exegesis in the Early Middle Ages'. In *Biblical Studies, the Medieval Irish Contribution*, Martin McNamara, ed., 74–160. Proceedings of the Irish Biblical Association 1. Dublin, 1976.

BISCHOFF, Bernhard and Josef HOFMANN. *Libri Sancti Kyliani. Die Würzburger Schreibschule und die Dombibliothek im VIII. und IX. Jahrhundert*. Quellen und Forschungen zur Geschichte des Bistums und Hochstifts Würzburg 6. Würzburg, 1952.

BITEL, Lisa M. *Isle of the Saints: Monastic Settlement and Christian Community in Early Ireland*. Ithaca, New York, 1990.

BLATHMAC. 'Poem to Our Lady'. In *Poems of Blathmac, Son of Cú Brettan, Together with the Irish Gospel of Thomas and a Poem on the Virgin Mary*, James Carney, ed. and tr., 1–88. Irish Texts Society. Dublin, 1964.

BOECKLER, A. 'Bildvorlagen der Reichenau'. *Zeitschrift für Kunstgeschichte* 12 (1949) 7–29.

BONNER, Campbell. *Studies in Magical Amulets, Chiefly Graeco-Egyptian*. Ann Arbor, Michigan, 1950.

BONNER, Gerald. *Saint Bede in the Tradition of Western Apocalyptic Commentary*. Jarrow, 1966.

BOURKE, Cormac. *Patrick: The Archaeology of a Saint*. Belfast, 1993.

BRAUNFELS, Wolfgang, ed. *Karl der Grosse, Lebenswerk und Nachleben*, 4 vols. Düsseldorf, 1965–7.

BREEN, Aidan. 'A New Irish Fragment of the *Continuatio* to Rufinus-Eusebius *Historia Ecclesiastica*'. *Scriptorium* 41 (1987) 185–204.

BROOKS, Nicholas. *The Early History of the Church at Canterbury*. Leicester, 1984.

BROWN, Michelle P. *The Book of Cerne: Prayer, Patronage, and Power in Ninth-century England*. The British Library Studies in Medieval Culture. London, 1996.
Cambridge University Library, MS Ll.1.10, The Book of Cerne. Ph.D. Thesis, University of London, University College, 1993.
'Echoes: The Book of Kells and Southern English Manuscript Production'. In O'Mahony, 333–43.
A Guide to Western Historical Scripts from Antiquity to 1600. London, 1990.
'The Lindisfarne Scriptorium from the Late 7th to the Early 9th Century'. In Bonner, 151–63.
'Paris, Bibliothèque Nationale, lat. 10861 and the Scriptorium of Christ Church, Canterbury'. *ASE* 15 (1986) 119–37.

BROWN, Peter. *The Body and Society: Men, Women and Sexual Renunciation in Early Christianity*. Lectures on the History of Religions, vol. 13. New York, 1988.

BROWN, T. J. 'The Irish Element in the Insular System of Scripts to Circa A.D. 850'. In *Die Iren und Europa im früheren Mittelalter*, Heinz Lowe, ed., 101–19. Stuttgart, 1982.
'Late Antique and Early Anglo-Saxon Books'. In *Manuscripts at Oxford. R. W. Hunt Memorial Exhibition*. Oxford, 1980.

'Northumbria and the Book of Kells'. Reprinted from Jarrow Lecture 1971. *ASE* 1 (1972) 219–46.

'The Oldest Irish Manuscripts and Their Late Antique Background'. In Ní Chatháin, 1984, 311–27.

BRUCE-MITFORD, Rupert. 'The Durham-Echternach Calligrapher'. In Bonner, 175–8.

BULLOUGH, Donald A. 'Alcuin and the Kingdom of Heaven: Liturgy, Theology, and the Carolingian Age'. In *Carolingian Essays, Andrew W. Mellon Lectures in Early Christian Studies*, ed. Uta-Renate Blumenthal, 1–69. Washington, D.C., 1983.

'Roman Books and Carolingian *Renovatio*'. In *Renaissance and Renewal in Christian History*, ed. Derek Baker, 23–50. Studies in Church History 14. Oxford, 1977.

CABROL, F. 'Bangor (Antiphonaire de)'. *DACL* 2.1, 183–91.

CAHILL, Michel. 'Is the First Commentary on Mark an Irish Work?' *Peritia* 8 (1994) 35–45.

CALKINS, Robert G. *Illuminated Books of the Middle Ages*. Cornell, 1983.

CALLEWAERT, C. 'La durée et le caractere du carême ancien dans l'église latine'. In *Sacris Erudiri, fragmenta liturgica collecta a monachis Sancti Petri de Aldenburgo in Steenbrugge ne Pereant*, 459–507. Steenbrugge, 1940a.

'Notes sur le carême primitif gallican'. In *Sacris Erudiri: Fragmenta liturgica collecta a monachis Sancti Petri de Andenburgo in Steenbrugge ne Pereant*, 529–47. Steenbrugge, 1940b.

CAMILLE, Michael. 'Mouths and Meanings: Toward an Anti-iconography of Medieval Art'. In *Iconography at the Crossroads*, Brendan Cassidy, ed., 43–57. Index of Christian Art Occasional Papers. Princeton, 1993.

CAMPBELL, Ewan, and Alan LANE. 'Celtic and Germanic Interaction in Dalriada: The 7th-Century Metal-working Site at Dunadd'. In Spearman, 52–63.

CAREY, John. 'Ireland and the Antipodes: The Heterodoxy of Virgil of Salzburg'. *Speculum* 64 (1989) 1–10.

CARNEY, James. 'The Deeper Level of Early Irish Literature'. *Capuchin Annual* 36 (1969) 160–71.

'The Earliest Bran Material'. In *Latin Script and Letters A.D. 400–900: Festschrift Presented to Ludwig Bieler on the Occasion of His 70th Birthday*, J. J. O'Meara and B. Naumann, eds., 174–93. Leiden, 1976.

CARRUTHERS, Mary. *The Book of Memory: A Study of Memory in Medieval Culture*. Cambridge Studies in Medieval Literature. Cambridge, 1990.

CASSIAN. *De Institutis Coenobiorum et de Octo Principalium Vitiorum Remediis*. PL 49–50.

CASSIODORUS. *Expositio Psalmorum*. CCL 97–8.

Institutiones, ed. R. A. B. Mynors, Oxford, 1973.

CATTIN, Giulio. *Music of the Middle Ages I*. S. Botterill, tr. Cambridge, 1984.

CAU, E. 'Ricerche sui codici in onciale dell'Italia settentrionale (secoli iv–vi)' *Ricerche medievali* 3 (1968) 1–26.

CECCHELLI, C., ed. *The Rabbula Gospels*. Olten and Lausanne, 1959.

CHAPMAN, John. *Notes on the Early History of the Vulgate Gospels*. Oxford, 1908.

CHARLES-EDWARDS, Thomas M. 'A Contract Between King and People in Early Medieval Ireland: *Críth Gablach* on Kingship'. *Peritia* 8 (1994) 107–19.

'The Pastoral Role of the Church in the Early Irish Laws'. In Blair, 63–81.

CHAVASSE, Antoine. 'Le carême romain et les scrutins prébaptismaux avant le IXe siècle'. *Recherches de science religieuse* 35 (1948) 325–81.

'L'organization stationnale du carème romain, avant le VIIIe siècle: une organization pastorale'. *Revue des sciences religieuses* 56 (1982) 17–32.

'La structure du carême et les lectures des messes quadragésimales dans la liturgie romaine'. *Maison-Dieu* 31 (1952) 76–119.

CLANCY, Thomas Owen, and Gilbert MÁRKUS. *Iona: The Earliest Poetry of a Celtic Monastery*. Edinburgh, 1995.

CLAYTON, Mary. 'Homiliaries and Preaching in Anglo-Saxon England'. *Peritia* 4 (1985) 207–42.

COLGRAVE, Bertram, ed. and tr. *Two Lives of Saint Cuthbert*. Cambridge, 1940.

Commentarius in Lucam. CCL 108C, 1–101.

CONSTANTINESCU, Radu. 'Alcuin et les "Libelli Precum" de l'epoque carolingienne'. *Revue de l'histoire de la spiritualité* 50 (1974) 17–56.

CORSANO, Karen. 'The First Quire of the Codex Amiatinus and the *Institutiones* of Cassiodorus'. *Scriptorium* 41 (1987) 3–34.

CUBITT, Catherine. *Anglo-Saxon Church Councils 650–850*. Studies in the Early History of Britain. Leicester, 1995.

CURRAN, Michael. *The Antiphonary of Bangor and the Early Irish Monastic Liturgy*. Dublin, 1984.

DALTON, O. M. 'A Note on the Alfred Jewel'. *Society of Antiquaries of London. Proceedings*, ser. 2, 20 (1904) 71–7.

DANIELOU, Jean. *Sacramentum Futuri: études sur les origines de la typologies biblique*. Paris, 1950.
'Le symbolisme du Temple de Jerusalem chez Philon et Josèphe'. In *Le symbolisme cosmique des monuments religieux*, 83–90. Rome 1957.

DAVID, Pierre. 'Un recueil de conférences monastiques irlandaises du VIIIe siècle. Notes sur le manuscrit 43 de la Bibliothèque du chapître de Cracovie'. *RB* 49 (1937) 62–89.

DAVIS-WEYER, Caecilia. 'Komposition und Szenenwahl im Dittochaeum des Prudentius' In *Studien zur spätantiken und byzantinischen Kunst Friedrich Wilhelm Deichmann gewidmet*, eds. Otto Feld and Urs Peschlow, vol. 3, 19–29. Forschungsinstitut für Vor- und Frühgeschichte, Monographien 10.1. Bonn, 1986.

de BRUYNE, Donatien. 'Les notes liturgiques du Codex Forojuliensis'. *RB* 30 (1913) 208–18.
Sommaires, divisions et rubriques de la bible latine. Namur, 1914.

DEKKERS, Eligius and Aemilius GAAR. *Clavis Patrum Latinorum a Tertulliano ad Bedam*, 2nd ed. Steenbrugge, 1961.

de PAOR, Liam. *Saint Patrick's World: The Christian Culture of Ireland's Apostolic Age*. Blackrock, Co. Dublin, 1993.

DESHMAN, Robert. 'Anglo-Saxon Art After Alfred'. *Art Bulletin* 56 (1972) 176–200.
The Benedictional of Aethelwold. Studies in Manuscript Illumination. Princeton, 1995.
'The Imagery of the Living Ecclesia and the English Monastic Reform'. In Szarmach, 261–82.

DESSLER, F., F. Mütherich and H. BEAUMANN. *Das Evangeliar Ottos III. CLM 4453 der Bayerischen Staatsbibliothek München*, vols. 1 and 2. Frankfurt a. M., 1977–78.

(DIDYMUS OF ALEXANDRIA). *Didyme L'Aveugle. Sur Zacharie texte inédit d'aprés un papyrus de Toura*. 3 vols. Louis Doutreleau, ed. and tr. Sources chrétiennes 83. Paris, 1962.

DODWELL, C. R. *Anglo-Saxon Art, a New Perspective*. Manchester, 1982.

DOHERTY, Charles. 'The Cult of St. Patrick and the Politics of Armagh in the Seventh Century'. In *Ireland and Northern France AD 600–850*, Jean-Michel Picard, ed., 53–94. Dublin, 1991.
'The Monastic Town in Early Medieval Ireland'. In *The Comparative History of Urban Origins in Non-Roman Europe: Ireland, Wales, Denmark, Germany, Poland and Russia from the Ninth to the Thirteenth Century*, H. B. Clarke and Anngret Simms, eds. BAR International Series. Oxford, 1985.
'The Use of Relics in Early Ireland'. In Ní Chatháin, 1984, 89–101.

DOLD, Alban. 'Spärliche, aber bedeutsame Bruchstücke dreier alter Perikopenbücher'. *Archiv für Liturgiewissenschaft* I (1950) 82–101.

DOTTIN, G. 'Les deux chagrins du royaume du ciel'. *Revue celtique* (1909) 349–87.

DOYLE, A. I. 'A Fragment of an Eighth-century Northumbrian Office Book'. In *Words, Texts and Manuscripts: Studies in Anglo-saxon Culture Presented to Helmut Gneuss on the Occasion of His Sixty-fifth Birthday*, Michael Korhammer, Karl Reichl, and Hans Sauer, eds., 11–27. Woodbridge, Suffolk, 1992.

DUMVILLE, David. 'Some British Aspects of the Earliest Irish Christianity'. In Ní Chatháin, 1984, 16–24.

DUCHESNE, Louis. *Origines du culte chrétien*, 5th ed., Paris, 1919.
Christian Worship, its Origins and Evolution. M. L. McClure, tr. London, 1923.

EDDIUS Stephanus. *Life of Wilfrid*. ed. and tr. Bertram Colgrave. Cambridge, 1927.

EDWARDS, Nancy. *The Archaeology of Early Medieval Ireland*. Philadelphia, 1990.

ENRIGHT, Michael J. *Iona, Tara and Soissons: The Origin of the Royal Anointing Ritual.* Arbeiten zur Frühmittelalterforschung: Schriftenreihe des Instituts für Frühmittelalterforschung der Universität Münster. Berlin, 1985a.
'Royal Succession and Abbatial Perogative in Adomnán's *Vita Columbae*'. *Peritia* 4 (1985b) 83–103.

ÉTAIX, Raymond. 'Un homéliaire quadragésimal du IXe siècle le Ms. CLM 14386'. *Scriptorium* 40 (1986) 3–15.
'Le lectionnaire de l'office de Cluny'. *Récherches augustiniennes* 11 (1976) 91–159.

ETCHINGHAM, Colmán. 'Bishops in the Early Irish Church: A Reassessment'. *Studia Hibernica* 28 (1994) 35–62.
'The Early Irish Church: Some Observations on Pastoral Care and Dues'. *Eriu* 42 (1991) 99–118.
'The Implications of *paruchia*'. *Eriu* 44 (1993) 139–62.

EUCHERIUS OF LYONS. *Formulae spiritalis intelligentiae*, PL 50.
The History of the Church from Christ to Constantine. G. A. Williamson, tr. New York, 1965.

EUSEBIUS. *The Ecclesiastical History*, 1 J. E. L. Oulton, tr., H. J. Lawlor, ed.; 2 K. Lake, tr., E. Schwartz, ed. 2 vols. London, 1926, 1932.

EVANS, G. R. *The Language and Logic of the Bible: the Earlier Middle Ages*. Cambridge, 1984.

FARMER, D. H., ed. *The Voyage of Saint Brendan.* J. F. Webb, tr. In *The Age of Bede*, D. H. Farmer, ed., 211–45. Harmondsworth, Middlesex, 1983.

FARR, Carol A. 'The Celtic Hero and the Arrest Scene in the Book of Kells', in *Minorities and Barbarians in Medieval Life and Thought*, Susan J. Ridyard and Robert G. Benson, eds., 235–48. Sewanee Mediaeval Studies 7. Sewanee, Tennessee, 1996.
'History and Mnemonic in Insular Gospel Book Decoration'. In *From the Isles of the North: Early Medieval Art from Britain and Ireland*, Cormac Bourke, ed., 137–45. Belfast, 1995.
Lection and Interpretation: the Liturgical and Exegetical Background of the Illustrations in the Book of Kells. Unpublished Ph.D. Dissertation. University of Texas at Austin, 1989.
'Liturgical Influences on the Decoration of the Book of Kells'. In *Studies in Insular Art and Archaeology*, Robert T. Farrell and Catherine Karkov, eds., 127–41. American Early Medieval Studies 1. Oxford, Ohio, 1991.
'Textual Structure, Decoration, and Interpretive Images in the Book of Kells'. In O'Mahony, 437–49.

FASSLER, Margot E. 'The Office of the Cantor in Early Western Monastic Rules and Customaries: A Preliminary Investigation'. *Early Music History* 5 (1985), 29–51.

FERBER, Stanley. 'The Temple of Solomon in Early Christian and Byzantine Art'. In *The Temple of Solomon, Archaeological Fact and Medieval Tradition in Christian, Islamic and Jewish Art*, ed. J. Gutmann, 21–43. American Academy of Religion and Society of Biblical Literature, 3. Missoula, Montana, 1976.

FISCHER, Bonifatius. 'Bedae de titulis psalmorum liber'. In *Festschrift Bernard Bischoff*, ed. J. Autenreith, 90–110. Stuttgart, 1971.
'Die Texte'. In *Der Stuttgarter Bilderpsalter, Bibl. fol. 23. Würtembergische Landesbibliothek Stuttgart*, ed. B. Bischoff, B. Fischer, F. Mütherich, et al, vol. 2, 226–85. Stuttgart, 1968.

FISHER, D. J. V. *The Anglo-Saxon Age, c.400–1042*. Harlow, Essex, 1973.

FOOT, Sarah. 'Anglo-Saxon Minsters: A Review of Terminology'. In Blair, 212–25.

FORRER, Robert. *Römische und byzantinische Seiden-Textilien aus dem Gräberfelde von Achmim-Panopolis*. Strassburg and Basil, 1891.

FOX, Peter, ed. *The Book of Kells: MS 58 Trinity College Library Dublin*. Facsimile and Commentary. Luzern, 1990.

FRIEND, A. M. 'The Picture of the Second Advent, Frontispiece of St. Jerome's Vulgate Gospels A.D. 384'. *American Journal of Archaeology* 30 (1926) 88–9.

FRIGULUS. [Commentary on Matthew, preserved in the *Expositio Libri Comitis* of Smaragdus of Saint-Mihiel]. PL 102, 1119–22 (incomplete).

GAMBER, Klaus. *Das Bonifatius-Sakramentar und weitere frühe Liturgiebücher aus Regensburg*. Textus Patristici et Liturgici 12. Regensburg, 1975.

Codices Liturgici Latini Antiquiores. Spicilegi Friburgensis Subsidia 1. Freiburg, 1963.

GAMESON, Richard. 'The Royal 1.B.vii Gospels and English Book Production in the Seventh and Eighth Centuries'. In Gameson, 24–52.

GANZ, David. 'Bureaucratic Shorthand and Merovingian Learning'. In *Ideal and Reality in Frankish and Anglo-Saxon Society, Studies Presented to J. M. Wallace-Hadrill*, Patrick Wormald, Donald Bullough and Roger Collins, eds., 58–75. Oxford, 1983.
'Mass Production of Early Medieval Manuscripts: The Carolingian Bibles from Tours'. In Gameson, 53–62.
'The Preconditions for Caroline Minuscule'. *Viator* 18, (1987), 23–46.

GARRISON, E. B. *Studies in the History of Italian Medieval Painting*. Florence, 1961.

GATCH, Milton McC. 'Piety and Liturgy in the Old English *Vision of Leofric*'. In *Words, Texts and Manuscripts: Studies in Anglo-Saxon Culture Presented to Helmut Gneuss on the Occasion of His Sixty-fifth Birthday*, Michael Korhammer, ed. Woodbridge, Suffolk, 1992.

GIBSON, Margaret. 'Carolingian Glossed Psalters'. In Gameson, 78–100.

GLORIEUX, Palémon. *Pour revaloriser Migne, table rectificatives.* Mélanges de science religieuse 9, Cahier supplémentaire. Lille, 1952.

GNEUSS, Helmut. 'Liturgical Books in Anglo-Saxon England and Their Old English Terminology'. In *Learning and Literature in Anglo-Saxon England, Studies Presented to Peter Clemoes on the Occasion of his Sixty-Fifth Birthday*, ed. Michael Lapidge and Helmut Gneuss, 91–141. Cambridge, 1985.
'A Preliminary List of Manuscripts Written or Owned in England up to 1100'. *ASE* 9 (1980) 1–60.

GODEL, Willibrord. 'Irisches Beten im frühen Mittelalter'. *Zeitschrift für katholische Theologie* 85 (1963) 261–381, 389–439.

GODU, G. 'Epîtres'. *DACL* 5.1, 245–344.
'Evangiles'. *DACL* 5.1, 852–923.

GOFFART, Walter. *The Narrators of Barbarian History (A.D. 550–800): Jordanes, Gregory of Tours, Bede, and Paul the Deacon.* Princeton, 1988.

GOLDSCHMIDT, Adolph. *German Illumination: vol. 2 Ottonian Period*. Florence, 1928.

GOODENOUGH, Erwin R. *Jewish Symbols in the Greco-Roman Period*. 13 vols. New York, 1953–65.

GORMAN, Michael M. 'The Diffusion of the Manuscripts of Saint Augustine's "De Doctrina Christiana" in the Early Middle Ages'. *RB* 95 (1985) 11–24.

GOUGAUD, Louis. *Les chrétientés celtiques*. Paris, 1911.
Devotional and Ascetic Practices in the Middle Ages, tr. G. C. Bateman. London, 1927.

GRABAR, André. *Christian Iconography, a Study of its Origins*. The A. W. Mellon Lectures in the Fine Arts, 1961. London, 1980.

GRANT, Michael. *Dawn of the Middle Ages*. New York, 1981.

GREEN, Eugene A. 'Enoch, Lent, and the Ascension of Christ'. In *De Ore Domini: Preacher and Word in the Middle Ages*, Thomas Amos, ed., 13–25. Studies in Medieval Culture. Kalamazoo, Mich. 1989.

GREGORY THE GREAT. *In Primum Regum Expositiones. PL* 10A–468B.
XLI Homiliarum in Evangelia. PL 76.

GREGORY OF TOURS. *History of the Franks*. Lewis Thorpe, tr. New York, 1974.

GUTMANN, Joseph. *Hebrew Manuscript Painting*. New York, 1978.

GWYNN, J. *Liber Ardmachanus: The Book of Armagh*. Dublin and London, 1913.

HADDAN, A. W., and W. STUBBS, eds. *Councils and Ecclesiastical Documents Relating to Great Britain and Ireland*. Oxford, 1871.

HALPORN, James W. 'Pandectes, Pandecta, and the Cassiodorian Commentary on the Psalms'. *RB* 90 (1980) 290–300.

HARBISON, Peter. *Pilgrimage in Ireland: The Monuments and the People*. Syracuse, New York, 1991.

'Review of Helen Roe, *Monasterboice and Its Monuments*'. *County Louth Archaeological and Historical Journal* 19, no. 4 (1980) 319–20.

'Three Miniatures in the Book of Kells'. *Proceedings of the Royal Irish Academy* 85, C, no. 7 (1985) 181–94.

HARMON, James A. *Codicology of the Court School of Charlemagne: Gospel Book Production, Illumination and Emphasized Script*. European University Studies ser. 28, History of Art 21. Frankfurt, 1984.

HARVEY, Anthony. 'Early Literacy in Ireland: The Evidence from Ogam'. *Cambridge Medieval Celtic Studies* 14 (1987) 1–15.

HENDERSON, George. *Bede and the Visual Arts*. Jarrow, 1980.
Early Medieval. Style and Civilization Series. New York, 1977.
From Durrow to Kells, the Insular Gospel-books, 650–800. London, 1987.
Losses and Lacunae in Early Insular Art. University of York Medieval Monograph Series 3. York, 1982.

HENDERSON, Isabel. 'The Book of Kells and the Snake Boss Motif on Pictish Cross Slabs and the Iona Crosses'. In Ryan, 56–65.
'Pictish Art and the Book of Kells'. In *Ireland in Early Mediaeval Europe, Studies in Memory of Kathleen Hughes*, eds. Dorothy Whitelock, Rosamond McKitterick and David Dumville, 79–105. Cambridge, 1982.
'The Shape and Decoration of the Cross on Pictish Cross-slabs Carved in Relief'. In Spearman, 209–18.

HENNIG, John. 'The Literary Tradition of Moses in Ireland'. *Traditio* 7 (1949–51) 233–61.
'Old Ireland and Her Liturgy'. In *Old Ireland*, ed. Robert McNally. New York, 1965.

HENRY, Françoise. *The Book of Kells*. New York, 1974.
Irish Art During the Viking Invasions. Ithaca, New York, 1967.

HERBERT, Maire. *Iona, Kells, and Derry: The History and Hagiography of the Monastic familia of Columba*. Oxford, 1988.

HERBERT, Maire, and Martin McNAMARA, eds. and trans. *Irish Biblical Apocrypha: Selected Texts in Translation*. Edinburgh, 1989.

HERITY, Michael. 'Early Irish Hermitages in the Light of the *Lives of Cuthbert*'. In Bonner, 45–63.

HIGGITT, John. 'A Strictly Limited Edition: The New Facsimile of the Book of Kells'. Review. *Art History* 14 (1991) 446–51.

HILARY OF POITIERS. *Commentarius in Matthaeum*. PL 9.

HILLGARTH, J. N. 'Ireland and Spain in the Seventh Century'. *Peritia* 3 (1984) 1–16.

HILEY, David. *Western Plainchant: A Handbook*. Oxford, 1993.

HOLDER, Arthur G., trans. *Bede: On the Tabernacle*. Translated Texts for Historians. Liverpool, 1994.

HOLLIS, Stephanie. *Anglo-Saxon Women and the Church: Sharing a Common Fate*. Woodbridge, Suffolk, 1992.

HOVEY, Walter Read. 'Sources of the Irish Illuminative Art'. *Art Studies* 6 (1928) 105–19.

HUGHES, Andrew. *Medieval Manuscripts for Mass and Office: A Guide to Their Organization and Terminology*. Toronto, 1982.

HUGHES, Kathleen. *The Church in Early Irish Society*. Ithaca, New York, 1966.
'The Distribution of Irish Scriptoria and Centres of Learning from 730 to 1111'. In *Studies in the Early British Church*, ed. N. K. Chadwick, 243–72. Cambridge, 1958.
'Some Aspects of Irish Influence on Early English Private Prayer'. *Studia Celtica* 5 (1970) 48–61.

HUGLO, Michel. 'Liturgia e musica sacrá Aquileiese'. In *Storia della cultura Veneta*, vol. 1: *Dalle origini al Trecento*, ed. G. Folena, 312–23. Vicenza, 1976.

IRVINE, Martin. 'Bede the Grammarian and the Scope of Grammatical Studies in Eighth-Century Northumbria'. *ASE* 15 (1986) 15–44.
The Making of Textual Culture: 'Grammatica' and Literary Theory. Cambridge, 1994.

ISIDORE. *Quaestiones in Vetus Testamentum*. PL 83, 207–423.

JAMES, Edward. *The Franks*. Oxford, 1988.

JEREMIAS, J. *The Unknown Sayings of Jesus*. London, 1957.

JEROME. *Commentariorum in Mattheum*. CCL 77.
  Commentariorum in Zachariam Prophetam, CCL 76A, 747–900.
  Tractatus in Psalmos. CCL 78.

JONAS. *Vita Columbani*. ed. Bruno Krusch. *Vitae Sanctorum Columbani, Vedastis, Iohannis*. Scriptores Rerum Germanicarum in Usum Scholarum ex Monumentis Germaniae Historicis Separatim Editi. Hanover, 1905.

JOSEPHUS. *The Jewish War*. H. St. J. Thackery, tr. The Loeb Classical Library, vol. 3. London, 1930.

JUNGMANN, Josef A. *The Early Liturgy to the Time of Gregory the Great*. Francis A. Brunner, tr. Liturgical studies. Notre Dame, Indiana, 1959.
  Symbolik der katholischen Kirche. Innsbruck, 1960.

KARKOV, Catherine. 'The Decoration of Early Wooden Architecture in Ireland and Northumbria'. In *Studies in Insular Art and Archaeology*, Catherine Karkov and Robert Farrell, eds., 27–48. American Early Medieval Studies 1. Oxford, Ohio, 1991.

KELLY, E. P. 'The Lough Kinale Shrine: The Implications for the Manuscripts'. In O'Mahony, 280–9.

KELLY, Joseph F. T. 'Augustine in Hiberno-Latin Literature'. *Augustinian Studies* 8 (1977) 139–49.
  'Books, Learning and Sanctity in Early Christian Ireland'. *Thought* 54 (1979) 253–61.
  'Hiberno-Latin Exegesis and Exegetes'. *Annuale Mediaevale* 21 (1982 for 1981) 46–60.
  'The Hiberno-Latin Study of the Gospel of Luke'. In *Biblical Studies: The Medieval Irish Contribution*. M. McNamara, ed. Proceedings of the Irish Biblical Association 1. Dublin, 1976, 10–29.
  ed. *Scriptores Hibernae Minores. CCL* 108C. Turnhout, 1974.
  'The Venerable Bede and Hiberno-Latin Exegesis'. In Szarmach, 65–75.
  'The Venerable Bede and the Irish Exegetical Tradition on the Apocalypse'. *RB* 92 (1982) 393–406.

KENDRICK, T. D., R. L. S. BRUCE-MITFORD, T. J. BROWN, eds. *Evangeliorum Quattuor Codex Lindisfarnensis*, 2 vols. Olten and Lausanne, 1956–60.

KENNEY, J. F. *The Sources for the Early History of Ireland; Ecclesiastical*. 2nd ed. Dublin, 1993 (reprint of 1968).

KEYNES, Simon, and Michelle P. BROWN. 'The Mercian Supremacy'. In *The Making of England: Anglo-Saxon Art and Culture AD 600–900*, Leslie Webster and Janet Backhouse, trs., 193–220. London, 1991.

KING, Archdale Arthur. *Liturgies of the Past*. London, 1959.

KITSON, Peter. 'Lapidary Traditions in Anglo-Saxon England: Part II, Bede's *Explanatio Apocalypsis* and Related Works'. *ASE* 12 (1983) 73–123.

KITZINGER, Ernst. 'The Coffin Reliquary'. In *The Relics of St. Cuthbert*, C. F. Battiscombe, ed., 228–73. Oxford, 1956.

KLAUSER, Theodor. *Das römische Capitulare Evangeliorum: Texte und Untersuchungen zu seiner ältesten Geschichte*, 2nd ed. Liturgiewissenschaftliche Quellen und Forschungen 28. Munster, 1972.
  'Studien zur Entstehungsgeschichte der christlichen Kunst'. *Jahrbuch für Antike und Christentum* 1 (1958) 20–51, 2 (1959) 115–45, 3 (1960) 112–33, 7 (1964) 67–76.

KLEINBAUER, W. Eugene. 'The Orants in the Mosaic Decoration of the Rotunda at Thessaloniki: Martyr Saints or Donors?' *Cahiers archéologiques* 30 (1982) 25–45.

KLOSTERMANN, Erich, ed. *Die griechischen christlichen Schriftsteller der ersten drei Jahrhunderte: Origenes Werke X, Origenes Matthäuserklärung I, Die griechisch erhaltenen Tomoi*. Leipzig, 1935.

KRINSKY, Carol. 'Representation of the Temple of Jerusalem Before 1500'. *Journal of the Warburg and Courtauld Institutes* 33 (1970) 1–19.

KÜHNEL, Bianca. *From the Earthly to the Heavenly Jerusalem: Representations of the Holy City in Christian Art of the First Millennium*. Römische Quartalschrift für christliche Altertumskunde und Kirchengeschichte. Supplementheft 42. Rome 1987.
  'Jewish Symbolism of the Temple and the Tabernacle and Christian Symbolism of the Holy Sepulchre and the Heavenly Tabernacle: A Study of their Relationship in Late Antique and Early Medieval Art and Thought'.

Jewish Art 12/13 (1986–87) 147–68.

KUYPERS, A. B., ed. *The Prayerbook of Aedelvald the Bishop, Commonly Called The Book of Cerne*. Cambridge, 1902.

LADNER, Gerhardt B. 'The Symbolism of the Biblical Corner Stone in the Medieval West'. *Mediaeval Studies* 4 (1942) 43–60. Reprinted in G. B. Ladner, *Images and Ideas in the Middle Ages*. Storia e letteratura, racolta di Studi e Testi 155. Rome 1983.

LAISTNER, M. L. W. 'The Library of the Venerable Bede'. In *Bede, His Life, Times and Writings*, A. H. Thompson, ed., 237–66. Oxford, 1935.

LAISTNER, M. L. W. and H. H. KING. *A Hand-List of Bede Manuscripts*. Ithaca, New York, 1943.

LAPIDGE, Michael, ed. *Anglo-Saxon Litanies of the Saints*. London, 1991.
    'The School of Theodore and Hadrian'. *ASE* 15 (1986) 45–72.
    'The Study of Greek at the School of Canterbury in the Seventh Century'. In *The Sacred Nectar of the Greeks: The Study of Greek in the West in the Early Middle Ages*, Michael Herren, ed., 169–94. London, 1988.

LAPIDGE, Michael and Richard SHARPE. *A Bibliography of Celtic-Latin Literature, 400–1200*. Royal Irish Academy, Dictionary of Medieval Latin from Celtic Sources, Ancillary Publications 1. Dublin, 1985.

LATHAM, R. E., ed. *Revised Medieval Latin Word-List From British and Irish Sources*. Oxford, 1965.

LAW, Vivien. *Wisdom, Authority and Grammar in the Seventh Century: Decoding Virgilius Maro Grammaticus*. Cambridge, 1995.

LECLERCQ, H. *Manuel d'archéologie chrétienne*. Paris, 1907.
    'Semaine sainte'. *DACL* 15.1, 1151–85.

LEO. *Tractatus*. *CCL* 138, 138A.

LEWIS, Suzanne. 'Sacred Calligraphy: The Chi Rho Page in the Book of Kells'. *Traditio* 26 (1980) 139–59.

LINDBLOM, John. 'Altchristliche Kreuzessymbolik'. *Studia Orientalia* (1925) 102–13.

LO BUE, Francesco, ed. *The Turin Fragments of Tyconius' Commentary on Revelation*. Texts and Studies, Contributions to Biblical and Patristic Literature, New Series 7. Cambridge, 1963.

LOWE, Elias Avery, ed. *The Bobbio Missal, a Gallican Mass-Book* (*Ms. Paris, Lat. 13246*). *HBS* 53, 58, 61. London, 1917–24.
    ed. *Codices Latinae Antiquiores: A Palaeographical Guide to Latin Manuscripts Prior to the Ninth Century*. 12 vols. Oxford, 1934–72.

LUCE, A. A., G. O. SIMMS, P. MEYER, L. BIELER, eds. *Evangeliorum Quattuor Codex Durmachensis*, 2 vols. Olten and Lausanne, 1960.

MACALISTER, R. A. S. *Monasterboice, Co. Louth*. Dundalk, 1946.

MAC NIOCAILL, Gearóid. 'The Background to the Book of Kells'. In Fox, *Commentary*, 27–33.

MAIBURG, Ursula. 'Christus der Eckstein, Ps. 118,22 und Jes. 28,16 im neuen Testament und bei den Lateinischen Vatern'. In *Vivarium: Festschrift für Theodor Klauser zum 90. Geburtstag*, 247–56. Jahrbuch für Antike und Christentum, Ergänzungsband 11. Münster, 1984.

MARSDEN, Richard. *The Text of the Old Testament in Anglo-Saxon England*. Cambridge Studies in Anglo-Saxon England 15. Cambridge, 1995.

MARSHALL, Edward, tr. *The Explanation of the Apocalypse*. Oxford and London, 1878.

MARTIMORT, A. -G. *Les Lectures Liturgiques et Leurs Livres*. Typologies des sources du moyen âge occidental. Louvain, 1992.

MARTIN, Dale B. *The Corinthian Body*. New Haven, 1995.

MAXIMUS OF TURIN. *Sermones*. *CCL* 23.

MAYR-HARTING, Henry. *The Coming of Christianity to Anglo-Saxon England*. 3rd ed. University Park, Pennsylvania, 1991.

The Venerable Bede, the Rule of St. Benedict and Social Class. Jarrow, 1976.

McCLURE, Judith. 'Bede's Old Testament Kings'. In *Ideal and Reality in Frankish and Anglo-Saxon Society, Studies Presented to J. M. Wallace-Hadrill,* ed. Patrick Wormald, Donald Bullough and Roger Collins, 76–98. Oxford, 1983.

McCONE, Kim. *Pagan Past and Christian Present in Early Irish Literature.* Maynooth Monographs 3. Maynooth, 1990.

McCORMICK, M. 'Un fragment inédit de lectionnaire du viiie siècle'. *RB* 86 (1976) 75–82.

McGINN, Bernard. 'Portraying Antichrist in the Middle Ages'. In *The Use and Abuse of Eschatology in the Middle Ages,* Werner Verbeke, Daniel Verhelst, and Andries Welkenhuysen, eds., 1–48. Mediaevalia Lovaniensia. Leuven, Belgium, 1988.

McGURK, Patrick. 'Citation Marks in Early Latin Manuscripts'. *Scriptorium* 15 (1961a) 3–13.
'The Gospel Book in Celtic Lands Before AD 850: Contents and Arrangement'. In Ní Chatháin, 1987, 166–89.
'The Gospel Text'. In Fox, *Commentary,* 59–152, 1990a.
'The Irish Pocket Gospel Book'. *Sacris Erudiri* 8 (1956) 249–70.
Latin Gospel Books From AD 400 to AD 800. Les Publications de Scriptorium 5. Paris, 1961b.
'The Oldest Manuscripts of the Latin Bible'. In Gameson, 1–23.
'The Texts at the Opening of the Book'. In Fox, *Commentary,* 37–58. 1990b.
'Two Notes on the Book of Kells and its Relation to Other Insular Gospel Books'. *Scriptorium* 9 (1955) 105–7.

McNALLY, Robert E. *The Bible in the Early Middle Ages.* Woodstock Papers 4. Westminster, Maryland, 1959.
ed. *Scriptores Hiberniae Minores* 1. *CCL* 108B. Turnhout, 1973.

McNAMARA, Martin. *The Apocrypha in the Irish Church.* Dublin, 1975.
ed. Glossa in Psalmos: *The Hiberno-Latin Gloss on the Psalms of Codex Palatinus Latinus 68 (Psalms 39:11–151:7).* Studi e testi. Vatican, 1986.
'Ireland and Northumbria as Illustrated by a Vatican Manuscript'. *Thought* 54 (1979) 274–9.
'Plan and Source Analysis of Das Bibelwerk, Old Testament'. In Ní Chatháin, 1987, 84–112.
'Psalter Text and Psalter Study in the Early Irish Church (AD 600–1200)'. *Royal Irish Academy. Proceedings* 73C (1973) 201–98.

McNEILL, John T. and Helena GAMBER. *Medieval Handbooks of Penance.* New York, 1938.

MEEHAN, Bernard. *The Book of Kells: An Illustrated Introduction to the Manuscript in Trinity College Dublin.* London, 1994.
'Dimensions and Original Number of Leaves'. In Fox, *Commentary,* 175–76. 1990a.
'Summaries of Text Incorporating Index to Folios'. In Fox, *Commentary,* 333–54. 1990b.

MERK, August. 'Das älteste Perikopensystem des Rabbulakodex'. *Zeitschrift für katholische Theologie* 37 (1912) 202–16.

MEYER, Kuno, ed. and trans. *Hibernica Minora: Being a Fragment of an Old-Irish Treatise on the Psalter.* Anecdota Oxoniensa, Mediaeval and Modern Series, Part VIII. Oxford, 1894.

MEYVAERT, Paul. *Bede and Gregory the Great.* Jarrow, 1964.
'Bede and the Church Paintings at Wearmouth-Jarrow'. *ASE* 8 (1979) 63–77.
'Bede, Cassiodorus, and the Codex Amiatinus', *Speculum* 71 (1996) 827–83.
'Bede the Scholar'. In *Famulus Christi, Essays in Commemoration of the 13th Centenary of the Birth of the Venerable Bede,* ed. G. Bonner, 40–69. London, 1976.
'The Book of Kells and Iona'. *Art Bulletin* 71 (1989) 6–19.

MORIN, Germain, ed. *Anecdota Maredsolana, I. Liber comicus sive Lectionarius Missae, quo Toletana ecclesia ante annos mille ducentos utebatur (Paris BN nouv. acq. 2171).* Maredsous, 1893a.
'L'année liturgique à Aquilée'. *RB* 19 (1902) 1–12.
'Un commentaire romain sur S. Marc de la première moitié du Ve siècle'. *RB* 27 (1910) 352–62.
Etudes, textes, découvertes. Anecdota Maredsolana, ser. 2, vol. 1. Oxford, 1913.
'Fragments inédits et jusqu'a present uniques d'antiphonnaire Gallican', *RB* 22 (1905) 329–51.
'Le lectionnaire de l'eglise de Paris au VIIe siècle'. *RB* 10 (1893b) 438–41.
'La liturgie de Naples au temps de saint Grégoire, d'apres deux évangiles du septième siècle'. *RB* 8 (1891) 481–93, 529–37.
'Liturgie et basiliques de Rome au milieu du VIIe siècle d'après les listes d'évangiles de Würzburg'. *RB* 28

(1911) 296–330.

'Les notes liturgiques de l'Evangélaire de Burchard'. *RB* 10 (1893c) 113–26.

'Un nouveau type liturgique'. *RB* 10 (1893d) 246–56.

'Le premier volume des Anecdota Maredsolana'. *RB* 9 (1892) 442–47.

'Un système inédit de lectures liturgiques en usage au VIIe/VIIIe siècle dans une église inconnue de la haute italie'. *RB* 20 (1903) 375–88.

MÜTHERICH, Florentine. 'Ausstatung und Schmuck des Handschrift'. in *Das Evangeliar Ottos III. CLM 4453 der Bayerischen Staatsbibliothek München*, vol. 2, ed. F. Dessler, F. Mütherich and H. Beumann. Frankfurt a. M., 1977–78.

'Les Manuscrits Enluminés en Neustrie'. In *La Neustrie: les pays au nord de la Loire de 650 à 850*, H. Atsma, ed., 319–38. Beihefte der Francia. Sigmaringen, 1989.

MÜTHERICH, Florentine and Joachim E. Gaehde. *Carolingian Painting*. New York, 1976.

MYTUM, Harold. *The Origins of Early Christian Ireland*. London, 1992.

NEES, Lawrence. 'A Fifth-Century Book Cover and the Origin of the Four Evangelist Symbols Page in the Book of Durrow, *Gesta* 17 (1978) 3–8.

The Gundohinus Gospels. Cambridge, Massachusetts, 1987.

'Ultán the Scribe'. *ASE* 22 (1993) 127–46.

NETZER, Nancy. *Cultural Interplay in the Eighth Century: The Trier Gospels and the Makings of a Scriptorium at Echternach*. Cambridge Studies in Paleography and Codicology. Cambridge, 1994a.

'Observations on the Influence of Northumbrian Art on Continental Manuscripts of the 8th Century'. In Spearman, 45–51.

'The Origin of the Beast Canon Tables Reconsidered'. In O'Mahony, 322–32. 1994b.

'Willibrord's Scriptorium at Echternach and Its Relationship to Ireland and Lindisfarne'. In Bonner, 203–12.

NEUMAN DE VEGVAR, Carol L. *The Northumbrian Renaissance: A Study in the Transmission of Style*. Selinsgrove, Pennsylvania, 1987.

NILGEN, Ursula. 'Evangelistensymbole'. *Reallexicon zur deutschen Kunstgeschichte* 6, 517–71.

NORDENFALK, Carl. 'Another Look at the Book of Kells'. in *Festschrift Wolfgang Braunfels*, eds. F. Piel and J. Träger, 275–9. Tübingen, 1977a.

'Before the Book of Durrow'. *Acta Archaeologia* 18 (1947) 141–74.

Celtic and Anglo-Saxon Painting. New York, 1977b.

'The Diatesseron Miniatures Once More'. *Art Bulletin* 55 (1973) 532–46.

'An Illustrated Diatesseron'. *Art Bulletin* 50 (1968) 119–40.

'One Hundred and Fifty Years of Varying Views on the Early Insular Gospel Books'. In Ryan, 1–6.

Die spätantiken Zierbuchstaben. Stockholm, 1970.

OAKESHOTT, Walter. *Classical Inspiration in Medieval Art*. London, 1959.

Ó CARRAGÁIN, Eamonn. 'Christ over the Beasts and the Agnus Dei: Two Multivalent Panels on the Ruthwell and Bewcastle Crosses'. In Szarmach, 377–403.

The City of Rome and the World of Bede. Jarrow Lecture 1994. Jarrow, 1994a.

'A Liturgical Interpretation of the Bewcastle Cross'. In *Medieval Literature and Antiquities, Studies in Honour of Basil Cottle*, eds. Myra Stokes and T. L. Burton, 15–42. Cambridge, 1987a.

'The Meeting of St. Paul and St. Anthony: Visual and Literary Uses of a Eucharistic Motif'. In *Keimelia, Studies in Medieval Archaeology and History in Memory of Tom Delaney*, Gearóid Mac Niocaill and Patrick F. Wallace, eds., 1–72. Galway, 1988.

'The Ruthwell Cross and Irish High Crosses: Some Points of Comparison and Contrast'. In Ryan, 118–28. 1987b.

'*Traditio evangeliorum*' and '*Sustenatio*'. The Relevance of Liturgical Ceremonies to the Book of Kells'. In O'Mahony, 398–436. 1994b.

Ó CORRÁIN, D. 'The Early Irish Churches: Some Aspects of Organisation'. In *Irish Antiquity: Essays and Studies Presented to Professor M. J. O'Kelly*, Donnchadh O Corráin, ed., 327–41. Cork, 1981.

'The Historical and Cultural Background of the Book of Kells'. In O'Mahony, 1–32. Dublin, 1994.

'Historical Need and Literary Narrative'. In *Proceedings of the Seventh International Congress of Celtic Studies, Oxford, 1983*, D. Ellis Evans, John G. Griffith, and E. M. Jope, eds., 141–58. Oxford, 1986.

'Irish Vernacular Law and the Old Testament'. In Ní Chatháin, 1987, 284–307.

Ó CORRÁIN, Donnchadh, Liam BREATNACH, and Aidan BREEN. 'The Laws of the Irish'. *Peritia* 3 (1984) 382–438.

Ó CRÓINÍN, Dáibhí. *Early Medieval Ireland 400–1200*. Longman History of Ireland. Harlow, Essex, 1995.

'The Irish Abroad'. Review of *Die Iren und Europa im früheren Mittelalter*, ed. Heinz Löwe, Stuttgart, 1982. In *Peritia* 5 (1986) 445–52.

'Is the Augsburg Gospel Codex a Northumbrian Manuscript?' In Bonner, 189–202.

'Merovingian Politics and Insular Calligraphy: The Historical Background to the Book of Durrow and Related Manuscripts'. In Ryan, 40–3.

'Pride and Prejudice'. Review of *The Durham Gospels* (*Durham Cathedral Library*, MS A.II.17), C.D. Verey et al., eds., Copenhagen, 1980. In *Peritia* 1 (1982) 352–62.

'Rath Melsigi, Willibrord and the Earliest Echternach Manuscripts'. *Peritia* 3 (1984) 17–49.

Ó LAOGHAIRE, Diarmud. 'Irish Elements in the *Catechesis Celtica*. In Ní Chatháin, 1987, 146–64.

O'DWYER, Peter. *Célí Dé, Spiritual Reform in Ireland, 750–900*. Dublin, 1981.

OGILVY, J. D. A. *Books Known to the English, 597–1066*. Cambridge, Mass., 1967.

The Place of Wearmouth and Jarrow in Western Cultural History. Jarrow, 1978.

O'NEILL, Timothy. *The Irish Hand*. Dublin, 1984.

O'REILLY, Jennifer. 'The Book of Kells, Folio 114r: A Mystery Revealed Yet Concealed'. In Spearman, 106–14.

'Early Medieval Text and Image: The Wounded and Exalted Christ'. *Peritia* 6–7 (1987–8) 72–118.

'Exegesis and the Book of Kells: The Lucan Genealogy'. In O'Mahony, 344–97.

'The Rough-Hewn Cross in Anglo-Saxon Art'. In Ryan, 153–8.

O'SULLIVAN, William. 'Insular Calligraphy: Current State and Problems'. *Peritia* 4 (1985) 346–59.

'The Lindisfarne Scriptorium: For and Against'. *Peritia* 8 (1994a) 80–94.

'The Palaeographical Background to the Book of Kells'. In O'Mahony, 175–83. 1994b.

OPENSHAW, Kathleen. 'Weapons in the Daily Battle: Images of the Conquest of Evil in the Early Medieval Psalter'. *Art Bulletin* 75 (1993) 17–38.

PAGE, Raymond I. *An Introduction to English Runes*. London, 1973.

PARKES, Malcom B. 'The Contribution of Insular Scribes of the Seventh and Eighth Centuries to the 'Grammar of Legibility''. In *Grafia e interpunzione del latino nel medioevo*, A. Maierù, ed., 15–31. Lessico intellettuale europeo. Rome, 1987.

Pause and Effect: An Introduction to the History of Punctuation in the West. Berkeley, Los Angeles, New York, and London, 1993.

The Scriptorium of Monkwearmouth and Jarrow. Jarrow Lecture. Jarrow, 1982.

PATTERSON, Nerys. *Cattle Lords and Clansmen: The Social Structure of Early Ireland*. 2d ed. Notre Dame, Indiana, 1994.

PAUL THE DEACON. *Homiliarius*. PL 95.

PEREZ DE URBEL, Justo and Atilano GOZALEZ Y RUIZ-ZORRILLA, eds. *Liber Commicus. Monumenta Hispaniae sacra, serie litúrgica 2, 3*. Consejo Superior de Investigaciones Cientificas, Escuela de Estudios Medievales Textos 13, 28. Madrid, 1950–55.

PERRER, Maria Luisa Gatti. *La Gerusalemme celeste dal III al XIV secolo. La Dimora di Dio con gli uomini*. Milan, 1983.

PHILO OF ALEXANDRIA. *Allegory of the Laws*. F. H. Colson, tr. Loeb Classical Library, vol. 1. London, 1935.

Every Good Man is Free (*Quod Omnis Probus Liber Sit*). F. H. Colson, tr. The Loeb Classical Library: Philo, vol. 9. London, 1935.

Moses I and II (*De Vita Mosis*). F. H. Colson, tr. The Loeb Classical Library: Philo, vol. 6, 273–595. London, 1935.

PLUMMER, Charles, ed. *Venerabilis Baedae Historiam Ecclesiasticam Gentis Anglorum; Historiam Abbatum, Epistolam ad Ecberetum, una cum Historia Abbatum Auctore Anonymo.* Oxford, 1896.

PORTER, Arthur Kingsley. *The Crosses and Culture of Ireland.* London, 1931.

PRAYON, Friedhelm. 'Zum salomonischen Tempelbau der Quedlinburger Itala und zu verwandten Darstellungen in der spätantiken Kunst'. In *Studien zur spätantiken und byzantinischen Kunst Friedrich Wilhelm Deichmann gewidmet,* Otto Feld and Urs Peschlow, eds., vol. 3, 1–9. Forschungsinstitut für Vor- und Frühgeschichte, Monographien Bd. 10.1 Bonn, 1986.

PSEUDO-BEDE. *De Titulis Psalmorum.* PL 93, 477–1098.
   Excerptiones Patrum, Collectanea. PL 94, 539–60.
   Quaestiones Super Exodum. PL 93, 363–88.

PSEUDO-GREGORY. *Expositio in Quattuor Evangelia.* PL 114, 861–916.

PSEUDO-ISIDORE. *In Apocalypsin.* ed. J. Hamman, *PL Supplementum* 4, 1850–63.

PSEUDO-JEROME. *Breviarium in Psalmos.* PL 26, 871–1346.
   Commentarius in Evangelium Marci. PL 30, 589–644.
   Expositio Quattuor Evangeliorum. PL 30, 531–90.

RANKIN, Susan. 'The Liturgical Background of the Old English Advent Lyrics: A Reappraisal'. In *Learning and Literature in Anglo-Saxon England: Studies Presented to Peter Clemoes on the Occasion of his Sixty-Fifth Birthday,* eds. M. Lapidge & H. Gneuss, 317–40. Cambridge, 1985.

RAPONI, Santino. 'Cristo tentato e il cristiano. La lezione dei Padri'. *Studia Moralia* 21 (1983) 209–38.

RAUH, Horst Dieter. *Das Bild des Antichrist im Mittelalter: von Tyconius zum deutschen Symbolismus.* Beitrage zur Geschichte der Philosophie und Theologie des Mittelalters, N.F. 9. Münster, 1973.

RAW, Barbara. *Anglo-Saxon Crucifixion Iconography and the Art of the Monastic Revival.* Cambridge Studies in Anglo-Saxon England. Cambridge, 1990.

REUDENBACH, Bruno. 'Säule und Apostel: Überlegungen zum Verhältnis von Architektur und architekturexegetischer Literatur im Mittelalter'. *Frühmittelalterliche Studien* 14 (1980) 310–51.

REVEL-NEHER, Elisabeth. 'Du Codex Amiatinus et ses rapports avec les plans du tabernacle dans l'art juif et dans l'art byzantin'. *Journal of Jewish Art* 9 (1982) 6–17.

ROE, Helen M. *Monasterboice and Its Monuments.* Longford, Ireland, 1981.

ROTH, Cecil. 'Jewish Antecedents of Christian Art'. *Journal of the Warburg and Courtauld Institutes* 16 (1953) 24–44.

SALMON, Pierre, ed. *Le Lectionnaire de Luxeuil,* 2 vols. Collectanea biblica latina 7, 9. Rome, 1944, 1953.
   L'Office divin, histoire de la formation du bréviaire. Lex Orandi, Collection du Centre de pastorale liturgique 27. Paris, 1959a.
   'Le système des lectures liturgiques contenu dans les notes marginales du Ms. Mp. th. Q. 1a de Würzburg'. *RB* 61 (1951) 38–53.
   'Le système des lectures liturgiques contenu dans les notes marginales du Ms. Mp. Th. q. 1a de Würzburg, additions et corrections'. *RB* 62 (1952) 294–96.
   Les 'Tituli Psalmorum' des manuscrits latins. Paris, 1959b.

SAXL, Fritz. 'The Ruthwell Cross'. *Journal of the Warburg and Courtauld Institutes* 6 (1943) 1–19.

SCHAPIRO, Meyer. 'The Image of the Disappearing Christ, the Ascension in English Art Around the Year 1000'. *Gazette des Beaux Arts,* series 6 (1943), 135–52, reprinted in Meyer Schapiro, *Late Antique, Early Christian and Mediaeval Art, Selected Papers,* New York, 1979, 267–87.
   'The Miniatures of the Florence Diatessaron (Laurentian Ms. Or. 81)'. *Art Bulletin* 55 (1973a) 494–531.
   Words and Pictures, on the Literal and the Symbolic in the Illustration of a Text. Approaches to Semiotics, Paperback Series, 11. Paris, 1973b.

SCHEFFCZYK, Leo. 'Vox Christi ad Patrem – Vox Ecclesiae ad Christum. Christologische Hintergrunde der beiden Grundtypen christlichen Psalmenbetens und ihre spirituellen Konsequenzen' In *Liturgie und Dichtung, ein interdisziplinäres Kompendium*. H. Becker and R. Kaczynski, eds., vol. 2, 579–614. Pietas Liturgica 1, 2. St. Ottilien, 1983.

SCHILLER, Gertrud. *Iconography of Christian Art*. 3 vols. Greenwich, Conn., 1972.

SCIASCIA, Pius. *Lapis Reprobatus*. Studia Antoniana 13. Rome, 1959.

SELMER, Carl, ed. *Navigatio Sancti Brendani Abbatis from Early Latin Manuscripts*. Blackrock, Co. Dublin, 1989 (reprint of Notre Dame, 1959).

SHARPE, Richard. 'Armagh and Rome in the Seventh Century'. In Ní Chatháin, 1984, 58–72. 1984a.
    'Churches and Communities in Early Medieval Ireland: Towards a Pastoral Model'. In Blair, 81–109.
    Medieval Irish Saints' Lives: An Introduction to Vitae Sanctorum Hiberniae. Oxford, 1991.
    'Palaeographical Considerations in the Study of the Patrician Documents in the Book of Armagh'. *Scriptorium* 36 (1982) 3–28.
    'Some Problems Concerning the Organization of the Church in Early Medieval Ireland'. *Peritia* 3 (1984b) 230–70.

SHERLEY-PRICE, Leo, ed. and tr. Bede, *A History of the English Church and People*. New York, 1968.

SIEGER, Joanne Deane. '*Pictor Ignotus*': The Early Christian Pictorial Theme of "Christ and the Church" and its Roots in Patristic Exegesis of Scripture'. Ph.D. diss., University of Pittsburgh, 1980.

SMALLEY, Beryl. *The Study of the Bible in the Middle Ages*, 3rd edition. Oxford, 1983.

SMYTH, Alfred P. *Warlords and Holy Men, Scotland AD 80–1000*. London, 1984.

STAFFORD, Pauline. *The East Midlands in the Early Middle Ages*. Studies in the Early History of Britain. Leicester, 1985.

STALLEY, Roger. 'European Art and the Irish High Crosses'. *Proceedings of the Royal Irish Academy* 90 C, no. 6 (1990) 135–58.

STANCLIFFE, Clare. 'Early "Irish" Biblical Exegesis'. In *Studia Patristica* 12 (1975), 361–70. Texte und Untersuchungen 115.
    'Red, White and Blue Martyrdom'. In *Ireland in Early Mediaeval Europe, Studies in Memory of Kathleen Hughes*, eds. D. Whitelock, R. McKitterick, D. Dumville, 21–46. Cambridge, 1982.

STEVENSON, Jane. 'The Beginnings of Literacy in Ireland'. *Proceedings of the Royal Irish Academy* 89 C, no. 6 (1989) 127–65.
    'Literacy in Ireland: The Evidence of the Patrick Dossier in the Book of Armagh'. In *The Uses of Literacy in Early Medieval Europe*, Rosamond McKitterick, ed., 11–35. Cambridge, 1990.

STEVICK, Robert David. *The Earliest Irish and English Bookarts*. Philadelphia, 1994.

STOKES, Whitley, ed. *The Martyrology of Gorman*. HBS 9. London, 1885.
    ed. *The Martyrology of Oengus the Culdee*. HBS 29. London, 1905.

TALBOT RICE, David. 'Britain and the Byzantine World in the Middle Ages'. In *Byzantine Art: An European Art*. Lectures, 30–1. Athens 1966.

THACKER, Alan. 'Bede's Ideal of Reform'. In *Ideal and Reality in Frankish and Anglo-Saxon Society: Studies Presented to J. M. Wallace Hadrill*, Patrick Wormald, Donald Bullough, and Roger Collins, eds., 130–53. Oxford, 1983.
    'Monks, Preaching and Pastoral Care in Early Anglo-Saxon England'. In Blair, 137–70.

THALHOFER, Valentin. *Erklärung der Psalmen und der im römischen Brevier vorkommenden biblischen Cantica mit besonderer Rücksicht auf deren liturgischen Gebrauch*. Regensburg, 1895.

THÉREL, Marie-Louise. *Les symboles de l'"Ecclesia" dans la création iconographique de l'art chrétien du IIIe au VIe siècle*. Rome, 1973.

THOMPSON, E. A. 'St. Patrick and Coroticus'. *Journal of Theological Studies* n.s. 31 (1980) 12–27.

THURSTON, Herbert. *Lent and Holy Week, Chapters on Catholic Observance and Ritual*. London, 1904.

TRONCARELLI, Fabio. 'Una pietà più profonda: Scienza e medicina nella cultura monastica medievale italiana', in Gian Carlo Alessio et al., *Dall'eremo al cenobio: La civiltà monastica in Italia dalle origini all'età di Dante*. Milan, 1987.

'Alpha e acciuga: Immagini simboliche nei codici di Cassiodoro', *Quaderni medievali* 41 (1996) 6–26.

TRONZO, William. *The Via Latina Catacomb, Imitation and Discontinuity in Fourth-Century Roman Painting*. University Park, Pennsylvania, 1986.

TYCONIUS. *Liber Regularum*. F. C. Burkitt, ed. *Texts and Studies, Contributions to Biblical and Patristic Literature* 3.1, 1–85. Cambridge, 1895.

TYRER, John W. *Historical Survey of Holy Week, Its Services and Ceremonials*. Alcuin Club Collection 29. London, 1932.

VAESEN, Jos. 'Sulpice Sévère et la Fin Des Temps'. In *The Use and Abuse of Eschatology in the Middle Ages*, Werner Verbeke, Daniel Verhelst, and Andries Welkenhuysen, eds., 49–71. Mediaevalia Lovaniensia. Leuven, Belgium, 1988.

VEREY, Christopher D., ed. *The Durham Gospels, Together with Fragments of a Gospel Book in Uncial: Durham, Cathedral Library, Ms. A.II.17*. Copenhagen, 1980.

VEZIN, Jean. 'Les divisions du texte dans les évangiles jusqu'à l'apparition de l'imprimerie'. In *Grafia e interpunzione del latino nel medioevo*, A. Maieru, ed., 55–68. Lessico intellettuale europeo. Rome, 1987.

von SIMSON, Otto. *Sacred Fortress, Byzantine Art and Statecraft in Ravenna*. Princeton, 1987, reprint of 1948 edition.

WALKER, G. S. M., ed. *Sancti Columbani Opera*. Scriptores Latini Hiberniae 2. Dublin, 1957.

WALLACE-HADRILL, J. M. *Bede's 'Ecclesiastical History of the English People': A Historical Commentary*. Oxford, 1988.

WALSH, Maura, and Dáibhí O CRÓINÍN. *Cummian's Letter De controversia paschali, Together with a Related Irish Computistical Tract De Ratione Conputandi*. Studies and Texts 86. Toronto, 1988.

WARNER, George F., ed. *The Stowe Missal: Ms. D. II. 3 in the Library of the Royal Irish Academy, Dublin*. Woodbridge, Suffolk, 1989 (reprint of *HBS* 31, 32, London 1906, 1915).

WARREN, F. E. *The Antiphonary of Bangor*, 2 vols. HBS 4, 10. London, 1893, 1895.
The Liturgy and Ritual of the Celtic Church; reprint of London, 1881, ed. Jane Stevenson. Studies in Celtic History 9. Woodbridge, Suffolk, 1987.

WEBSTER, Leslie E. 'Stylistic Aspects of the Franks Casket' In *The Vikings*, ed. Robert T. Farrell, 20–31. Phillimore, 1982.

WEBSTER, Leslie, and Janet BACKHOUSE, eds. *The Making of England: Anglo-Saxon Art and Culture AD 600–900*. Toronto, 1991.

WEIS, Adolf. 'Die spätantike Lektionar-Illustration im Scriptorium Reichenau'. In *Die Abtei Reichenau*, ed. H. Maurer, 311–62. Sigmaringen, 1971.

WEITZMANN, Kurt. *Late Antique and Early Christian Book Illumination*. New York, 1977.

WERCKMEISTER, O. K. 'Die Bedeutung der 'Chi'-Initialseite im Book of Kells'. In *Das erste Jahrtausend, Kunst und Kultur im werdenden Abendland an Rhein und Ruar*, ed. V. H. Elbern, vol. 2, 687–710. Dusseldorf, 1964. *Irisch-Northumbrische Buchmalerei des 8 Jh. und monastische Spiritualität*. Berlin, 1967.

WERNER, Martin. '*Crucifixi, Sepulti, Suscitati*: Remarks on the Decoration of the Book of Kells'. In O'Mahony, 450–88.
'The *Madonna and Child* Miniature in the Book of Kells'. *Art Bulletin* 54 (1972) 1–23, 129–39.

WHITE, Henry Julian. *The Four Gospels from the Munich Manuscript now Numbered Lat. 6224 in the Royal Library at Munich*. Old Latin Biblical Texts 3. Oxford 1888.

WILLIS, Geoffrey G. *Further Essays in Early Roman Liturgy*. Alcuin Club Collections 50. London, 1968.

WILMART, André 'Transfigurare'. *Bulletin d'ancienne littérature et d'archéologie chrétienne* 1 (1911) 282–92.

WILSON, David M. *Anglo-Saxon Art from the Seventh Century to the Norman Conquest*. Woodstock, New York, 1984.

WILSON, H. A., ed. *The Calendar of St. Willibrord*. *HBS* 55. London, 1918.

WORMALD, Patrick. 'The Age of Bede and Aethelbald'. In *The Anglo-Saxons*, ed. James Campbell, 70–100. Oxford, 1982.

WRIGHT, Charles D. *The Irish Tradition in Old English Literature*. Cambridge studies in Anglo-Saxon England 6. Cambridge, 1993.

YOUNGS, Susan. *'The Work of Angels': Masterpieces of Celtic Metalwork, 6th–9th Centuries AD*. London, 1989.

INDEX

OF MANUSCRIPTS CITED

INDEX

OF BIBLICAL CITATIONS

189

INDEX